Sport in the UK

Leona Trimble, Babatunde Buraimo,
Clint Godfrey, David Grecic, and Sue Minten

LearningMatters

First published in 2010 by Learning Matters Ltd
© 2010 Leona Trimble, Babatunde Buraimo, Clint Godfrey, David Grecic, and Sue Minten.

British Library Cataloguing in Publication Data

A CIP record for this book is available from the British Library

ISBN: 9781844453832
Cover design by Toucan Design

Text design by Toucan Design

Project Management by Swales & Willis Ltd, Exeter, Devon

Typeset by Swales & Willis Ltd, Exeter, Devon

Printed and bound in Great Britain by TJ International Ltd, Padstow, Cornwall

Learning Matters Ltd

33 Southernhay East

Exeter EX1 1NX

Tel: 01392 215560

E-mail: info@learningmatters.co.uk

www.learningmatters.co.uk

Sport in the UK

Active Learning in Sport – titles in the series

To order, please contact our distributor: BEBC Distribution, Albion Close, Parkstone, Poole, BH 12 3LL. Telephone: 0845 230 9000, email: learningmatters@bebc.co.uk. You can find more information on each of these titles and our other learning resources at www.learningmatters.co.uk.

Contents

About the authors

Leona Trimble is Senior Lecturer and Course Leader for Sports Development at the University of Central Lancashire. Areas of interest include sport and community capacity building, volunteering, club development and sports development delivery systems and policies. Leona began her career in health club management before working as a sports development office in Cheshire focusing on Active Sports, club development and youth games. Leona has been a university lecturer for six years.

Babatunde Buraimo is Senior Lecturer in Sports Management and Sports Economics at the University of Central Lancashire. His research areas include demand for football, economics of sports broadcasting, competitive balance in sports and the econometric analysis of sports. He has published a number of articles in peer reviewed journals including *Journal of Sports Economics*, *Journal of the Royal Statistical Society* and *Journal of the Operational Research Society*.

Clint Godfrey is Senior Lecturer for Sports Development and Coaching at the University of Central Lancashire. Areas of interest include community sports development, training and development in the sports development sector, community coaching, sports finance and international sports development. Prior to joining the University of Central Lancashire in August 2007, he worked in the sports development sector for nine years. This was spent working in local authority sports development teams for five and a half years and for Sport England for three and a half years.

David Grecic is a Senior Lecturer at the University of Central Lancashire and the Director of the International Institute for Golf Education. Areas of interest include sports participation demographics, sport development intervention strategies, and sport programme planning and implementation. David began his career in education before moving into sports management and then into higher education. He has worked closely with county sports partnerships both in a consultancy role and as part of their management team. He also works with golf's national governing bodies in order to deliver their national and community objectives.

Sue Minten is a Senior Lecturer at the University of Central Lancashire. Her PhD examined the employability of sports graduates, particularly focusing on their transition into the workplace. She also lectures and researches human resource management in sport. She has worked in higher education for 18 years, prior to that she worked in sports facility management for five years. Between 2002 and 2005 she was seconded to Advantage West Midlands to facilitate the development of links between higher education and leisure businesses. She has also undertaken consultancies for a range of organisations.

Foreword

This book will encourage readers to develop an understanding of the key drivers which underpin and shape the sporting landscape of the UK across the public, private and voluntary sectors. In Part 1, issues surrounding implementation, funding, capacity and governance will be examined. Part 2 will explore the differing environments in which sport and physical activity takes place: school, community and elite settings. Part 3 will outline the influences in the commercial sports sector and debate contemporary sport issues emerging in the UK such as London 2012. The issues surrounding active participation and those of the spectator will also be looked at. These issues will be seen from as wide a sporting context as possible with examples from football, tennis, cycling, Formula 1, golf and the NBA to name but a few. Part 4 will inform readers about the sports labour markets within UK sport; training, career opportunities and the professional athletes market. Throughout the text some underlying themes will also be explored such as equity, international perspectives and partnership working to see what impact they are having on sport in the UK.

This is an ideal book for anyone wishing to gain an understanding of the fundamental aspects of sports infrastructure in England, Scotland, Wales and Northern Ireland whilst acknowledging the influences of the international context. Regardless of the programme of study this book will provide an essential foundation of knowledge through a series of learning actives, case studies and reflections.

Acknowledgements

The team would like to thank Anthony Haynes for getting the project up and running and providing much support in the early stages. We would also like to express our gratitude and appreciation to the hard work of Helen Fairlie who has provided fantastic editorial support and kept us moving along until we crossed the finish line.

Acronyms and abbreviations

ATP	Association of Tennis Professionals
BASEM	Association of Sport and Exercise Medicine
BASES	British Association of Sport and Exercise Sciences
BBC	British Broadcasting Corporation
BMRB	British Market Research Bureau
BOA	British Olympic Association
BSF	Building Schools for the Future
BSkyB	British Sky Broadcasting
CCPR	Central Council of Physical Recreation
CCT	Compulsory Competitive Tendering
CIS	Chartered Institute for Sport
CPD	Continued Professional Development
CSP	County Sport Partnerships
CSR	Comprehensive Spending Review
CTF	Coaching Task Force
DCAL	Department for Culture, Arts and Leisure
DCMS	Department of Culture, Media and Sport
DCSF	Department for Children, Schools and Families
DENI	Department of Education for Northern Ireland
DfES	Department for Education and Skills
DTH	direct-to-home
DTT	digital terrestrial broadcasting
EBU	European Broadcasting Union
EFDS	English Federation of Disability Sport
EFSMA	European Federation of Sports Medicine Associations
EHFA	European Health and Fitness Association
EIS	English Institute of Sport
EITC	Everton in the Community
EM	ethnic minority
EPG	England Golf Partnership
ESPN	Entertainment and Sports Programming Network
EU	European Union
FA	Football Association
FIA	Fitness Industry Association

FIFA	Fédération Internationale de Football Association
FPP	Fast-Track Practitioner Programme
FTA	free to air
GAA	Gaelic Athletic Association
GB	Great Britain
GHS	General Household Survey
HD	high definition
HM	Her Majesty's
IAAF	International Association of Athletics Federations
IBM	International Business Machines Corporation
ICT	information and communication technologies
ID	identification
ILAM	Institute of Leisure and Amenity Management
IOC	International Olympic Committee
IRB	International Rugby Board
IS	Institutes of Sport
ISPAL	Institute of Sport, Parks and Leisure
ISRM	Institute of Sport and Recreation Management
ITV	Independent Television
IVR	Institute for Volunteering Research
LOCOG	London Organising Committee for the Olympic Games
MLB	Major League Baseball
MP	Member of Parliament
NASD	National Association for Sports Development
NBA	National Basketball Association
NDPB	non-departmental public body
NFL	National Football League
NGB	national governing bodies
NHS	National Health Service
NSAS	National Skills Academy for Sport
NSF	National Sports Foundation
ODA	Olympic Delivery Authority
PE	Physical Education
PESS	Physical Education and School Sport
PESSCL	PE, School Sport and Club Links
PESSYP	Physical Education and School Sport for Young People
PGA	Professional Golfers' Association
QCDA	Qualifications and Curriculum Development Authority
REPs	Register of Exercise Professionals
SAF	SportsAid Foundation
scUK	sports coach UK
SCW	Sport Council for Wales

SDO	Sport Development Officer
SIRC	Sport Industry Research Centre
SNI	Sport Northern Ireland
SSC	Sector Skills Councils
SSDA	Sector Skills Development Agency
TASS	Talented Athlete Scholarship Scheme
UCI	International Cycling Union
UEFA	Union of European Football Associations
UK	United Kingdom
UKCC	United Kingdom Coaching Certificate
UKCF	United Kingdom Coaching Framework
UKSI	United Kingdom Sports Institute
VDA	Volunteer Development Agency
WCVA	Wales Council for Voluntary Actions
WSFF	Women's Sports and Fitness Foundation
WSP	Whole Sport Plans
WTA	Women's Tennis Association
YST	Youth Sport Trust

Part One
The strategic direction of UK sport

Chapter 1
Shaping the vision for sport and physical activity in the UK: the role of central government

Learning Objectives

This chapter is designed to help you:

- understand the political context and drivers across the UK which influence and shape the vision for sport and physical activity;
- investigate central government funding and how national agencies gain funding to achieve their objectives;
- explore the trends in participation and gain better understanding of the challenges faced by those constantly striving to increase mass participation.

Historically, the role of central government has been interwoven into the sporting landscape of the UK. Policy making, funding, delivery agencies and target setting have been significantly influenced and guided by central governments. The development of government involvement in sport has been haphazard at best. Generally, central governments have been reluctant to intervene in matters of sport and many interventions have tended to be reactive rather than the outcome of a strategic overview (Houlihan 1997: 92). The purpose of this chapter is to provide an overview of the role that central governments have played in shaping the vision for sports and physical activity in each of the four home nations. It will also look at participation trends, targets and interventions which have often been at the forefront of government policy.

In little over 100 years, sport has been transformed from an activity arousing only a small interest among governments to a global phenomenon demanding the attention of presidents, prime ministers and monarchs (Houlihan 1997: 1). There is an acknowledgement that physical activity by its very nature is a cross-cutting government responsibility and a range of departments are leading in creating more opportunities to get physically active. Houlihan (1997: 2) commented that 'most industrial countries have reached a position where sport and government are inextricably linked across a wide and diverse range of policy issues'. All government departments across the UK therefore know the importance of promoting a lifelong adoption of a healthy lifestyle and are continually looking to raise participation levels and encourage people to be more physically active.

Learning Activity 1.1

If a government is going to promote a healthy lifestyle and encourage more people to be physically active, a number of agencies will need to be involved and considerable action taken.

1   Which do you consider to be the most important agencies to be involved in increasing participation levels by 2020 in England, Scotland, Wales and Northern Ireland?

2   What roles to do you think each of the agencies will play in achieving the targets set?

3   Think about the different settings in which sport and physical activity takes place, such as school, community and clubs.

1960	The Wolfenden Report 'Sport in the Community'
1966	Council of Europe adopted the 'Sport for All' slogan
1972	The GB Sports Council formed under royal charter
1975	The first government sport policy 'Sport and Recreation'
1979	Margaret Thatcher elected Prime Minister: sport under her administration characterised by monitoring of performance, target setting and privatisation
1980s	CCT introduced by Conservative government
1982	*Sport in the Community: The Next Ten Years* published
1983	National Coaching Foundation formed as a sub-committee of the then (GB) Sports Council
1992	Conservative government with John Major as Prime Minister: sport under his administration characterised by focus on school sport and limited acknowledgement of wider community participation through local authorities
1994	Youth Sport Trust established and National Lottery launched
1995	*Sport Raising the Game* published
1996	Atlanta Olympic Games (GB finished tenth in medal table, pressure to give elite sport more priority)
1996	*England: A Sporting Nation* published
1997	Twenty years of Tory rule ended by the election of Tony Blair's New Labour into power. Sport under Blair's administration characterised by 'sport for good' and social welfare/exclusion issues
1999	Policy Action Team 10 (PAT 10) focuses on the contribution sport and the arts can potentially make towards neighbourhood renewal
2000	*A Sporting Future for All* – confirmed central role of school sport, outlined the fragmented organisation and management of sport
2002	*Game Plan*: mass participation, sporting talent and international success, hosting mega sporting events and the sporting infrastructure. Participation, the target set was 70 per cent of the population being physically active for thirty minutes three times per week
2008	*Playing to Win: A New Era for Sport*: capitalise on the once in a lifetime opportunity presented by London winning the bid to host the Olympic and Paralympic Games in 2012 to inspire a generation to take part and succeed in sport
2012	Olympic and Paralympic Games: London

Figure 1.1 A timeline of the political contexts and drivers in England

Political context and drivers – England

The Wolfenden Report (1960) was the first significant independent report on 'sport in the community'. The Conservative government had an indifference to sport, with many MPs seeing it as a private pastime and something that government should avoid (Collins 2008: 61). Although central government took a key role in shaping national policies they had few executive responsibilities. Throughout the 1970s there was an increasing devolution of responsibilities for service delivery to semi-independent agencies such as the Sports Council (Houlihan 1997: 45). The Council was responsible for encouraging participation, facility development and international performance (Collins 2008: 61). And so in 1975 the first ever government sport policy document, 'Sport and Recreation' was published, its significant content relating to the role that sport could play in wider society. The Labour government of the time was keen to promote sporting opportunities as an integrated part of the welfare state and during this time we saw the introduction of the 'Sport for All' campaign (Bramham 2008: 20).

The Thatcher era (1979–1990) was characterised by monitoring of performance, target setting and privatisation. Central objectives of the Conservative governments of the 1980s were: to reduce the scope of central government and to introduce a market approach to public services. Thus, Compulsory Competitive Tendering (CCT) was introduced, which gave private investors the opportunity to run leisure services and forced the public sector to consider adopting strategies and policies of the market sector (Houlihan 1997: 94). The devolution of responsibility for policy implementation and service delivery from central government to the Sports Council and then to local government (local authorities) continued to gather momentum throughout the Thatcher administration (Houlihan 1997: 46).

From 1992 to 1997 there was a Conservative government under John Major which was characterised by a 'back to basics' approach to sport. Major actually voiced an interest in sport (Collins 2008: 66) and his government pragmatically breathed new life into the Sports Council through National Lottery funding and with its commitment to excellence (Bramham 2008: 21). Major's aim was to reverse the decline in school sport and importantly to re-establish competitive sport in schools. His significant policy document was *Sport: Raising the Game* (1995), which reasserted the intrinsic benefits of team sports (Bramham 2008: 21), encouraged a renewed interest in extra-curricular sport and school–club links, and provided a stronger focus on elite sport (Collins 2008: 66). A criticism would be its limited reference to wider community participation promoted by local authorities.

New Labour swept into power in 1997 and promised widespread changes. There was immediate pressure placed upon Sport England, NGBs and local authorities to demonstrate how their sporting outcomes were contributing to broader social objectives (Bramham 2008: 22).

Through the Department for Culture, Media and Sport (DCMS) the government continued to stress the importance of sport in addressing society-wide inequalities and the gains that sport could make in tackling national cross-cutting 'wicked' issues (Collins 2008: 69). The most significant publication was *Game Plan* in 2002. It was produced by a team of non-sports people and gave an independent and objective review of sport's place in society and government policy. It identified four key areas in which targets should be set, resources channelled and action taken. These areas were: mass participation, sporting talent and international success, hosting mega sporting events, and the sporting infrastructure. In terms of participation, the target set was 70 per cent of the population being physically active for 30 minutes three times per week (DCMS 2002: 81). This has been viewed with some scepticism in many quarters but it has nevertheless provided a target at which to aim (Jackson 2008: 34). In June 2008 the government launched its latest strategic document, *Playing to Win: A New Era for Sport*. One of the main objectives was to capitalise on the once in a lifetime opportunity presented by London winning the bid to host the Olympic and Paralympic Games in 2012 to inspire a generation to take part and succeed in sport.

> *Our ambition is simple – we want to become a truly world leading sporting nation. We are committed to providing access to sport and work to encourage the take-up of sport across communities and by children and young people in particular. We will ensure that everyone has the chance to take part, while focusing special support for world-class sportspeople.*
>
> (DCMS 2008b: 5)

Key to achieving the targets set is the role of the Department of Culture, Media and Sport (DCMS). This department is responsible for government policy on the arts, sport, the National Lottery, tourism, libraries, museums and galleries, broadcasting, creative industries including film and the music industry, press freedom and regulation, licensing, gambling and the historic environment. It is also responsible for the 2012 Olympic Games and Paralympic Games (DCMS 2008a). This responsibility manifests itself through the publication of strategic policy documents, target setting and the allocation of funding to the key delivery agencies. Its role is supported by the Olympic Delivery Authority (ODA) and the London Organising Committee for the Olympic Games (LOCOG). The role of the Olympic agencies will be discussed further in Chapter 7. There has long since been the recognition that sport has an unmatched ability to unite the nation and excite people in their millions and this has been significantly exaggerated since London 2012 was secured. Within the new DCMS strategy, the new vision sets out a shared goal – maximising English sporting success by expanding the pool of talent in all sports, providing more coaching and enabling more competitive sport for all young people.

Funding in England

The new vision set out in *Playing to Win* outlines a single funding approach which replaces the range of funding streams at a national and regional level. A more streamlined system will free up £20m for investment into frontline sports development (DCMS 2008b: 2). In terms of investment in community sport, Sport England has the responsibility of distributing government funding. Since 1994 they have invested more than £550m of government funding to maintain the sporting infrastructure in England and £2.8 billion of National Lottery funding to develop sport and physical activity at grassroots level. Since 1997, UK Sport has operated a world class development programme to support leading Olympic and Paralympic athletes. Owing to limited resources, funding has been directed towards those athletes who can demonstrate they have the capability to deliver medal winning performances at the highest level of competition. In 2006, UK Sport assumed full responsibility for all Olympic and Paralympic performance-related support and adopted a 'no compromise' approach to funding. The current athlete funding package towards 2012 stands at £600m, with £300m coming from the national lottery, £200m coming directly from the Exchequer and £100m coming from private investment and sponsorship.

Sportsmatch is government funded to support the development of grassroots sport in England, and they have approximately £3m per year to award. The principle behind Sportsmatch is that organisations find sponsorship for projects from £1,000 to £50,000 and then the government will match the amount. Since it started in 1992, Sportsmatch has awarded over £48m to almost 6,000 projects across England and has brought in over £58m from the private sector (Sport England 2009c).

Political context and drivers – Scotland

Proposals for a devolved Scottish government were brought forward by the UK government in 1997. Following a referendum in support of devolution, the Scottish Executive (officially referred to as the Scottish government since 2007) was established. In 2007 the Scottish National Party won power in the Scottish parliament and soon after became the official party of the Scottish government. The primary aim of the Scottish National Party is to take Scotland forward to independence, which would mean that the Scottish parliament would have full control over Scottish affairs, a voice on the world stage and greater freedom within a society built on common interests (Scottish National Party 2009). At present, the Scottish government has wide legislative powers over a range of devolved issues including sport. It has autonomy to develop its own policies and initiatives, which allows it to build on the nation's strong sporting tradition (The Scottish Government 2009). The government's aim is to encourage participation in a diverse cultural life and widen access to sport. It believes that it is essential for everyone to have the opportunity to participate, and it is committed to removing all barriers which discourage people from taking part in activity at all levels (The Scottish Government 2009). The government is fully aware of the rewards of hosting mega sporting events. It continues to engage with the UK government and the London Organising Committee for the Olympic and Paralympic Games to ensure that all opportunities available to Scotland are secured and that all valuable lessons are learnt, especially as Glasgow will be hosting the Commonwealth Games in 2014. In terms of sport policy, the Scottish government provides leadership, strategic direction and administers all the policies. The most recent sport strategy was published in 2007: *Reaching Higher – Building on the Success of Sport 21*. This outlines the vision, outcomes, priorities and targets from 2007 to 2020 (The Scottish Executive 2007). Within *Reaching Higher* the Scottish government outlined its vision to increase participation and improve performances in Scottish sport. It also outlined a vision to 'focus on the promotion, delivery, playing and enjoyment of sport. Key to this is developing a culture where sport is valued for the pleasure and quality it brings to people's lives and for the pride and recognition it brings to our nation' (The Scottish Executive 2007: 11).

Case Study
Dundee, Scotland

In 2008 the Scottish government challenged NHS Tayside in Dundee to cut the number of smokers in the disadvantaged areas of the city. The health service responded to the challenge by piloting a project in which participants were given £12.50 a week in groceries if they were able to prove they had not smoked. Sandy Watson, chairman of the health board, said, 'Smoking in Dundee is a difficult problem to tackle but we are hopeful that this innovative approach will encourage smokers to stop smoking for good and therefore make a real difference to their long term health' (BBC 2009a).

Despite this pilot project involving smoking it highlights the role of a government in creating a healthier nation. It also raises the prospect of similar projects which could relate to obesity, drug use and participation levels in sport/physical activity.

Learning Activity 1.2

1   To what extent do you think that NHS Tayside should be congratulated on their innovative response to the Scottish government's challenge by offering these incentives?
2   To what extent do you think that NHS Tayside should be criticised for effectively offering bribes to people to stop smoking?

Funding in Scotland

The government believes Scotland can be healthier and that the benefits of a healthier lifestyle will lead to a higher quality of life for all communities across Scotland (The Scottish Government 2009). It also acknowledges that improving the nation's health is a significant challenge. In 2007–8 £12m was invested in physical activity initiatives in schools, workplaces, homes and communities. A planned £11.5m a year will be invested in diet and physical activity for health and to help prevent obesity. Government funding is channelled through **sport**scotland and is available to sports which are recognised by **sport**scotland and the UK Sports Council. The Scottish government also provides funding to local authorities through Quality of Life and Community Regenerations funds. As the agency responsible for delivering the government's vision for sport, **sport**scotland has awarded 8,436 grants with a total value of £249,318,681 from the National Lottery Good Causes fund. In their corporate plan, **sport**scotland identifies investments for £47.4m (2009), £53.9m (2010) and £54.9m (2011) in sport to increase participation and improve sporting performance, contributing to a range of outcomes including better physical and mental health. This includes £4.1m, £6.6m, and £11.6m (2009–11) respectively, which will be invested in delivering a successful Commonwealth Games in Scotland in 2014 (**sport**scotland 2009a: 17)

Political context and drivers – Wales

As in Scotland, the referendum in 1997 led to the establishment of the Welsh Assembly. The role of the Welsh Assembly is to make decisions on matters which affect people's lives and to develop and implement policy: 'we are working to help improve the lives of people in Wales and make our nation a better place in which to live and work' (Welsh Assembly Government 2009a). Its policies reflect its commitment to sustainability, fairness, social justice and continual improvement to local services. The Government of Wales Act 1998 established the National Assembly for Wales. This is a democratically elected body that represents the interests of Wales. At the heart of its role is to hold the Welsh government to account and scrutinise spending and policy implementation (National Assembly for Wales 2009). The National Assembly is made up of elected members for all the political parties in Wales.

The Welsh Assembly's aim for its culture and sport strategies is to help make Wales a confident, creative and physically fit nation. It is committed to making sport and physical activity a priority and aims to:

- improve the health of our nation;
- encourage more people to take part in sport and physical activity regularly; and
- help more of our athletes and sports people to be more successful.

(Welsh Assembly Government 2009b)

The 10-year Culture Strategy for Wales is called *Creative Future* and was published in 2002. In terms of sports policy the Welsh Assembly government set out its policies and priorities in its strategy *Climbing Higher* 2005. The Assembly government is totally committed to bringing sport and physical activity into the centre stage of its administration and its priorities focus on increasing rates of participation in sport and physical activity along with achieving sporting success on the world stage (*Climbing Higher* 2005: 4). The strategy outlines three areas for action: active young people; a successful sporting nation; and active communities (Welsh Assembly Government 2009c).

Funding in Wales

The Welsh Assembly provides funding to help in its aim to strengthen Wales's cultural identity and promote sport and physical activity, health and well-being. Total Assembly funding for culture and sport in 2007/08 was nearly £110m (Welsh Assembly Government 2009c).

The Sports Council Wales is responsible for the distribution of funds made available for sports and physical activity by the Welsh Assembly. The government set out its 20-year vision for sport and physical activity in its strategy *Climbing Higher* (2005). In response to this, Sports Council Wales launched its framework for the development of sport and physical activity, which was designed to translate the government's vision into action:

- The Welsh Assembly allocated £27.15m to sport to be distributed by Sports Council for Wales (SCW). SCW is also responsible for distributing National Lottery funds to sport in Wales. To date they have awarded 6,670 grants to the tune of £141,922,267.
- The Assembly is committed to investing over £3.7m in the Coaching Plan for Wales.
- Community facilities are to be improved through Lottery and local authority funding (over £160m of Lottery funding).

In 2007 a cash injection from the Welsh Assembly helped to establish the North Wales Regional Institute of Sport, which is a network of facilities, coaches and support services working together to support world class talent for the future. It provides the tools and support services needed to help athletes fulfil their potential achieve success at elite level.

Political context and drivers – Northern Ireland

The Northern Ireland Assembly was established as part of the Good Friday Agreement in 1998. Devolution to Northern Ireland was suspended in 2002 but restored again in 2007. Since then the Northern Ireland Assembly and Executive has been responsible for all the devolved issues in Northern Ireland including the economy, culture, sport, education, social services and health (Directgov 2009a). The Northern Ireland Assembly has the responsibility for making laws on transferred matters in Northern Ireland (Northern Ireland Assembly 2009). The assembly debates and makes laws, scrutinises and makes decisions on the work of the Northern Ireland government departments.

In terms of policies for sport, this function was under the remit of the Department of Culture, Arts and Leisure (DCAL) along with policies on inland waterways and inland fisheries, museums, lottery and Northern Ireland's involvement in the London 2012 Olympics.

DCAL aims to establish the key priorities for the future development of sport and physical recreation in Northern Ireland and to inform the direction of future investment. The Northern Ireland Strategy for Sport and Physical Recreation 2007–2017, *Sport Matters,* outlines the vision and objectives of the government for enhancing the impact of sport and physical recreation in Northern Ireland, and for building a legacy from the Olympic and Paralympic Games. The vision is expressed as 'a culture of lifelong enjoyment and success in sport' (DCAL 2009: 6).

Reflection Point 1.1

Reflect on the information you have read so far in this chapter. Consider the following two statements and construct arguments in support of each statement.

- It is the government's responsibility to set targets, provide public funding and incentives to create a healthier nation.
- It is an individual's responsibility to ensure they are sufficiently active to lead a healthy lifestyle. If they neglect this, they should deal with the consequences.

Funding in Northern Ireland

In its Strategy for Sport and Physical Recreation in Northern Ireland 2007 to 2017, *Sport Matters,* Sport Northern Ireland identified ten pillars to focus their funding on in order to reach their targets. The aim is that by 2019 it will have 'secured a world class system for athlete development consisting of services, facilities and competition following the hosting of the Olympic and Paralympic games in London 2012' (Sport Northern Ireland 2009a). From 2009 to 2013, Sport Northern Ireland plans to invest £13.2m of its performance budget on strengthening the ten pillars it deems necessary to achieve successful athlete development, which includes: modern, fit-for-purpose delivery organisations; talent identification systems; quality coaching; athlete support; and participation initiatives. To date, Sport Northern Ireland has awarded 3,213 grants totalling £143,955,516 to support sport from the National Lottery Good Causes funding (Sport Northern Ireland 2009b).

In terms of supporting elite sport development, Sport Northern Ireland awarded 35 sports £6m each from 2009 to 2011 directly to the NGBs to create pathways for talented athletes and increase participation. This funding will build the foundations of a world class sporting system as each sport had to demonstrate through their plans that they could achieve targets for participation, talent identification, high performance, coaching and modernisation. Some of the sports to benefit are: Cricket Ireland, the Irish FA, the Ulster Council GAA and Ulster Hockey (Sport Northern Ireland 2009b).

Participation

Increasing participation is the fundamental reason why individuals and organisations get involved in sports development activities. The target set by the government is 2m adults taking part in more sport/physical activity by 2012–13 (DCMS 2008b). Participation can be defined in a number of ways but for the purposes of this book the definitions from Sport England's Active People Survey will be used.

Sports participation – the number of adults (aged 16 and over) participating in at least 30 minutes of sport at moderate intensity at least three times per week.

Individual sports participation – participation in each sport and activity is defined as the percentage of the adult population (aged 16 and over) who have participated at least once in the last four weeks.

(Sport England 2009)

Reflection Point 1.2
Reflect on your sport and physical activity history.

- What would you consider to be the significant influencing factors on your participation choices throughout your life?
- Take one of these factors and in 100 words reflect on its significance: why, how and when was it significant?

Young people and participation

Young people continue to appear to have strong beliefs in the value of activity – at least at a basic level (Sport England 2005: 30). In England, approximately 82 per cent of young people take part in sport 'regularly' in their free time (at least 10 times in the previous 12 months) (Sport England 2003: 2). The trends in PE and leisure-time sport and physical activity among youth reflect a broadening and diversification of participation (Green et al. 2005: 30). However, the most recently available data in Northern Ireland reports that only 36 per cent of children under 16 participate in sport/physical activity 3–5 times per week (Children and Young People's Unit 2006: 54). In England, 95 per cent of young people agreed it was important to 'keep fit' (Sport England 2005: 30) and the shift towards 'lifestyle activities' appears to suggest that overall levels of participation is higher than is commonly assumed, but also that participation patterns are somewhat more complex' (Sport England 2003b: 2). Given this research, Green et al. (2005: 32) concluded that co-occurring increases in participation in games that might be deemed lifestyle or recreational activities – such as tenpin bowling – alongside those that are more stereotypically sporting in orientation – such as basketball – reflect the complexity of the youth participation picture. The significance of participation at an early age cannot be underestimated. In England, childhood obesity levels have doubled in the last 10 years with recent figures pointing to 24 per cent of boys and 26 per cent of girls aged 11–15 being classed as obese. In Northern Ireland more than 5 per cent of children were obese, with 22 per cent classified as being overweight or obese (Department Health, Social Services and Public Safety and Dept of Education 2005: 6). These figures would suggest that there is a huge challenge for providers to overcome the 'health timebomb' that awaits (BBC 2006). Roberts (2006: 157) commented that 'the best predictor of any individual's future uses of leisure is that same person's past behaviour'. Therefore the challenge is to change the inactive culture and build upon the positive participation trends because young people's early experiences are likely to have profound implications for their subsequent patterns of participation in sport and physical activity generally (Green et al. 2005: 32).

Measuring adult participation

Measuring participation levels in sport and physical activity in the UK has evolved over time. For many years the General Household Survey (GHS) was the tool used to measure activity levels.

The GHS found that in 2002 walking, keep fit, swimming, cycling and snooker were the top five activities for women and walking, snooker, cycling, swimming and soccer were the top five activities for men. There was an increase in participation rates over the previous 10 years, however women were still less likely to participate than men. The largest gap was in the 17–19 age group with 64 per cent of women taking part compared to 91 per cent of men. A number of ethnic minority groups had lower participation rates than the national average, including Pakistanis and Afro-Caribbeans. Gender differences also existed amongst EM groups particularly in the Asian population. However, the baseline data available from the GHS was fairly limited so to measure participation rates more accurately Sport England commissioned a more extensive survey that was specifically designed for sport and physical activity. The Active People Survey is the largest ever survey of sport and active recreation to be undertaken in Europe. It provides by far the largest sample size ever established for a sport and recreation survey and allows levels of detailed analysis previously unavailable (Sport England 2009a). The first survey was in 2005/06, the second in 2007/08 and the third in 2008/09. In Active People Survey 3, the sports participation indicator that measures Sport England's 1m target is the number of adults (aged 16 and over) participating in at least 30 minutes of sport at moderate intensity at least three times a week (referred to as '3 × 30 sport'). The current data reveals that 6,902,000 adults (21.17 per cent) of the population in England are doing the recommended 3 × 30. There has been no statistically significant change in participation when compared with the results of Active People Survey 2 covering the period October 2007 to October 2008 (Sport England 2009b). For more information regarding the Active People results and trends go to www.sportengland.org.

Learning Activity 1.3

Take some time to complete a participation diary over a few weeks. Document activity, duration, place of activity, whether it was individual/group activity, what types of involvement (player, spectator, coach, volunteer, teacher), total hours spent participating and total hours spent as a spectator.

1   What can you learn about your participation levels and involvement in sport/physical activity from your diary?

2   To what extent can you discover trends in your participation?

3   What implications do these trends have on the organisations and agencies who provide opportunities for sport and physical activity, for example sport development agencies?

Challenges to increasing participation

The challenges faced when trying to increase participation in sport and physical activity across the country are varied and well established. Despite participation levels rising slowly over the last decade, the challenge for delivery agencies is to overcome inequality and barriers to participation. Key influences on participation include: disposable income, educational attainment, social class, culture, ethnicity, age and ability. All of these influences can either empower or discourage sports participation (Hylton and Totten 2008: 52). Participation is also hampered by difficulty in accessing facilities, poor facilities and the cost of joining clubs and gyms (Sport England 2005: 5). Challenges to identity such as having to show others an unfit body, incompetence or, for women, appearing overly masculine are also identified as barriers to participation (Sport England 2005: 5).

All of the home nation governments and key delivery agencies acknowledge the importance of increasing participation in their respective areas primarily for health benefits but also to strengthen communities, promote economic growth, build a post 2012 sporting legacy and achieve a successful country. The challenges they face are complex and well established because of the social fabrics of society and the barriers to participation which exist in all countries. These physical, economic, motivational, cultural and political barriers are what sport agencies have to grapple with in order to promote inclusion and increase participation (Hylton and Totten 2008: 52). Girls and young women have, for many years, been identified as a target group and many barriers have been identified which affect their participation levels. Transitions, including lifestyle changes, have a negative impact on participation. Psychological and social issues were very important when explaining participation. Family and friends have the greatest influence on participation. Those that never participate commonly came from inactive families and had inactive friends. Self-confidence and perception of ability played a significant role on not participating (Sport England 2006: 8).

Aside from the traditional 'target groups' the government has questioned fundamentally the culture in English sport (DCMS 2008b: 1) and whether the sporting landscape in England is good enough to create opportunities for everyone to do more sport and physical activity. It identified in 2002 that a significant behavioural change was required, and participation needed to be linked to health benefits, community

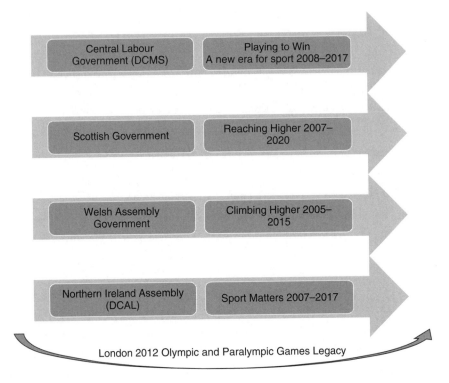

Figure 1.2 UK Governments and their current sport strategies

cohesion, teamwork, leadership and having fun (DCMS 2002: 15). Those same challenges are still very much relevant and are summed up well by Alan Pugh, Minister for Culture, Welsh Language and Sport who said 'we are blessed with a natural environment and a climate well suited to sport and physical activity. Yet participation is still a minority pursuit. In sharp contrast to other parts of the EU, only around 30 per cent of the adult population of Wales take enough exercise to gain a health benefit' (Pugh, cited in The Welsh Assembly Government 2005: 3).

Chapter Review

The aim of this chapter was to develop an understanding of the political context and drivers which help to influence and shape the vision for sport and physical activity across the UK.

Houlihan (1997: 2) commented that 'most industrial countries have reached a position where sport and government are inextricably linked across and wide and diverse range of policy issues'. Hopefully this chapter has helped to gain a better understanding of this. In all of the home countries, the role of central government often involves target setting, strategic direction and funding allocations. Once targets have been set then central government guides the various delivery agencies on how the targets will be achieved. A fundamental target for all governments has been the desire to increase the participation rates for the whole nation. Rowe (2004: 3) suggests that in terms of participation we find ourselves in the position that participation rates have remained stubbornly static and inequities in participation between different social groups have continued largely unchanged over the last 30 years or so with perhaps the exception of more women taking part in fitness related activities.

After reading this chapter and attempting the learning activities you should now be able to answer the following questions:

1   What are the political drivers which influence and shape the vision for sport and physical activity across the UK?
2   In England, how did the views of sport and government differ between the Conservative and Labour governments throughout the 1980s and 1990s?
3   How do the governments in Scotland, Wales and Northern Ireland intend to prioritise their funding in the coming years?
4   What challenges face government and delivery agencies when trying to increase mass participation across the UK?

Further Reading

For an overview of government policy:
- Collins, M. (2008) Public policies on sports development: can mass and elite sport hold together?, in V. Girginov (ed.) *Management of Sports Development*. Oxford: Elsevier.

For a historical look at governments' involvement in sport:
- Houlihan, B. (1997) *Sport, Policy and Politics: A Comparative Analysis*. London: Routledge, Chapter 3.

For a contextual overview of participation issues:
- Rowe, N., Adams, R. and Beasley, N. (2004) Driving up participation in sport: the social context, the trends, the prospects and the challenges, in *Driving up Participation: The Challenge for Sport*. London: Sport England, Chapter 3.

Chapter 2
National sports organisations and their priorities

Learning Objectives

This chapter is designed to help you:

- understand the role, strategic direction, and objectives of the key sport agencies across the UK sporting landscape;
- understand how partnership working helps the national sports agencies turn government strategy into implementation.

The sporting landscape in the UK is ever-changing and complex in nature. It is important to have an understanding of the key sport agencies that are responsible for responding to government targets and vision and to understand their strategic direction and objectives. The purpose of this chapter is to provide an overview of the agencies, their priorities and how partnership working helps to turn strategy into implementation.

The sporting landscape – England

There are three key sporting landscape partners in England: Sport England, Youth Sport Trust and UK Sport. They work together to fulfil the vision set by the DCMS and to try and achieve a number of joint targets within a shared goal of 'maximising English sporting success in all its forms' (Sport England 2008: 1). Each organisation has its own area of responsibility and targets within the landscape and those will be explored in more detail as we go through this chapter.

Sport England is a non-departmental public body (NDPB) responsible for advising, investing in and promoting community sport to create an active nation. A NDPB is defined as follows:

> A non-departmental public body (NDPB) is a national or regional public body, working independently of ministers to whom they are nevertheless accountable. They are not staffed by civil servants. An executive NDPB (such as Sport England) are those with executive, administrative, commercial or regulatory functions. They carry out set functions within a government framework, but the degree of operational independence varies.

(Directgov 2009b)

Sport England is focused on the creation of a world-leading community sport system. They invest National Lottery and government funding in organisations and projects that will grow and sustain participation in grassroots sport and create opportunities for people to excel at their chosen sport (Sport England 2009d). They are accountable to the Department of Culture, Media and Sport and have introduced a plethora of initiatives over the years to increase participation levels of the nation. They invest expertise, resources and both government and Lottery money into community sport – each year £480m is invested directly through 46 national governing bodies of sport (Sport England 2009eb). Their ambition is to get 2m people doing more sport by 2012 – and to make sure that participation is sustained (Sport England 2008: 4). Following the objectives set out in *Playing to Win: A New Era for Sport*, Sport England has also taken a new direction.

*To take a strategic lead for **community sport**, developing a world leading community sport system to sustain and increase participation and develop sporting talent at all levels.*

(DCMS 2008a: 8)

Grow	One million people taking part in more sport
15% of investment	More children and young people taking part in five hours of PE and sport a week
Sustain	More people satisfied with their sporting experience
60% of investment	25% fewer 16–18 year olds dropping out of at least five sports
Excel	Improved talent development in at least 25 sports
25% of investment	

Table 2.1: Sport England's outcome targets 2008–11 (Sport England 2009)

The directional change to focus exclusively on sport is partly down to trying to address the needs for sport in the lead up to and beyond the Olympic and Paralympic Games in 2012 (Sport England 2008: 8). The new strategic direction means that Sport England will focus exclusively on sport and not get drawn into meeting the targets and agendas in other associated areas such as health and community cohesion. This is in direct contrast to previous strategies whereby Sport England worked in partnership to achieve targets in these areas.

Learning Activity 2.1

1 To what extent do you think it is right that Sport England should focus less on the health and community cohesion agendas to concentrate exclusively on sport?
2 What do you consider to be the most important actions that Sport England needs to take at grassroots level to ensure that they develop a world-leading community sport system?
3 How do you think that Sport England could help reduce the number of 16 year olds who drop out of sport?

To strengthen the links between community sport and school sport, Sport England needs to work closely with the Youth Sport Trust (YST) to help schools gain the support of community sport providers to meet the five hour offer. Since they were established in 1994 the YST has aimed to build a brighter future for young people by enhancing the quality of their physical education (PE) and sporting opportunities (Youth Sport Trust 2009a). A more detailed look at the role of school sport in the sporting landscape will follow in Chapter 3. Kirk (2004: 76) suggests that quality early learning experiences are crucially important if young people are to continue to enjoy participating in physical activities. The YST focus their attention and resources on the school part of the sporting landscape by implementing national strategies and working in partnership to achieve joint objectives. Flintoff (2008: 393) suggests that the phased implementation of a national strategy is transforming the infrastructure of PE and school sport through a number of inter-related policy initiatives.

High quality PE and school sport produces young people with the skills, understanding, desire and commitment to continue to improve and achieve in a range of PE, sport and health-enhancing physical activities in line with their abilities.

(DfES/DCMS 2003: 3)

PE, school sports and club links implemented 2003	PE and sports strategy for young people implemented 2008
Aim to increase the percentage of school children in England who spent a minimum of two hours each week on high quality PE and school sport within and beyond the curriculum (YST 2009) Initial target was 75% which was increased to 85% and exceeded YST expectations (YST 2009)	Aims are aligned to the vision of DCMS who have called for the Youth Sport Trust to lead the way in the creation of a world class system for PE and sport for all children and young people
Government invested over £1.5bn from 2003 to 2008 (DCMS 2008a)	Backed by £783 million investment from DCMS in order to deliver the five hour sport offer for young people (DCMS 2008a:10)
National structure has been created which has enabled more children and young people to take part in a wider range of sports for more time (DfES/DCMS 2003)	

Table 2.2: Youth Sport Trust's recent strategies for PE and school sport

---

Learning Activity 2.2

Read the PE and School Sport for Young People Strategy, available at www.teachernet.gov.uk

Answer the following questions:

1   Which two government departments were involved in developing the PE and Sport Strategy for Young People?
2   What are the current estimates of how many 5–16 year olds and 16–19 year olds participate in five hours of sport each week?
3   The new ambition from this strategy is to create a new 'five hour offer' for all 5–16 year olds. What is this?
4   To make the strategy successful the government needs to work with a number of delivery partners, can you name them?

The third key agency within the sporting landscape in England is UK Sport. In terms of elite sport, the UK, like many Western nations has had a gradual, inclusive approach to excellence programmes, with a growing emphasis on offering the opportunity to achieve excellence to a large number of people (Hill 2007: 8). Since 1997 the organisation tasked with developing sporting excellence in the UK has been UK Sport. They were established after the inception of the National Lottery and since then have been operating world class programmes designed to support leading Olympic and Paralympic athletes. Their mission is to 'Work in partnership to lead sport in the UK to world-class success' (UK Sport 2008a).

Use the platform of London 2012 to accelerate the quality and impact of everything we do, by:

1. Building a team of agile, open-minded, high-calibre people, hungry to learn, evolve and excel.
2. Operating effective and innovative business processes to support and simplify our activities.
3. Promoting the UK Sport brand to win and maintain the respect, trust and engagement of everyone with whom we interact.

Table 2.3: UK sport strategic priorities

They were established at the time when New Labour swept into power. At that time the government continued to support the view that the only means of Britain achieving success in the global sporting arena was through a systematic and professional approach (Hill 2007: 38). This professional approach meant that in 2006 UK Sport assumed full responsibility for all Olympic and Paralympic performance-related support in England. To achieve this, a 'no compromise' approach was taken, targeting resources and activity primarily at those sports and athletes capable of delivering medal-winning performances (UK Sport 2008b). The 'no compromise' approach has led to the creation of the World Class Performance Programme which sits at the heart of the UK Sport decision-making process. UK Sport has also received additional funding and endorsement from the government in order to enable the best athletes to realise their medal ambitions

(UK Sport 2008). As the body responsible for elite sport at a UK level, UK Sport will work in partnership with the other home country sports councils and institutes as well as key delivery partners such as the British Olympic and Paralympic Associations to meet their targets (DCMS 2008: 18).

> We have raised our own game, and 'Mission 2012' – introduced this year – is our prime focus now for supporting the aspirations of our Governing Bodies and athletes. It is an innovative approach that will ensure we leave no stone unturned in the search for success.

(UK Sport 2007: 1)

In addition to its funding role, UK Sport is also the UK's appointed national anti-doping agency. It co-ordinates a comprehensive testing programme across more than 50 sports. It is responsible for ensuring compliance among sports bodies with the World Anti-Doping Code and through this the implementation and management of the UK's anti-doping policy.

Learning Activity 2.3

1 To what extent do you think that UK Sport should focus their resources on those sports that win medals at major competitions rather than those sports that do not?
2 UK Sport wants to encourage the next generation of sporting champions to get involved and enjoy sport cleanly and fairly. To what extent do you agree that
   a those athletes found taking drugs should be banned from competitions for life?
   b those athletes found taking drugs should be given a second chance after being banned?

Equity partners

Sport has the potential to reach out to a wide range of people with different abilities and cultural backgrounds. Much time, effort and finance has been spent by the sport delivery agencies in an attempt to address the balance of opportunities for those people who face specific barriers preventing participation in sport.

The work of the delivery agencies is supported by, amongst others, three organisations which have a specific remit to ensure equitable opportunities for the individuals and organisations that they support. They work in partnership and provide a voice for specific populations within our communities. A brief overview of each is provided below.

English Federation of Disability Sport

Launched in 1998 the English Federation of Disability Sports (EFDS) is the umbrella organisation for disability sport in England. The English Federation of Disability Sport brings together the nine regional federations and five national disability sports organisations recognised by Sport England: British Amputees and Les Autres Sports Association; British Blind Sport; WheelPower-British Wheelchair Sport; Mencap Sport; and UK Deaf Sport. Their mission is:

To be the united voice of disability sport seeking to promote inclusion and achieve equality of sporting opportunities for disabled people.

(EFDS 2009)

Women's Sports and Fitness Foundation

The aim of the Women's Sports and Fitness Foundation (WSFF) is to increase the health, fitness and well-being of women and girls by making physical activity an integral part of their lives, where physical activity is defined as sport and exercise. The main focus of its campaign is to make sport as appealing to women and girls as it is to men and boys, to make women aware of the importance of being active, and to make fit and healthy women and girls social and cultural role models (WSFF 2009).

Sporting equals

Sporting Equals exists to promote ethnic diversity across sport and physical activity, and is the only organisation in the UK to do so. Set up in 1998 by Sport England, in partnership with the Commission for Racial Equality, but now an independent body, it informs, influences and inspires in order to create an environment in which:

- BME communities can influence and participate in all aspects of sport and physical activity.
- The governors and providers of sport and physical activity recognise and value a fully integrated and inclusive society.
- Ethnic diversity is recognised and celebrated.

(Sporting Equals 2009)

These three organisations support the first ever equality standard for sport which was launched in November 2004. The standard is a framework and a tool that can be used to address some of the barriers that prevent participation and access within sport. Particularly, it focuses on addressing the balance for women and girls, ethnic minority groups and disabled people. The standard has been developed by the four home country sports councils and UK Sport. They have made it a mandatory condition as part of their funding agreements with national governing bodies and other funded partners that each must demonstrate progress through the four stages (foundation, preliminary, intermediate, advanced). The standard is based around these organisations developing their services.

Reflection Point 2.1

In the context of a sport that you may have played or been involved with, consider what changes could be made to help ensure that the sport is equitable.
Also, consider what organisations could do to provide greater opportunities for all.

The sporting landscape – Scotland

Delivery of sport comes in the form of **sport**scotland which is the national agency, a non-departmental public body responsible through ministers to the Scottish Parliament. **sport**scotland distributes Scottish government and National Lottery resources to develop sport across Scotland. Its mission is:

> *Encourage everyone in Scotland to discover and develop their own sporting experience, helping to increase participation and improve performances in Scottish sport.*

(**sport**scotland 2009b)

In terms of trying to achieve the aims of the national strategy, **sport**scotland has a dual role to play: planning and delivering its contribution, putting in place the building blocks of the strategy, and supporting local authorities, Scottish governing bodies and other partners in planning, developing and sustaining their contributions to the strategy. To effectively contribute to the challenges and building blocks of the national strategy, **sport**scotland produced a corporate strategy for 2009–2011 which has 7 priorities: quality facilities; strong partners; a stronger **sport**scotland; coaching and volunteering; high performance sport; performance development; and school and community (**sport**scotland 2009b).

In Scotland, physical education, physical activity and sport is delivered through the Health and Wellbeing outcomes within Scotland's Curriculum for Excellence Strategy. Support for both sport and physical activity comes from within the Sports Division in the Public Health and Wellbeing Directorate of the Scottish Government (Youth Sport Trust 2009b).

The sporting landscape – Wales

The Sports Council for Wales (SCW) is the Welsh Assembly's main delivery agent for implementing its *Climbing Higher* strategy. It develops and administers the programmes which deliver the Welsh Assembly's policies and translates the strategy into action. It is the national organisation responsible for developing and promoting sport and active lifestyles. It is the main adviser on sporting matters to the Welsh Assembly and is responsible for distributing funds from the National Lottery to sport in Wales (Sports Council Wales 2007a). In Wales, the Physical Education and School Sport (PESS) programme is managed by the Sports Council with a budget from the government's Children, Education, Lifelong Learning and Skills Department. The PESS programme aims to raise standards of the quality of learning and teaching in education across primary and secondary schools. The Sports Council is advised on the direction of the PESS programme by the National Implementation Team made up of PE advisors, teachers and lecturers (Youth Sport Trust 2009b).

The sporting landscape – Northern Ireland

To achieve its objectives the government works through Sport Northern Ireland (SNI), which is the key delivery agency and an executive non-departmental public body. It was established on 31 December 1973 under the provisions of the Recreation and Youth Service (Northern Ireland) Order 1973. Its aim is to create a culture of lifelong enjoyment and success in sport (DCAL/SNI 2007: 5) There is also a strategic priority to maximise on the benefits for Northern Ireland from the 2012 Olympic and Paralympic Games in London (DCAL/SNI 2007: 6). In response to the strategy, Sport Northern Ireland has produced its corporate plan 2008–2011. In it Sport Northern Ireland stresses how keen it is to promote the message that sport and physical recreation is for everyone, regardless of age, gender or ability and that the benefits of an active lifestyle should be fully embraced and enjoyed by all (Sport Northern Ireland 2009c: 5). In Northern Ireland, the governance for physical education and sport sits within two different government departments. PE sits within the Department of Education for Northern Ireland (DENI) but sport sits within the Department of Culture Arts and Leisure where Sport Northern Ireland is the main driver.

Reflection Point 2.2

Can you explain the role that out-of-school or community sports clubs played in your sporting pathway?

Explain the organisation of the club you were involved with. (How many teams were there? Who took training? How often did training occur?)

Now think in terms of how your club was run – how was it financed? Were there new facilities that had just been funded by grants? Were there club roles assigned to various members?

Were there various grassroots initiatives that happened in your club or around the area that helped promote sport? Who was involved in organising these?

sports coach UK

sports coach UK is a charitable organisation and is the agency tasked to lead, develop and support the implementation of a world-leading coaching system in the United Kingdom. sports coach UK is dedicated to guiding the development and implementation of a coaching system, recognised as a world leader, for all coaches at every level in the UK (sports coach UK 2009). It has been the lead agency in the development of the UK Coaching Framework. The vision of the UK Coaching Framework is to create a cohesive, ethical, inclusive and valued coaching system where skilled coaches support children, adults, players and athletes at all stages of their development in sport, and one that will be world-leading by 2016 (sports coach UK 2009). sports coach UK plans to work in close partnership with governing bodies of sport and each of the home country sports councils to enhance the quality and quantity of coaches at all levels of sport, leading to increased and sustained participation and improved performance. This will be underpinned by:

- clear career structures for coaches as part of a professionally regulated vocation, recognising volunteer and part/full-time roles;
- a cohesive and world-leading coaching system.

(sports coach UK 2009)

National governing bodies and their strategic plans

Each NGB has responsibility for managing its sport in terms of administration, coaching and playing from grassroots to international level and, in particular, for stimulating the development of its sport (Houlihan and White 2002). NGBs are expected to deliver and operate at high standards of internal organisation and democracy, ensuring that the voices of all levels and participant groups are heard (Sport England 2008: 2). In Northern Ireland there are over 70 operating NGBs, and they are affiliated to either the UK Governing Body of Sport or the Irish Governing Body of Sport. Sport Northern Ireland implements a policy on the recognition of sporting activities and governing bodies of sport jointly with the Sports Councils in England, Wales and Scotland (Sport Northern Ireland 2009b).

It is worth noting that governing body objectives are often primarily concerned with the survival and prosperity of their sport, with a view to attracting and retaining the most talented players (Reid 2003). In view of the new strategy by DCMS and the change in strategic direction of Sport England, NGBs will find themselves with greater freedom and control of funding. However, they will be challenged to expand participation and provide more quality coaching for more people (DCMS 2008a: 1). It is important that NGBs recognise their changing role and reach and serve all sectors of society (Sport England 2008: 2). In order for DCMS to monitor and evaluate the successes or failures of the NGBs, individual sports are being held accountable to Sport England and have been asked to submit a plan for their sports development. Such plans have existed in a number of guises since the early years of the home country sports council's grant distributing responsibilities. NGBs still had to bid for funding and had their accounts audited, even in the early days. However, Beech and Chadwick (2004: 36) point out that, during the first two decades (1973–1993) of the then Sports Council's grant aiding to NGBs, efficiency and other aspects of corporate governance were not required. This has changed somewhat with what appears to be a far tighter and more stringent process, with NGBs being held accountable, based on key performance indicators, for their public spending.

Houlihan and White (2002: 164) state that 'public funding is available to governing bodies to help them run and develop their sport, but it comes with strings attached'. This issue is still prevalent today as the NGBs have greater accountability when it comes to spending and meeting targets. Sports operating in the additional three home countries of Wales, Scotland and Northern Ireland can access additional funds directly from each individual Sports Council. For example, in Scotland, the Scottish governing bodies work with **sport**scotland to develop a single plan for their sport. On a sport by sport basis **sport**scotland will agree investment and support against the shared objectives of this plan (**sport**scotland 2009).

Reflection Point 2.3

Try and think of yourself as an employee of a particular national governing body. You have been asked for your ideas about how the organisation could help people grow, sustain and excel in their sport.

1   Consider what plans/initiatives you could suggest to enable this to happen.
2   Now think about what the key headings would be in a plan for your sport. A starting point might be your vision for the sport. What else do you think Sport England, **sport**scotland, SportNI, Sports Council Wales would expect to see in your plan?

Central Council of Physical Recreation

In 1935 a physical educationalist by the name of Phyllis Colson had a 'vision' in which:

every youngster had a chance to take part in enjoyable and health-giving physical activity and in which all people and associations worked together, pooling their knowledge, experience and resources, helping each other and tackling their problems by joint effort.

(CCPR 2007)

This vision led to the Central Council of Physical Recreation (CCPR) being established in 1935. The original objectives of the CCPR in 1935 were to:

- encourage as many people as possible to participate in all forms of sport and physical recreation;
- to provide the separate governing bodies of the individual sports with a central organisation that would represent them;
- promote their individual and collective interests;
- to increase public knowledge and awareness of the importance of sport.

According to Houlihan and White (2002: 18) the CCPR by the early 1960s had established itself as the primary advocate for sport. The CCPR organised coaching courses for national governing bodies as far back as 1945 and utilised grants offered by the Ministry for Education for salaries of national coaches to work at national, regional and local levels to train coaches and leaders in sport and recreation (CCPR 2007). Considering this information, it could be argued that these were the forerunners to the sports development profession and that the foundations of the sector lay here.

The assets of the CCPR were eventually transferred to a newly formed Sports Council in 1972, although the CCPR remained as an independent body to represent the views of its members. Today, the CCPR represents a national alliance of bodies of sport and recreation, representing 150,000 clubs across the UK and some 8m regular participants. It provides these organisations with a single, independent voice ensuring that their interests are represented and that they have the skills and capacity to deliver high quality sport and recreation across the country (CCPR 2008).

Learning Activity 2.4

If the role of the CCPR is to represent the views of its members and to lobby other organisations to secure resources for its members (mainly NGBs), who do you think they would target to voice their opinions?

Visit: http://www.ccpr.org.uk/ourcampaigning/ to develop your understanding.

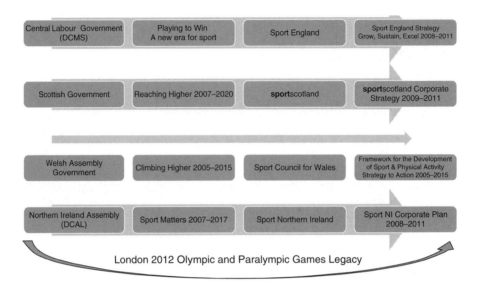

Figure 2.1 UK governments, their current sport strategies, which feed into the key delivery agencies, and their implementation plans

Partnership working

Throughout this chapter many references have been made to partnership working within the UK sporting landscape. Sports organisations work together on target setting, funding, strategic plan delivery and achieving goals.

> *A partnership is a cross-organizational group working together towards common goals which would be extremely difficult, if not impossible, to achieve if tackled alone.*

(Armistead and Pettigrew 2004: 571)

Partnerships require the involvement of at least two agencies with at least some common interests and require a relationship between them that involves some degree of trust (Powell and Glendinning 2002: 3). **sport**scotland (2009) advocates partnership working to help achieve their objectives and their legacy. They stress that what they are planning to achieve could not happen without strong partnerships. Collins (2004) argues 'that in order to make any sort of substantial breakthrough with their targets [sports organisations] need partnerships to replace the single-silo isolated approach seen so often in recent times'. This approach is supported by Sport Northern Ireland (2007) who state that a genuine partnership approach needs to be implemented across the country because no single individual or organisation can deliver the vision for sport on their own. There is a realisation within most sports organisations that they must be prepared to join a growing international movement that promotes 'inter-professional collaboration' (Lawson 2005: 145). The role of partnership working is reinforced to sport agencies that are trying to create opportunities for community development, social meaning levels of competence and personal satisfaction (Sport England 2004a). DCMS in a recent policy document commented on the role of partnership in this quest:

Strong and motivated partnerships, which represent the different groups in a community, emerge from effective local consultation and needs assessment. Solid partnership development offers a better chance of making best use of the funding that is available.

(DCMS 2004: 6)

Partnerships can be the key vehicle that enables the resources of government to be brought to bear on improving health, reducing inequalities and improving services in a co-ordinated and coherent manner (Barnes and Sullivan 2002). In sport, partnership working is evident at several levels to meet several agendas. The school sport co-ordinator programme is an example of the government's attempts to produce 'joined up thinking' between departments – in this case between sport (the Department of Culture, Media and Sport, DCMS) and education (the Department for Education and Skills, DfES), as well as a number of other agencies (Flintoff 2003). The success of this programme rests on the development of partnerships between the different agencies involved in the delivery of youth sport in addition to building partnerships between schools and wider community sports clubs. In the case of the home nations' sports councils working with NGBs to deliver their strategic plans, there would appear to be a number of joint objectives that can be achieved by working together including increasing grassroots participation and working on the 'Sport for All' agenda.

Case Study
The Sporting Chance Project, Cheshire, England

In Cheshire, the county sports partnership developed working relationships with a wide range of partners to facilitate the delivery of several national and regional initiatives across the county. As an organisation they have outlined the important role that partnership working plays in achieving their vision and acknowledged the potential that can be unlocked by working in this way. 'Our aim is to create a "single system" whereby all agencies work together more effectively to widen access, increase participation, create clear pathways and improve levels of performance in sport and physical activity' (Cheshire and Warrington Sport Partnership 2009a). The Sport Cheshire 'Sporting Chance' programme (2002–6) identified and supported young people as volunteers, coaches and leaders in sport. By working closely with the Connexions Service, Sports Network North West (SNNW), voluntary organisations and local community groups, this programme linked young people 13–19 years with sports leadership, coaching and volunteering opportunities. The goal of the programme was to increase the sport and leisure opportunities available to young persons, to develop their personal life-long skills, such as improving self-image and awareness, building confidence, improving communication skills, personal development and citizenship. The programme aimed to go beyond just engaging with disaffected, disadvantaged and excluded young people to actively supporting them and giving them what they needed to be the best that they could be. The model (see Figure 2.2) was developed out of a holistic multi-agency approach (Crabbe 2000: 385), which incorporated many of the elements associated with broader community capacity building models. At its height there were seven programmes running weekly sessions across the county with up to 80 young people taking part. One of the main goals was to increase the opportunities available for young people by working closely in partnership with other agencies such as local education authorities, Connexions, youth services and local authority sport and leisure departments. This partnership approach was relatively uncharted territory for many of the agencies mentioned and particularly working with a sports organisation. 'There were definitely changes in policy and changes in attitudes from many of the agencies who were involved in the project' (Healey 2006). The strengths of the partnership approach were that local forums were used to engage local people in decision making, young people were given the chance to take a leading role in their community and the partnerships were initiated to seize upon funding opportunities. The weaknesses of the partnership working were that more clearly stated objectives were needed, better communication would have helped the partnership to achieve objectives and better understanding and respect for other partners from different sectors was needed to improve collaborative working.

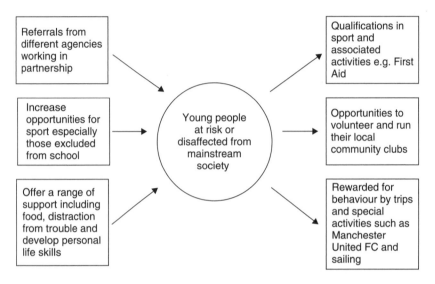

Figure 2.2 A model illustrating the objectives and outcomes of the Sporting Chance Project

Chapter Review

The aim of this chapter was to develop an understanding of the role and objectives of the key agencies that provide strategic direction for sport across the UK. As we approach the London 2012 Olympic Games, sport appears to be gaining momentum and is high up on the political agenda. This chapter has explored the role and priorities of the four home country sports councils and other key sport agencies in the UK and discussed their contribution in relation to the emerging priorities. The role of UK Sport has been considered in relation to London 2012 and an overview of the future funding priorities has been given. This work is underpinned by the national governing bodies of sport and the equity partners that support the implementation of the Equality Standard. The NGBs have seen themselves slightly marginalised towards the early part of this century with sport being used, alongside physical activity, to support wider societal issues. DCMS (2008a: 13) are now suggesting that the NGBs will now find themselves with greater freedom and control of funding, all of which, undoubtedly, supports the government with making London 2012 a successful Olympic Games, of which the UK population can be proud. A picture of these agencies and how they work in partnership should now be emerging and this will be discussed in further chapters, particularly the role of the sports agencies in three key sport settings: school, community and elite.

After reading this chapter and attempting the learning activities you should now be able to answer the following questions:

1   What are the key agencies that support this development and what are their priorities?
2   How do these key agencies work together in order to achieve their shared priorities?
3   What does the future hold for the national governing bodies of sport up until 2013?

Further Reading

For a general overview of the new strategic direction of DCMS:
- DCMS (2008a) *Playing to Win: A New Era for Sport*, London: DCMS.

For an exploration of partnership working in sport:
- Partnerships in sport, in K. Hylton, P. Bramham, D. Jackson and M. Nesti (2001) *Sports Development: Policy, Process and Practice,* 2nd edn. London: Routledge, Chapter 6.

For a better understanding of sport delivery in England, Scotland, Wales and Northern Ireland:
- Sport England (2008) *Grow, Sustain, Excel: Sport England Strategy 2008–2011*. Available www.sportengland.org.
- The Scottish Government (2008) *Reaching Higher*. Available www.scotland.gov.
- Sports Council for Wales (2007) *Climbing Higher*. Available www.sports-council-wales.org.
- Sport Northern Ireland/DCAL(2007) *Sport Matters*. Available www.dcalni.gov.uk.

For a contextual overview of participation issues:
- Rowe, N., Adams, R. and Beasley, N. (2004) Driving up participation in sport: the social context, the trends, the prospects and the challenges, in *Driving Up Participation: The Challenge for Sport*. London: Sport England.

Part Two

Bringing the
vision to life

Chapter 3
School sport

Learning Objectives

This chapter is designed to help you:

- understand the role that schools play in the delivery system of sport and physical activity;
- investigate the provision for sport and physical activity within and beyond the national curriculum which is driven by the Youth Sports Trust;
- explore the challenges faced for those involved in school sport who try to get young people active from an early age.

The context in which this study of school sport takes place is against the backdrop of striving for excellence, particularly in the run up to the London Olympic Games in 2012. In order to have a world class talent development programme which supports excellence, all the important delivery agencies need to have a clear understanding of the role that they play in that process. This chapter will focus on the role of school sport and the importance of a national curriculum for PE and school sport. It will also look at the challenges faced by those on the front line of delivery who are striving to get children and young people active during their time at school so they adopt a lifestyle of lifelong participation in physical activity.

Role of school sport in the delivery system – England

The foundation of any sport development system is school sport. It is the place where so many people get their first experiences of organised physical activity and sport and where the player pathway journey begins. Since the New Labour administration was elected in 1997 there has been a commitment to making 'education its stated top priority' (Bache 2003: 300). While other issues have at times risen to the top of the political agenda, most notably increased funding to the National Health Service (NHS), education has remained the government's top long-term priority (Houlihan and Green 2006: 73). School sport and PE also emerged as a significant cross-departmental vehicle for Labour's broader social policy objectives which were evident in 'A sporting future for all', 'Game Plan' and 'Learning through PE and sport' (Houlihan and Green 2006: 74). Within *Playing to Win: A New Era for Sport*, the DCMS have outlined the role and targets for school sport development and more specifically for the Youth Sports Trust for 2017. These targets include: a world leading system for PE and school sport, the 'five hour offer' for 5–16 year olds, three hours of sport each week for 16–19 year olds and competition and coaching at the heart of school sport system (DCMS 2008a: 4).

> ### PE, school sport and club links (PESSCL) 2002
>
> In 2002, only around 25% of 5–16 year olds took part in at least two hours of high quality PE and sport each week. PESSCL's ambition was to increase this to 75% by 2006 and to 85% by 2008. The 2008 target was met a year early, with 86% doing at least two hours in 2006/07 (DCMS 2008a:10).

> ### School Sport Co-ordinator programme
>
> A national school sports infrastructure was created within the PESSCL Strategy (2002) which built a network of 402 sports colleges and 450 school sport partnerships (Teachernet 2009). The vision was to raise standards of achievement in physical education and sport and build an ethos throughout the school and within the local community. The underlying philosophy of the programme was one of social inclusion. A central premise was the strategic development of networks and partnerships to maximise the quality, quantity and coherence of youth sport and PE opportunities through 'joined up policy thinking' (Flintoff 2003).

> ### Specialist sports colleges
>
> Specialist sports colleges were at the hub of the government's strategy to enhance young people's opportunities to participate in a wide range of activities as well as raising standards in school sport (Teachernet 2009). The aim was that these specialist colleges would have a good understanding of young people and an appreciation of their different motivations and attitudes towards physical activity and sport involvement. A key question for the School Sport Co-ordinator programme was not just what new opportunities would be opened up for young people, but who would be involved in their delivery, and what philosophies they would bring (Flintoff 2003). Physical education is at the heart of their curriculum and the infrastructure of families of schools that received additional funding from the government to come together, share good practice, facilities and other resources to ensure that learning opportunities are improved for all (Teachernet 2009).

Figure 3.1 Summary of key recent developments in school sport

The PE and School Sport for Young People Strategy

The PE and School Sport for Young People Strategy (PESSYP) forms part of a public service agreement to 'deliver a successful Olympic Games and Paralympics Games with sustainable legacy and get more children and young people taking part in high quality PE and sport' (DCMS/DCSF 2008a: 1). It follows on from the PE, School Sport and Club Links Strategy (PESSCL) which was launched in 2002. Central to the strategy is the target that all young people will achieve five hours of activity each week (it is envisaged that this 'five hour offer' will be two hours within the curriculum and three hours outside the curriculum). To achieve the targets set and to illustrate the government's commitment to school sport and creating a world class education system they have pledged £755m of investment from 2008 to 2011(DCMS/DCSF 2008a: 1). This investment will be channelled into the following areas:

- increasing the number of specialist sport colleges;
- to extend the school sport partnership network;
- to invest in facilities, coaching and competition framework;

- establish a network of multi-skill clubs for pupils with a disability;
- extend the work on supporting gifted and talented young people.

(DCMS/DCSF 2008a: 2)

The Youth Sports Trust (YST) has developed a wide range of programmes to deliver high quality PE and sport to all young people regardless of ability. The programmes delivered with partners reflect the objectives of the government in terms of participation, talent ID/competition, leadership/volunteering and international development. There are also a range of programmes focusing on coaching which aim to create a step change in the recruitment, training and deployment of sports coaches working in school sport. It also aims to increase the number of coaching hours delivered through school sport by 675,000 hours per year (Youth Sports Trust 2009c). These objectives correlate to the work of sports coach UK and their aim of creating a coaching framework to enhance the quality of coaching across the sporting landscape. To support the objective of creating sport and physical activity opportunities that are accessible to all, the YST also have a range of programmes which are designed to encourage specific groups to engage in school sport. Training, support and guidance is given to those who are working with young people with a disability or with special educational needs. The National Curriculum for PE includes a detailed statement on inclusion, which instructs schools to modify their study programmes to provide relevant and appropriately challenging work across the spectrum (Youth Sports Trust 2009d). The inclusion agenda is an important area of work for the key sporting agencies across the sporting landscape. The Youth Sports Trust, in partnership with the EFDS, have outlined in their playground to podium framework the interventions needed to support the achievement of the five hour offer for young disabled people, and ensure that those with a higher level of ability are identified and are able to access a talent pathway (Youth Sports Trust 2009e). To support the objective of talent identification and maximising the London 2012 legacy, the YST have a number of programmes specifically designed for young people who are gifted in PE and talented in sport. The YST will work closely in partnership with UK sport within these programmes to guide and provide support for talented young performers in sport, so they can realise both their sporting and academic potential (Youth Sports Trust 2009f).

The YST are uniquely placed as the central co-ordination point to ensure that schools play their part in the development continuum. Key partners that work alongside the YST to meet the targets set within the objectives above include UK Sport, home nation sports councils and national governing bodies of sport. As mentioned in Chapter 2 an essential component of the key sporting agencies across the sporting landscape is partnership working. The school sport infrastructure has been considerably strengthened by the development of the school sport partnership framework. Across the country models of good practice are being implemented as local partners including CSPs, NGBs, clubs, coaches and school partnerships adopt a co-ordinated approach to delivery and planning in achieving the five hour offer.

Case Study
Preston school sports partnership

In 2010, Preston school sports partnership consists of 11 high schools and 68 infant and special schools. There are good structures for PE, sport and physical activity in the city and a number of strong clubs. The SSP works with a range of strategic partners to reduce barriers to young people's access within and beyond the curriculum. The strong, strategic structure in Preston helps to support this partnership working. A key element of this is the sport and physical activity alliance (SPAA) which includes Preston City Council (cultural services and sports development), Lancashire County Council, Lancashire Sport, the University of Central Lancashire, the PCT, the police, the youth service, Age Concern, NGBs, Preston North End FC and the SSP. An important objective of the SSP in the last year has been the school sports coaching programme. This programme focuses on nine sports: basketball, swimming, dance, gymnastics, athletics, rugby union, squash, cycling and tennis. Each sport has its own plan for implementation, funding and delivery. To help fund these projects the SSP has received £21,000 over three years to allow them to contribute as a funding partner to support a number of coaches used across the city in partnership with the local authority. There has been an immediate impact in terms of increasing participation. Coaching is of a higher quality and there is greater cohesion across the partnership which can be attributed to the strength of the local structures and networks. The partnership has also received Sport Unlimited funding to help achieve the five hour offer targets. It is envisaged over the next few years in the lead up to London 2012 the demand for activity and therefore coaches will increase significantly as schools try to increase activity levels from two to five hours. The school sport partnership is in a strong position to support the physical activity targets set in the city and will be an influential partner in the challenge to get more young people physically active by 2012.

www.youthsporttrust.org/coaching

Reflection Point 3.1

Reflect on your experiences of school sport and how your school managed the delivery of sport and physical education. What do you consider to be the most important actions that schools have to take in order that they meet the challenge of delivering a world class system for PE and school sport?

The National Curriculum

In tandem with the production of sport policies has been the increasing state intervention in education policy and the implementation of a National Curriculum (Houlihan and Green 2006: 74). Introduced in 1992, its explanation on how the different subjects should be delivered was generalised. By early 2002 the curriculum had modified to include evasion games, striking games, net games, athletics, dance, outward bound and swimming. The new National Curriculum for England was first published by QCA in 2007 and came into force in schools in September 2008.

The importance of physical education is illustrated through the new PE syllabus which stresses the value, in today's society, of the introduction of a healthy lifestyle and the adoption of an active lifestyle during and after leaving school. This variation in approach has given students greater opportunity and choice in the activities they participate in and study.

Physical education develops pupils' physical competence and confidence and their ability to use these to perform in a range of activities. It promotes physical skilfulness, physical development and knowledge of the body in action. Physical education provides opportunities for pupils to be creative, competitive and to face up to different challenges as individuals as individuals and in groups and teams. It promotes attitudes towards active and healthy lifestyles and informs them about making choices for a lifelong involvement in physical activity (Qualifications and Curriculum Authority 2009).

Learning Activity 3.1

Based on your experiences of PE and school sport within and beyond the national curriculum design a term of activities for Key Stage 4 pupils. The curriculum should be challenging, enjoyable and meet the objectives outlined above.

Role of school sport in the delivery system – Scotland

sportscotland was allocated £12m per year between 2004 and 2007 to develop the Active Schools network; this was extended to 2008 and continues to feature in the latest **sport**scotland corporate strategy 2009–11 (**sport**scotland 2009c). The fundamental aim was to offer all children the opportunities and motivation to adopt active, healthy lifestyles now and into adulthood (**sport**scotland 2009c). By the end of year three 2,500 schools were involved and network staff reached 680. Over 60 different activities were offered through Active Schools.

Within **sport**scotland's latest corporate strategy 2009–11, school and community sport is one of the seven priorities with objectives to:

- continue to develop Active Schools and improve pathways between schools and community sport;
- build and support the capacity of Scotland's network of sports clubs and support other community organisations to deliver quality and accessible sporting opportunities for everyone in our communities.

(**sport**scotland 2009a: 11)

sportscotland has recognised that Active Schools is a vehicle in which to 'target' the 'hard to reach' groups and try to engage them. A key role of the Active School co-ordinators is to encourage girls, people with a disabilities, ethnic minorities, people from areas of socio-economic disadvantage and young people not currently involved in any physical activity to become more active.

Schools in Scotland have been planning throughout 2009–10 for implementation of the new Curriculum for Excellence in 2010–11. The aim of the new curriculum is to provide relevant, inspiring, engaging education for every child and young person in Scotland (Learning and Teaching Scotland 2009a) PE, physical activity and sport are central to the Health and Wellbeing section of the new curriculum. 'It enables learners to develop the concepts and skills necessary for participation in a wide range of physical activity, sport, dance and outdoor learning, and enhances their physical wellbeing in preparation for leading a fulfilling, active and healthy lifestyle' (Learning and Teaching Scotland 2009b).

Role of school sport in the delivery system – Wales

The Sports Council for Wales manages the PE and School Sport (PESS) project which was set up in 2000. The aim of the project was to raise standards in physical education by ensuring that schools work towards a number of objectives including:

- managing PE within curriculum;
- set challenging targets;
- develop understanding of health and fitness;
- establishing CPD programmes for teachers;
- extend after school opportunities.

(Sports Council Wales 2007b)

The PE and School Sport partnership involves a co-ordinated approach to delivery from the local authorities, project line managers, PE School Sport Co-ordinators and Higher Education Institutes. All of these agencies work together to ensure the programme is rolled out successfully across Wales. Within the PESS programme, there are number of curriculum areas which have been deemed to need extra resources and attention which include: gymnastics, health and fitness, dance, ICT in PE, inclusion and adventurous activities. For more information, refer to the Sport Council Wales website.

Central to the delivery of PE and school sport in Wales is the 5 × 60 programme. The Welsh Assembly has invested £7.6m (£600k in 2006–7, £3m in 2007–8 and £4m in 2008–9) in the programme. The programme aims to increase the number of secondary age pupils taking part in sport or physical activity for 60 minutes, at least five times a week. The Sports Council Wales (2007c) reports that only 24 per cent of secondary age pupils take part in 5 × 60 minutes of sport and physical activity per week. By targeting children and young people who do not take part in sport or physical activity they hope to increase that to 90 per cent by 2020 in line with Climbing Higher. They want young people to leave school with the necessary skills to continue to enjoy sport throughout their life.

The programme is managed locally by local authority 5 × 60 officers, who are based in designated schools. They work with local stakeholders to create opportunities that meet the needs and choices of the pupils. Officers involve parents, students, and local coaches and sports club personnel in developing activities. The 5 × 60 programme complements existing sport and PE provision in schools by offering a range of activities to all children regardless of ability. A key principle is that the pupils chose the activities themselves. Activities include:

- competitive sport;
- informal recreational activity (such as dance, aerobics, etc.);
- coached activities; and
- outdoor activities.

(Sports Council Wales 2007c)

Role of school sport in the delivery system – Northern Ireland

Northern Ireland has a strong tradition of school sport and there is the belief that schools are the critical locations for introducing and developing sport, providing an extension of the compulsory curriculum in physical education and acting as a gateway to sport outside school (Sport Northern Ireland 2002: 4). As in the rest of the UK, schools in Northern Ireland are required to provide young people with at least two hours of quality PE per week and there is a demand for school club links to be developed and sustained (Sport Northern Ireland 2002: 7).

Sport Northern Ireland is the lead agency for developing sport in Northern Ireland, including school sport. It launched in 2009 an initiative, Activ8, to encourage Key Stage 2 pupils to take part in 60 minutes of physical activity per day, before, during and after school. The initiative was a partnership with the local education authorities (education and library boards) and the health promotion agency. Teachers can register their primary schools to take part and parents are also encouraged to take part in family activities in their local community. The project is based on eight steps to getting active and healthy which are: move your body; be part of a team; create your own game; involve your family; eat well; go outdoors; be a leader; and measure your success. This school sport initiative was awarded the London 2012 Inspire Mark and forms part of the programme of utilising the Olympic and Paralympics Games to promote a healthy and active lifestyle. For more information visit the Sport Northern Ireland website.

National Council for School Sport

This is an umbrella body for national school sports associations and its primary focus is on competition within the school sport framework. The main outputs have been the development of a national competition framework and the UK School Games in partnership with the Youth Sports Trust. The UK Games is a multi-sport event for the UK elite young athletes at school. The event comprises four days of competition in ten sports. It is an integrated programme with disability events in athletics, swimming and table tennis, which means that in 2009 there were over 1,500 athletes competing.

The national competition framework was launched in 2005 in order to transform the content and structure of competitive opportunities for young athletes. The aim was to develop single competitive frameworks for each sport that includes competitions in schools and clubs. To support the development of the framework, competition managers work with NGBs, national school associations and county sport partnerships to increase the number of young people engaged in regular competition. The development of the national competition framework supports the overall objectives of the government in trying to identify and nurture talent from the playground to the podium. School sport plays a pivotal role in the sporting landscape in getting young people started on the player pathway and is it essential that if targets are to be met that all the key delivery agencies across the sporting landscape work in partnership to embed a healthy and active culture across the UK. The other key partners and agencies in the sporting landscape will be discussed in Chapters 4 and 5.

Challenges faced for those involved in school sport who try to get young people active

In their recent strategy, *Playing to Win: A New Era for Sport*, the DCMS outlined their objective: extending the five hour offer to 5–16 year olds and three hours to 16–19 year olds (DCMS 2008a: 10). They also highlighted their concerns generally for PE and Sport for Young People:

- Are schools providing children with a high quality introduction to sport?
- Are all children getting the chance to try a wide range of sports?
- Are we too reliant on football?
- Are there enough coaches in enough sports?
- Are young people of all abilities coached and encouraged?
- Does the competition structure work?

(DCMS 2008a: 7)

The challenges to get young people active from an early age are complex and varied. On the one hand young people continue to appear to have strong beliefs in the value of activity – at least at a basic level (Sport England 2005: 30). The trends in PE, sport and physical activity among youth reflect a broadening and diversification of participation (Green et al. 2005: 30) and many young people enjoy up to five hours of physical activity per week. On the other hand with childhood obesity levels doubling in the last 10 years and recent figures pointing to 24 per cent of boys and 26 per cent of girls aged 11–15 in England classed as obese and 1 in 3 young people in Northern Ireland overweight or obese (Department of Health, Social Services and Public Safety and Dept of Education 2005: 6) there is a huge challenge for providers to overcome the 'health time bomb' that awaits (BBC 2006). It is so important to get young people active from an early age because as Roberts (2006: 157) commented 'The best predictor of any individual's future uses of leisure is that same person's past behaviour'. Therefore the challenge is to change the inactive culture and build upon the positive participation trends because young people's early experiences are likely to have profound implications for their subsequent patterns of participation in sport and physical activity generally (Green et al. 2005: 32).

The Youth Sports Trust (2009a) outlined what it sees as their challenges in the near future when driving forward with the challenge of the five hour offer. They highlight the need for teacher training particularly for new teachers so they are equipped to deliver the new curriculum. They also identify the need for a commitment from head teachers to put PE at the heart of the curriculum. They call for NGBs and school sport associations to make tough decisions in order to transform competitive systems in the school network system. They outline the need for improved facilities, transport and the allocation of resources. In the wider community, and continuing to improve school club links, they also stress the need for more junior clubs, more quality coaches and more opportunities for new and different types of people to deliver sport to young people at a local level (Youth Sports Trust 2009a).

Reflection Point 3.2

Think back to your experiences of PE and school sport and consider the following:

How would you describe your experiences in terms of the choices of activities you participated in within the curriculum?
How did the opportunity and choices you made at school influence and shape your player pathway?
How would you describe the opportunities created at your school with the outside community (school-club links)?
How would you describe your school's ability to identify and develop talent?

Chapter Review

The aim of this chapter was to develop an understanding of the role that schools play in the delivery system across the UK. With education remaining one of the government's top long-term priorities (Houlihan and Green 2006: 73) and continuing to be a significant cross-departmental vehicle for Labour's broader social policy objectives it is not surprising that schools have received heavy investment in recent years. It is important to understand that the foundation of any sport development system is school sport. It is the place where so many people get their first experiences of organised physical activity and sport and where the player pathway journey begins. Therefore it is also important to reflect on past experiences to gain a better understanding of current participation behaviour because early experiences are likely to have profound implications for their subsequent patterns of participation in sport and physical activity generally (Green et al. 2005: 32). The Youth Sports Trust is at the forefront of driving forward the agenda for improving the quality and quantity of PE and school sport within and beyond the curriculum. The challenge for them and all involved in the school sport partnerships is to achieve the targets set for the five hour offer. These challenges are particularly relevant in the current context of the build up to London 2012 and the uphill struggle of trying to combat the rising levels of childhood obesity.

After reading this chapter and attempting the learning activities you should now be able to answer the following questions:

1   What targets have the DCMS outlined in their new strategy for the Youth Sports Trust?
2   What is the 'five hour offer'?
3   How do school sport partnerships work?
4   What school sport programmes operate in Scotland, Wales and Northern Ireland?

Further Reading

For school sport and government policy:

- Houlihan, B. and Green, M. (2006) The changing status of school sport and physical education: explaining policy change. *Sport, Education and Society,* 11 (1): 73–92.

For a review of the school sport co-ordinator programme:

- Flintoff, A. (2003) The school sport co-ordinator programme: changing the role of the physical education teacher? *Sport, Education and Society,* 8 (2): 231–250.

For a better understanding of young people's participation in physical education:

- Green, K., Smith, A. and Roberts, K. (2005) Young people and lifelong participation in sport and physical activity: a sociological perspective on contemporary physical education programmes in England and Wales. *Leisure Studies,* 24 (1): 27–43.

Chapter 4
Community sport

Learning Objectives

This chapter is designed to help you:

- consider the meaning of community sport;
- understand the impact that sport can have within local communities;
- develop an understanding about how community sport has developed and is delivered in the UK;
- raise awareness of specific community sports development initiatives at national and local level.

As discussed in Chapters 1 and 2, sport in the UK is supported by a wide range of national agencies. Some have a specific remit or a responsibility to develop sport within communities across the UK. Community sport in the UK is also supported by a host of local sporting organisations and these will be considered in this chapter. At a national level community sport in the UK is led by the home country sports councils and national government bodies of sport. They work in partnership with a variety of organisations at a regional, county and local level. The purpose of this chapter is to introduce you to some of the work/initiatives that are being delivered by these agencies and to consider the impact that they are having within local communities.

What is community sport?

There are various definitions of what constitutes a community. There are also many attempts to define sport and what it means. A community can be drawn from people residing in a specific geographical area; it can be a means to define a group of people with shared possessions or interest. With the advent of accessible transport, communities have developed and become much more global. Similarly, sport has been defined in many forms and has evolved over a long period of time. It could even be argued that sport is one of the main benefactors of this global community of which we all form a part. So what does the term community sport mean to you? Try the exercise on the next page before reading the next section.

Learning Activity 4.1

Reflect upon your experiences of participating in sport outside school or college. Write down a list which identifies the following:

1   When did you take part in these activities during your sporting experience? Consider what age you were and also what time of day these activities took place.

2   Where did you participate in the activities?

3   Did you take part at a local club, leisure centre or another venue/facility?

4   Who delivered the sessions that you participated in?

5   Was it a professional paid person, a local volunteer or maybe somebody's parent?

The previous exercise is useful just to get you thinking about the settings and activities that begin to make up the meaning of community sport. Community sport can be interpreted very differently by people based upon their own experiences and perceptions. Although many organisations claim to work in the area there does not appear to be an agreed definition. However, the meaning can be attributed to any sporting activities that do not take place during somebody's school/college/work time or within a performance or elite setting.

Community sport for the purpose of this book is being considered in relation to grassroots sport. This is based upon the key work areas that sporting organisations focus upon under their community sport headings. Community sport although focusing on grassroots sport is not mutually exclusive to young people. It is concerned with people of all ages, abilities and backgrounds who have a shared passion to play and participate in sport. It is supported by a variety of agencies, whether it is a government department like the Department for Culture, Media and Sport, a health agency such as a local Primary Care Trust, a sports governing body such as UK Athletics or more locally a secondary school or local community sports club. Their roles within developing sport and their objectives may well be different but somewhere amongst their priorities will be a common purpose, to encourage people to be active and to participate in sport.

Also, for the purpose of this chapter the concept of community sport will be viewed as a term that supports both the development of people wishing to take part in sport for the enjoyment or perceived health benefits, and as a concept that can impact on wider social imperatives, such as community safety and education.

The traditional sports development continuum model

Under the traditional sports development continuum model (Casey, 1988, cited in Houlihan and White, 2002: 41) the considerations above would be referred to as the foundation and participation stages.

Figure 4.1 The traditional sports development continuum

The sports development continuum, otherwise known as the performance pyramid, offers a basic overview about how a person can progress through sport and how organisations prioritise their strategies and resources into distinct areas of sports development.

The **Foundation** level refers to the development of basic skills and movement. It is widely accepted that this will occur during the school years but this may not be the case for those new to sport or a particular sport in later years. The **Participation** level identifies those people taking part in sport on a regular basis. The primary motivation may vary from socialising to improving health and well-being. In a school setting it might refer to those playing for school teams or attending after school clubs. The **Performance** level relates to those playing competitively and attempting to improve their skills. Finally, the **Excellence** level relates to elite performers and generally means those competing or performing at a high level in sport with some form of monetary gain or elite award such as an Olympic medal.

Learning Activity 4.2

Think again about your past sporting experiences and any sport that you participate in at present. Where would you categorise these experiences on the continuum and why?

The evolution of community sport programmes

Community sport and the way in which it has been developed has evolved over the years. This next section will explore this development in England over the last 30 years. It is not an in-depth evaluation but simply acts as a way to highlight some key milestones. You will be signposted to further reading at the end of the chapter to develop further your understanding about the historical context across the UK. As discussed in Chapter 1, in 2008 Sport England released its new strategy in response to *Playing to Win* from the DCMS. *Playing to Win* provided Sport England with a renewed focus, not a complete change in direction, but certainly a shift in the prioritisation of their resources. This was a shift from previous Sport England strategy which saw sport being heavily utilised as a tool to contribute towards social change. However, such shifts have occurred many times throughout recent history and are likely to continue in future years. At a local level much of this policy and the strategy from the home country sports councils is delivered by local voluntary sports clubs and local authority sports development teams. Both have evolved significantly in recent times and are key stakeholders within the delivering of national policy at a local level. The voluntary sports clubs and local authority sports development units co-exist and work in partnership to provide sporting opportunities across communities.

It is difficult to highlight a specific date or period that can be attributed to being solely responsible for the concept of community sports development, and in particular the emergence of local authority sports development teams. What is without doubt, though, is that a number of key milestones both periodically and conceptually have contributed to developing the concept as we know it today. Much of this has been covered in Chapter 2 with local implementation being heavily influenced by national policy and strategy. We will explore a few of the programmes that have emerged as a result of such policy and strategy next in this chapter.

Government intervention

The Sports Council was established in 1972 to promote sport and physical activity. The status of the Sports Council was strengthened by the 1975 Government White Paper *Sport and Recreation*. This alluded to sport as being a vital component of the physical and mental well-being of the population and that sport was a useful tool to reduce boredom and urban frustration. The paper legitimised the role of sport as part of the fabric of the welfare state and identified specific target groups who could benefit from sport. This resulted in greater investment into sport, particularly aimed at the local community.

This was supported by Lord Scarman who, reporting on the Brixton riots in the early 1980s (see Carrington and Leaman 1982: 10), suggested that:

in order to secure social stability there will be a long term need to provide useful, gainful employment and suitable educational, recreational and leisure opportunities for young people, especially in the inner city.

In 1982 the Action Sport project was established in the aftermath of such riots at Brixton and in the West Midlands and Liverpool. The programme was funded directly by central government and the initiative was launched via a partnership between the Sports Council and Manpower Services. The priorities for the Manpower Services Commission would not have been to develop highly skilled sports development workers, but rather to ensure adequate numbers were employed to deliver the initiative and to ensure that the long-term unemployed had opportunities to seek meaningful employment.

The programme was launched initially across London, and the West Midlands with £3m being invested into the appointment of 90 'community sports leaders', who wherever possible would be recruited from the unemployed and have a knowledge of and a profile within the local area. Carrington and Leaman (1982: 11) describe the role of these people as 'to organise and develop sports and recreational activities to benefit people living in inner cities, particularly those with large multi-racial communities'.

The title sports development officer at this stage had not yet been widely accepted, with the majority of development workers still operating in the more traditional surroundings of national government bodies of sport. According to Houlihan and White (2002), by 1987 there were 300 sports leaders employed by local government. Although they were employed by the local authorities their salaries were still covered by the Sports Council and this would be an issue that would restrict the development of the profession for some years. The sector at this stage was immature and, as highlighted by Rigg (1986), the main thrust of the early Action Sport work was the setting up of sports sessions aimed at specific target groups. Although the work was seen as positive, it did not go so far as to create links within the community.

Rigg (1986) also suggested in a review of the programme that there needed to be a central training resource for this type of scheme, and that although local authorities had aimed to provide local training, there is a compelling case for coordination and investment in training at a national level. Such issues still exist today in the sector and, although work is being developed to professionalise coaching through the UK Coaching Framework, it is difficult see where this direction is coming from within the sports development sector.

After the introduction of Action Sport, local authorities began to realise the value of sport to their wider social policies. Many of the Action Sport workers had opportunities to gain employment beyond the fixed-term contracts on which they had initially been employed, through additional 'top-up' grants from the English Sports Council. Hylton et al. (2001) highlight the mid-1980s as the beginning of 'sports development' as many understand it today. They suggest that this period was the first time that local authority leisure budgets were allocated to this area of work. However, these budgets provided only a proportion of the funding for the sports development workers and they were certainly not common practice across all local authorities.

A change in government

In 1997 Tony Blair and the Labour Party defeated the Conservative government and brought to office a period of social reform. By 1998 the Labour government had established 18 policy action teams (PATs) to investigate the disparity of opportunities in poorer neighbourhoods. Each PAT was made up from a wide range of stakeholders, including government officials, industry experts and people from academia. The teams were born from the recommendations of the Social Exclusion Unit's (1998) strategy for neighbourhood renewal called *Bringing Britain Together*. The report recognised the inequality of opportunities for some people living in the most deprived neighbourhoods across the United Kingdom.

The Policy Action Team (PAT) 10 was required to consider how to maximise government's arts, sports and leisure spend in these poorer areas. Chris Smith (1998: 2) who was the then Secretary of State for Culture, Media and Sport stated that:

This report shows that art and sport can not only make a valuable contribution to delivering key outcomes of lower long-term unemployment, less crime, better health and better qualifications, but can also help to develop the individual pride, community spirit and capacity for responsibility that enable communities to run regeneration programmes themselves.

Sport Action Zones

As a direct result of the findings from PAT 10, Sport Action Zones were established. In 2000 Sport England announced £750m of investment over 10 years in the development of Sport Action Zones (SAZ).

The first 12 areas designated by Sport England as Sport Action Zones were:

- Birmingham
- Bradford
- Cornwall and the Isles of Scilly
- East Manchester
- Leicester
- Liverpool
- London South Central
- Luton
- North Derbyshire and North Nottinghamshire Coalfields Area
- South Yorkshire Coalfields Area
- Wear Valley
- West Cumbria – the Districts of Barrow, Copeland and Allerdale

The intention in these areas of poverty was to increase low levels of participation in sport and to utilise sport to contribute towards improving health and social well-being. A key element of the work in these areas was to ensure programmes were delivered based upon the needs of local communities through consultation and not dictated by policy.

Learning Activity 4.3

You are employed as a Community Sports Development Worker and have some funding to develop a local sports project/initiative. The project has to be developed based upon the needs of local people.

1   What sort of information would you require?
2   Who would you ask?
3   What techniques would you employ to ensure that your programme met the needs of local people?

In 2006 Sport England commissioned consultants Ipsos MORI to conduct an evaluation of the work within Barrow-in-Furness, Liverpool, Bradford and Luton SAZ areas. Two of the four areas (Liverpool and Barrow) demonstrated significant increases in participation; however, the two other Zones (Bradford and Luton) did not see the levels of increase across the whole population.

The research did identify some success factors that had led to increases in participation in sport. Amongst these were:

- appointment of a highly motivated charismatic leader who can quickly establish local credibility and respect;
- building strong partnerships – to include sport and non-sport – the more partnerships and the more diverse the partnerships the better; have 'a foot in both camps' by working closely with people from a number of different organisations;
- investment in facilities to provide the opportunities for participation but focus on people as the keys to success; take a whole environment approach to include parks and informal open spaces.

This report can be viewed at the following link:
www.sportengland.org/research/idoc.ashx?docid=8aa3e9b4-3edb-48f5-ae06-3f00d50db79a&version=1

The changes kept coming

Numerous sports programmes, sporting initiatives and new sporting bodies were launched and developed at both a national and local level in order to support the development of local communities after Labour came into power. These included schemes such as Champion Coaching, Coaching for Teachers, the TOPs programmes and the Active Programmes. Whilst it is not intended to review each in turn throughout this chapter, we will consider how the role of the Community Sports Development Worker has changed. The role of the original Action Sport workers, which was to deliver coaching/sporting sessions, had evolved into that of a deliverer and a facilitator. It is generally more accepted that the role of community sport development workers is to add capacity within communities and to develop a strategic approach in a particular geographical area. This is not without problems, with programme delivery reliant on a predominantly volunteer workforce.

County Sports Partnerships

County Sports Partnerships were established in 2000, initially to deliver the now-defunct Sport England programme Active Sports. They continue to operate and provide strategic direction at a county level, working in partnership with local authorities, national governing bodies and other non-sporting partners. There are 50 in operation across the country. Their role, too, has been changing because of reliance upon government funding. Core funding has been reprioritised in line with Sport England priorities and they are now expected to form strategic alliances with national governing bodies and to continue to support local authority sports development. In many cases, they take a lead in workforce development across a particular county. This would include the development of volunteers and coaches.

Coaching Task Force

In 2002 the Coaching Task Force (CTF) was established in order to review coaching in the country and as a result the Community Sports Coaching Scheme was initiated. This has seen the appointment of nearly 3,000 paid coaches across the country in either a part-time of full-time capacity. This represented a major shift in the culture of working in coaching and community sports development. For the first time, community coaching could be viewed as a profession and there was a substantial workforce 'on the ground'. SkillsActive (2006), in the Sport and Active Leisure Skills and Productivity Alliance (SALSPA) action plan, suggest that this area of work will experience significant increases in employment opportunities over the next 10 years. However, as with other programmes, the scheme appears no longer to be gaining support and local authorities and other employing bodies are expected to source other monies to continue such posts. This would appear to be in contrast with the recommendations in PAT 10 which indicated the need to reduce the reliance on parachute solutions. Community sports development still suffers from a lack of any real identity and an absence of any long-term, continued support. The analogy of a winning sporting team can be used; it is very rare that a team experiences long-term success with a constant change in players, coaches and other personnel.

Sports Development Officers

Sports Development Officers are employed within local authorities, national governing bodies, county sport partnerships and sports clubs. Others do the work of an SDO but are perhaps employed under different job titles: Community Development Officer, Activity Officers, and so on. The sector has grown from the original 90 Action Sports Leaders to a sector that now boasts 36,500 people employed in the sport and recreation sector (SkillsActive 2006), 7 per cent of these working as SDOs. This equates to approximately 2,555 people employed as a Sports Development or Community Development Officer.

Although the role of the original Action Sport Leader appears to have evolved into modern day SDOs it would seem that the role of the activity leader or coach is increasingly becoming more important. SkillsActive (2006), in the North West Sector Skills Agreement, forecasts that the occupations most likely to grow in the sector over the next three years will be coaching and instructing. Sport England North East has recently awarded £1.3m to fund coaching. The funding will create 69 new coaching posts, in partnership with the County Sports Partnerships in the region (Leisure Opportunities 2007). Nationally Sport England has injected £38.3m into funding improved sports clubs and training 654 coaches between 2007 and 2010 in order to get more people active (Sports Management 2007). This recent investment into the coaching field could suggest that in time the role of the Action Sport Leader may turn full circle.

The delivery system

With a wide range of stakeholders, evolving programmes and initiatives it is important that local organisations have a means to be proactive. Local organisations need to be able to respond to their local communities and to the changes in government policy and strategy. In the *Review of National Sport, Effort and Resources* (2005), Lord Carter of Coles identified that with so many interested parties, it is vital to develop a system for the delivery of sport in England which is simple, systematic and joined up, overcoming the inefficiencies identified in Game Plan (Sport England 2006a: 4). The justification of a sporting delivery system was furthermore strengthened with the findings from the National Audit Office (2006) report *Delivering Efficiently: Strengthening the links in Public Service Delivery Chains*. The findings suggested that delivery chains were needed in order to join up central and national government priorities and those of the private and third (voluntary) sectors. The delivery system was sport's attempt to do this.

The delivery system was intended to join up the work of national, regional and local partners. At the heart of the system on a regional level would be the Regional Sports Boards. These Boards have now been dissolved by Sport England and it is unclear what the future holds for the delivery system in its current guise. What is certain though, is that many local organisations have united to form Community Sports Networks (CSNs), otherwise known as Sport and Physical Activity Alliances (SPAAs). These partnerships are intended to serve the organisations, people taking part and those delivering opportunities (coaches and volunteers) in a city or borough. The work of the Preston SPAA is profiled as a case study later in this chapter.

Learning Activity 4.4

Consider the challenges faced by individuals who have a remit to increase participation levels and develop sport in communities.

1   How do you think they go about developing programmes and initiatives that will encourage people to play more sport?

2   We have already considered consultation, but what other steps would you need to take once you have established the views and wishes of a local community in order to increase participation levels. How can you be certain if your programme is making a difference?

Here follows a series of case studies which demonstrate how particular organisations have attempted to develop such programmes to meet the needs of their local communities.

Case Study
Preston Sports Development Team

Preston is located in Lancashire, in the North West region of England. It was awarded city status by the Queen in April 2002, as part of her Golden Jubilee celebrations. The city has a population of just over 129,000 residents made up of 22 wards (Office for National Statistics, 2009a). Like many other cities or towns, Preston has its share of crime, anti-social behaviour and social issues. Preston is home to a multi-cultural society.

In the mid-1990s the then Borough Council of Preston developed a Sports Development Unit to work across its local communities. This Unit has evolved into a team of 31 staff, a mix of full time and part time. Only four of the staff are employed on a permanent basis, funded directly by the city council. The remaining members of staff are employed on fixed term contracts, part funded by external agencies. The remit of the development team has evolved over the years, in line with local, regional and national policy directives. For example, in 2000 the council appointed an Active Communities Officer, an Active Schools Officer, and an Active Sports Officer. This was in line with the now-defunct Sport England programmes previously mentioned in this chapter. At present the team is led by a Sports Development Manager along with three Senior Sports Development Officers. One is responsible for clubs/schools and sport, the second overseeing health and physical activity, and the third facilities. The Senior Sports Development Officer for Clubs, Schools and Sport manages a number of staff including an Early Years and Skills Coach, the Club Development Officer, and the Volunteer Support Co-ordinator.

The team has been instrumental in providing support to a wide range of partners in the city and developing specific projects and interventions that engage people in sport. An example of this is the Streetwise Soccer Initiative launched in 2005. Within Preston sport has become a crucial ingredient in the fight against crime. This particular scheme relies upon a strong partnership approach between the city council and other partners such as the police, Lancashire Sport, Positive Futures, Preston Group Intervention Panel, Preston Youth Offending Team, Preston Tenants Umbrella group. The programme is designed to use football as a means to engage young people in Preston between the ages of 10 and 16 years of age. Twenty-three sites across the city now receive holiday football coaching from the army of streetwise volunteers, with over 740 attending across all programmes. A league has been developed to offer a sustainable solution, with many players taking part on a competitive basis for the remainder of the year. During the holiday programmes, there has been evidence from the Preston Streetwise Analysis Report, 2005, that the amount of youth nuisance in particular hotspots has reduced, in some cases up to 31 per cent. Stephen Daley, Sports Development Manager for Preston City Council, says that

> The philosophy of Sports Development is to create a framework in which to increase and sustain lifelong participation in physical activity and sport, to promote the continuous improvement in the delivery of sporting opportunities and services at a local level for all the community. Also to identify gaps in provision for those most at risk of social exclusion and inequalities.
>
> (Personal communication)

The Sport and Physical Activity Alliance

In addition to Streetwise Soccer the team have supported the inception and development of the Preston Sports and Physical Activity Alliance (SPAA). The SPAA was established in 2006 in line with Sport England's new delivery system, as mentioned previously in this chapter. The SPAA consists of representatives from the council, the Central Lancashire Primary Care Trust, the University of Central Lancashire, local colleges and schools, the Lancashire Constabulary, Preston Sports Forum and representatives from the private sector. The SPAA was successful in securing £820,965 worth of investment: £310,387 was offered by Sport England, partnership funding of £352,524 was secured and in-kind commitment from the partners amounted to £158,054. The monies are be utilised to support the SPAA in contributing to the targets laid down in the Framework for Sport (2004). The intention in 2004 was to ensure that 50 per cent of the adult population is active (3 × 30) by 2020. This equates to an annual increase in Preston of 1,054 new participants per year. The SPAA has developed six projects based upon consultation with a wide range of stakeholders in order to contribute towards this increase, with five of the projects being led by the Sports Development Team. Pathways to Sport is an initiative that will aim to offer a variety of sport and physical activity opportunities to those members of the community who are inactive or those who might like to participate in physical activity but find traditional settings such as leisure centres a barrier.

These types of interventions support several of the seven key objectives in the city's Corporate Plan for 2009–12. Priorities in the Corporate Plan for Preston include, connecting better with Preston's communities, helping to make Preston a much safer place, and removal of multiple deprivation and social disadvantages. The sports development team have to contribute heavily towards achieving the outcomes of this local plan, along with satisfying the national priorities that securing funding from Sport England brings. A commonly used term in local government is the 'Golden Thread'. This implies the joining up of local services, with local priorities, regional and national policy. The work of the sports development teams is therefore, wide and varied, challenging and exciting.

The Preston Sports Forum

In addition to supporting the SPAA, Preston City Council provides financial support and expert advice to the Preston Sports Forum. PSF is a voluntary organisation and is represented from a variety of local Preston community sports clubs and other voluntary organisations that have an interest in sport. Members include Preston Harriers Swimming Club, etc. They see their role as being the representatives of the voluntary sports sector in Preston and to liaise closely with organisations like Preston city council to make a difference in their local communities. PSF receives an annual leisure grant from the city council of approximately £10,000. They distribute these funds to individuals and community organisations that are interested and best placed to develop sporting opportunities. Individual awards are given to talented performers and group awards to organisations that can increase sports participation in Preston in line with the aims and objectives of the Sports Development Team and the SPAA.

Case Study
Hindley St Peter's Pavilion Ltd
Background

Hindley is located in Wigan, Greater Manchester which has a population of approximately 300,000 (Office for National Statistics, 2009b) and the borough is based around two main towns (Wigan and Leigh) and consists of a number of smaller towns including Hindley.

Wigan is ranked as the sixty-seventh most deprived local authority in England. Twenty-nine of Wigan's 200 neighbourhoods fall within the 10 per cent most deprived neighbourhoods in England.

Hindley St Peter's Pavilion Limited was formed in 2005, the founder members being Hindley St Peter's Church, Hindley St Peter's Cricket Club, Hindley ARLFC, St Peter's Boys' Brigade and St Peter's Girl Guides. The group was formed to attempt to develop a new community and sports facility. Each of the partners was already established in their own right. The existing cricket club pavilion was built in 1965 and extended in 1998. The pavilion boasted two changing rooms and a bar area. The uniformed groups that helped form Hindley St Peter's Pavilion Ltd did not have their own facilities and had to utilise St Peter's Primary School for their activities. This resulted in clashes with school events and a lack of space. The rugby club used local authority pitches behind the cricket pavilion but had no changing accommodation. This resulted in some teams having to change in local public houses.

The club was the first cricket club in Wigan to obtain Clubmark in 2003. The rugby league club followed in 2005. Clubmark is an accreditation scheme for clubs with junior sections. Clubmark awards are based around a set of core criteria. Clubs have to adopt minimum operating standards in order to achieve them. The accreditation scheme was introduced by Sport England in 2002. It is also intended to recognise the better clubs that provide a friendly and safe environment for young people to play sport.

Learning Activity 4.5

1 What criteria do you think the clubs would need to achieve in order to be Clubmark accredited? First, they need to have a Child Protection Policy.
2 What are the benefits for the club in obtaining accreditation?
3 What are the benefits for young people/parents?

More information about Clubmark can be obtained from the following website: http://www.clubmark.org.uk/

Project description

The aim of the partnership was to procure funding to develop a brand new pavilion, which would include changing rooms and a community hall for the local community. The club has worked closely with their respective NGBs. Both the Rugby Football League and the English Cricket Board have provided support and funding to develop the project.

The prime objective of St Peter's Pavilion is to foster and promote community development by providing opportunities for recreation, leisure, social interaction and sport for the local and wider community that can be undertaken in a safe and non-threatening environment irrespective of age, ability, sex, race or religion (Hindley St Peters Pavilion Limited, 2005).

The new pavilion was to consist of four changing rooms for cricket and rugby, match officials' changing, a first aid room, treatment room and a large community space. They also planned to develop a multi-use games area, a children's play area, improved car parking and a woodland trail.

Funding secured

After a lengthy process beginning in 2005 the group were successful in securing £927,020 towards the development of their new pavilion. It opened in summer 2009. The following organisations provided the funding:

- Sport England – £273,000
- Coalfields Regeneration Trust – £261,718

- The English Cricket Board – £153,828
- The Rugby Football League – £80,000
- Biffaward – £49,860
- Virridor – £50,000
- Garfield Weston – £10,000
- Church and Community – £10,000
- St Peter's Church – £10,000
- Wigan MBC Brighter Borough Fund – £9,500
- Liverpool Diocese – £10,000
- Own funds – £1,704

Results and achievements

Clearly the level of engagement from a variety of funding partners demonstrates the ability of the project and the ability of sport to be able to contribute to a wide range of sporting and non-sporting priorities. Only three of the funders could be classified as sporting organisations. Sport has to reach out and grasp resources from elsewhere and this is evident in this project and within much of the literature in this book.

The club have added other sports to their portfolio including cycling and table tennis. They have worked closely with the Wigan and Leigh Leisure Culture Trust Active Living Team to provide a cycle pod and bicycles (including bicycles for disabled people) which enables people to hire bicycles from the club and explore the local cycle ways within the area. They have also developed a table tennis evening for existing members of the partners and other people from the local community. The rugby league section alone has increased junior membership by 30 per cent, from 135 to 175. They have doubled the number of active coaches at the club from 12 to 24, and increased the number of active volunteers from 24 to 52. The club was also successful in obtaining funding to employ a Facility Manager for a two and a half year period. This has led to the pavilion being heavily utilised by a wide range of other community organisations throughout the week.

The Revd Stephen Mather, who has played a vital role in developing the partnership, stated:

The new changing facilities and multi-use games area enable us to offer a wider range of sports to a greater number of young people and in particular, girls.

Community organisations, sport and recreation underpin people's quality of life. We believe that our development has provided a well designed scheme that will help to improve the lives of the people who live in this locality.

The club is continuing to plan for the future with plans to improve training facilities at the site, particularly for the rugby league section. The club is managing to make an annual profit of approximately £20,000 and some of this may be utilised to develop a new artificial training surface or an indoor training barn. The strength of the partnership has been the key to the success of this project, along with the dedication of the volunteers from each of the partner organisations that represent St Peter's Pavilion Ltd.

Chapter Review

The aim of this chapter was to introduce you to the concept of community sport. This area of work is constantly evolving and relies upon programmes and funding which appear to have a quick turnover. This area of work is widely supported by a number of key stakeholders but none more so than the numerous sports development teams and local clubs that operate across the UK. They face many challenges at local, regional and national levels. They attempt to engage their local communities by providing, developing and facilitating a number of interventions to encourage participation in sport. They attempt to utilise sport as a means to support wider societal issues such as crime, drug misuse, juvenile nuisance, rising obesity levels and more. At a regional and national level they work in partnerships with County Sports Partnerships and national government bodies. Case studies have been used to bring this work to life and to develop your understanding of the work that actually happens on the ground. Such work is happening in similar guises across the UK, albeit branded as a different programme or being delivered in a slightly different manner.

Further Reading

To develop a more in-depth understanding of community sports development programmes:
- Bloyce, D. and Smith, A. (2009) *Sport, Policy and Development: An Introduction*. London: Routledge.
- Collins, M. (2009) *Examining Sports Development*. London: Routledge.
- Hylton, K. and Bramham, P. (2008) *Sports Development: Policy, Process and Practice*, 2nd edn. London: Routledge.

Websites

- Sport England: http://www.sportengland.org
- Lancashire Sport (County Sport Partnership): http://www.lancashiresport.org.uk/
- Preston City Council – Sport and Leisure: http://www.preston.gov.uk/leisure-and-culture/sport-and-leisure/

Chapter 5
Elite sport

Learning Objectives

This chapter is designed to help you develop an understanding about:

- the support systems in place for elite sports development;
- the funding and finance invested in elite sports development within the public sector;
- programmes and initiatives that are being developed in order to support talent and elite sports performers leading up to London 2012 and beyond;
- the challenges faced by individual athletes when striving for success.

Introduction

When we switch on our television sets and watch elite performers competing at a national or international level, when we are rejoicing or commiserating their performance we do not tend to think about their support systems, the finance invested in that person or team, and the dedication of numerous people behind the scenes striving for excellence. Jenson Button was crowned the world champion in Formula 1 motor racing in October 2009, and by following Lewis Hamilton, it made it the first time in 40 years that Britain had enjoyed back-to-back successes. Those familiar with Formula 1 have a general acceptance that the role of the car, the engineers, the designers and other external factors outside the driver's control play a huge factor in success. The British cyclists who enjoyed much success in the Beijing Olympics in 2008 (14 medals: 8 gold, 4 silver, 2 bronze) rode bicycles that may be considered by the International Cycling Union (UCI) as illegal equipment next year, as they consider a new rule in 2010 that only bicycles which are on sale to the general public can be used in competition (Speck 2009: 79). The 2009 World Swimming Championships were dominated by world record times but plagued by accusations that new performance-enhancing clothing contributed significantly to the new improved times. Perhaps this notion of equipment to aid performance is less considered when we think about the successes in sports such as athletics and sports seemingly less reliant upon technology in the actual performance. A 100m runner simply needs a kit and a lane. There is very little reliance upon technology to aid performance in the actual race.

However, the actual race or performance that we see on the screen, regardless of the sport, is the culmination of days, weeks, months and in some cases years of training and practice. The performance may be reliant on technology or simply a person running in a lane, but their pathway to that performance has probably been aided and supported, both financially and scientifically, by a system striving for success.

Therefore, the aim of this chapter is to consider the current systems in the UK and to develop your understanding based around the learning objectives above.

Elite sports development

Since 1996 the way in which elite sport has been driven within the public sector across the UK has changed somewhat. UK Sport has become the leading agency which is responsible for distributing government and Lottery monies into the elite end of the sports development continuum. If you revisit the sports development continuum on page 45 you will see the top two tiers are excellence and performance. It could be argued that UK Sport only had the responsibility for the excellence level up until more recent times, with the performance level being considered and developed by the home country sports councils. Either way, the top two tiers which represent the more elite end of sport have been driven by these agencies in partnership with national governing bodies of sports. From 1983 until 1996, SportsAid (previously known as the SportsAid Foundation, which was founded in 1976) was a major source of funding for most of Britain's leading athletes, both able-bodied and disabled. Its principal function was to raise funds from the private sector to provide financial assistance to Britain's amateur sportsmen and women. Its changing role will be considered later in the chapter.

The catalysts for change within elite sports development came after poor performances by the Great Britain team in the 1996 Olympic Games in Atlanta. After the Los Angeles Games in 1984, subsequent Games leading up to Atlanta in 1996 suggest that the quality of performances at the Summer Olympics, which acts as a benchmark to compare international success, was diminishing. The following table summarises the medals count for Team Great Britain since the Los Angeles Games in 1984. The information is taken from the British Olympic Association website which can be found at http://www.olympics.org.uk.

	Gold	Silver	Bronze	Total	Position
1984: Los Angeles	5	11	21	36	11th
1988: Seoul	5	10	9	24	12th
1992: Barcelona	5	3	12	20	13th
1996: Atlanta	1	8	6	15	15th
2000: Sydney	11	10	7	28	10th
2004: Athens	9	9	12	30	10th
2008: Beijing	19	13	15	47	4th

Table 5.1: Great Britain medal count at the Summer Olympics (1984–2008)

Learning Activity 5.1

Why do you think performances dropped after the Olympics in 1984 and began to get better after the Atlanta Games in 1996? Write down your thoughts and consider the reasons behind the drop in performances and some suggestions for the improvements.

The poor performances in Atlanta followed the inception of the National Lottery in 1994, which has allocated just over £23bn to good causes to date (The National Lottery 2009). Further information supplied on their website suggests that 16.67 per cent of this funding has gone into sport. The combined expenditure that has been allocated to sport in the UK by the home country sports councils and UK Sport is just over £4.5bn.

At government level the focus on elite sport was strengthened with the production of various strategies from 1995, including *Sport: Raising the Game* (1995) and *A Sporting Future for All* (2000). More recently the DCMS have provided a renewed focus with their latest strategy, *A New Era for Sport: Playing to Win* (2008). These have been discussed in previous chapters but are mentioned again here to emphasise the political will to develop elite sport as a key policy area, alongside the will of those within sport.

Funding in elite sport

The current level of investment that sports will receive for the London 2012 Olympic and Paralympic Games currently stands at just over £303m. This covers the four years from the end of the Beijing Games to London 2012, otherwise known as an Olympiad. This includes all Olympic and Paralympic sports except for tennis and football as they are deemed as being able to fund themselves (UK Sport 2009a) and equates to just over an annual investment of £75m per year leading up to the Olympic and Paralympic Games. These levels of investment have risen significantly over the last 10 years with UK Sport distributing £17m to 24 sports at a UK level during its first year, in 1999 (Green and Houlihan 2005: 59). This comparison may be slightly distorted with the Games 'being in town' but what is without question is that the level of investment by UK Sport in Olympic related sport has risen significantly over the last 10 years. One has to also consider that UK Sport invested only in the top end of elite performance before 2006, with the home country sports councils investing in development and talented athletes.

How is the money spent?

Since 1997, UK Sport has operated world class programmes designed to support leading British Olympic and Paralympic athletes in their mission to win medals at the world's biggest sporting events. They have developed the World Class Performance pathway which operates at three levels (UK Sport 2009b):

World Class Podium

This supports those athletes in sports with realistic medal capabilities at the next Olympic/Paralympic Games. Support is provided through a performance programme with the governing body and an athlete personal award.

World Class Development

This is the next category immediately beneath the podium level. It is aimed at athletes who have demonstrated that they have realistic medal-winning capabilities for 2016. It will also embrace those sports with realistic capabilities to be competitive in 2016 but where medal achievement is unlikely.

World Class Talent

Identification and confirmation of athletes who have the potential to progress through the World Class pathway with the help of targeted investment. Olympic athletes will be a maximum of 8 years away from the podium.

Funding the World Class Performance pathways

There is a significant difference in the funding levels that athletes can acquire depending upon their status in these pathways. For example, an athlete on the podium level can expect to receive up to £55,000 worth of support from UK Sport compared to around £33,000 for those on the development programme. The athletes do not receive this money directly, but their respective national governing body is allocated the money to provide the programme of support services. This is overseen by a performance director within a particular sport. An example of this would be the role currently held by Dave Brailsford at British Cycling. In addition to these support services athletes can receive a personal award which can go towards living costs. Again this is dependent upon performance with podium athletes receiving up to £27,000 a year and development athletes receiving approximately £20,000. The allocations are means tested and athletes that receive additional income totalling just over £61k lose £1 for every pound over (UK Sport 2009c).

British Cycling

The role of Dave Brailsford and the British Cycling Performance Team involves developing selection criteria for representative teams of British Cycling at major events. An example of this would be the selection criteria that were developed for the 2009 World Road Championships which were held in Switzerland in September. Riders were considered for selection based upon a number of factors including current UCI ranking and race performances from February to August 2009 (British Cycling 2009a). Prior to the world track championships in 2007 the Performance Director stated:

> Our analysis and data collection is so good nowadays, that the team selects itself as it's all done on objective data. As a result, the coach's job is simply to help our riders be the best they can be so the objective data means that the team will pick itself. Wherever possible we have moved totally away from having to rely on subjective decisions when it comes to selections. This is especially important with the number of quality riders we now have competing for places and it's too tight to call on gut feelings alone.

(British Cycling 2009b)

British Cycling and the performance director receive support in the preparation and identification of their cyclists from the English Institute of Sport. Their role will be discussed later in this chapter.

The approach adopted by the sport is proving extremely successful with 22 gold medals being secured by British Cycling riders in word events in 2008. Table 5.2 illustrates the significant improvements that have been made in past Olympics and in recent world track championships.

Year	Olympics	World track
2004	2G/1S/1B	1G/1S/1B
2005	No event	4G/1S/1B
2006	No event	1G/4S/1B
2007	No event	7G/2S/1B
2008	8G/4S/2B	9G/2S/1B

Table 5.2: British Cycling medal overview

This is combined with medals being secured in other cycling disciplines and the more recent achievements of British cyclists Mark Cavendish and Bradley Wiggins in the 2009 Tour de France. Bradley Wiggins, already a triple Olympic gold medallist, finished in a remarkable fourth place, just under one minute behind the legendary Lance Armstrong. Mark Cavendish won the final stage at the Champs Elysées to claim a record-equalling sixth stage victory in the Tour de France. The profile of British cyclists has never been higher and further evidence is offered with Chris Hoy, four times Olympic gold medallist, receiving a knighthood and winning the popular vote by securing the BBC Sports Personality of the Year award for 2008. The British Olympic cycling team was named team of the year and Dave Brailsford won the coach of the year award.

This success has paved the way for cycling to develop a partnership with Sky TV. In July 2008 British Cycling announced a multi-million pound sponsorship deal, with Sky being confirmed as the principal partner of British Cycling for the next five years, leading up to London 2012 (British Cycling 2008). The intention is that the sponsorship will benefit the sport at every level, but inevitably a significant proportion will be channelled into the performance end of the sport. This was apparent with the announcement in February 2009 that BSkyB was developing a professional British road cycling team, Team Sky, to be managed by Great Britain Olympic performance director Dave Brailsford.

The intention is that Team Sky will build on the principles that make British riders a consistent success on the track and will support Sky's work as principal partner of British Cycling, fuelling the sport from grassroots to elite level.

Team Sky will aim to:

- create the first British winner of the Tour de France, within five years;
- inspire people of all ages and abilities to get on their bicycles, through the team's positive profile, attitude and success;
- add further support to competitive cycling in Great Britain.

(BSkyB 2009)

The heights that have been achieved within the sport in what is a relatively short period of time demonstrate the importance of developing the right system to meet the needs of the performers. It will be interesting to see if the sport can continue its success, be successful in London 2012 and perhaps create that first winner in the Tour de France.

Learning Activity 5.2

Write a list of support services that you would expect an individual athlete or cyclist to require if they are striving for success at the next Olympic Games.

The price of success and failure

The differences in funding levels can have a significant effect on an athlete's ability to perform and to reach their potential. Mark Lewis-Francis (aged 27), a Great Britain international sprinter, has had much success over the years in athletics. He won 100m gold at the World Junior Championships in 2001 and anchored Great Britain to gold at the 2004 Olympic Games (British Olympic Association 2009a). Unfortunately for him, he was injured and was not available for selection for the Beijing Games. After an unsuccessful comeback in 2008, attempting to qualify for the IAAF World Championships in Berlin, he has been dropped from receiving any world class programme funding and will no longer qualify for either medical care or physiotherapy (Hart 2009). Obviously this will have a significant impact on his ability to train and to prepare for future athletics events. Perhaps the biggest barrier will be that he will have to generate income from elsewhere, which will result in less time in the day for training and preparation. Similar issues were faced by Jenny Meadows (aged 28) who has recently been promoted to podium level funding after her bronze medal in the 800m at the IAAF World Championships in Berlin. In a recent interview with the BBC (2009b) she explained the challenges that she faced due to receiving a limited amount of funding from UK Athletics. For the past two years she has received approximately £7,500 from UK Athletics from their world class programme but had to supplement this with working full time for Manchester City Council as their Head Athletics Coach. She is quoted as saying:

> I was so unhappy working hard during the day, driving for an hour and then having to train. It was a nightmare. My candle was burning at both ends and I was getting really run down. I wasn't giving myself a chance to compete properly.

(BBC 2009b)

She finally gave up her job to concentrate on her training leading up to the World Championships and was rewarded with the bronze and increased funding from UK Athletics of just less than £27,000 based upon her successful performance. As a podium athlete she may now operate as a full-time athlete and can adopt a completely different approach to training and her preparations. Mark Lewis-Francis may not be able to afford such a luxury along with many other athletes who have had their funding reduced when they have failed to deliver.

A no compromise approach towards London 2012 and beyond

UK Athletics's approach, which has just been outlined in the previous section, fits in with the no compromise strategy developed by UK Sport for their world class funded programmes. Essentially, they will only fund those who meet the strict criteria of the world class programmes, and individual athletes and performers are accountable by their successes or failures. Whilst some might argue that this will discard talent and not allow some athletes to recover from injury, others would perhaps conclude that it offers value for money and ensures that finances are being spent on those best placed to deliver. Alongside the individual accountability is a renewed focus on the partnership with the national governing bodies. As previously stated, the eligible sports receive funding for individual performers, teams on world class programmes and this is overseen by the sports' performance directors. UK Sport have developed Mission 2012, which requires sports to monitor their own progress. They have to consider the following:

- their athletes' performance and development;
- the performance system that sits behind them;
- the leadership and climate that exists within the sport.

Sports have to conduct their own assessments based upon their strengths and weaknesses and to find solutions to any problems they encounter. UK Sport oversees this process and checks on all Olympic and Paralympic sports via quarterly updates. This accountability echoes the approach taken with the monitoring of the Whole Sport Planning process which was discussed in Chapter 2. NGBs are having to identify clearer aims and objectives for their sport and recognise that they must be successful in order to continue to receive the same levels of financial support.

The Institutes of Sport

Earlier on in this chapter you were asked to consider what support services an individual athlete or cyclist would require in order to be successful at an Olympic Games. British Cycling along with other NGBs works

---

Timeline of the English Institute of Sport

1995

Plans for a British Academy of Sport were first announced by the then Prime Minister, John Major.

1997

Initiative re-launched as the UK Sports Institute (UKSI) with Sheffield selected as the central hub site.

1999

Sport England announced plans to develop a £120m network of English Institute Centres.

2000

A central services operation, supported by UK Sport, was launched after the Sydney Olympics – an 18 month trial period for the English Institute of Sport (EIS) began.

2002

The EIS was officially 'launched' – providing sports science and medical support services to elite athletes in England through a network of regional centres.

2005

London won the bid to host the 2012 Olympiad.

2006

Transfer of EIS ownership from Sport England to UK Sport. The EIS became a wholly owned subsidiary of UK Sport – grant funded through the UK Sport Lottery Fund.

---

closely with the Institutes of Sport (IS) in order to develop such services. The inception and evolution of the English Institute of Sport (EIS) can be seen in the above timeline (English Institute of Sport 2009).

The EIS works in partnership with individual sports in order to ensure the following support services are delivered effectively: sports medicine, physiotherapy, strength and conditioning, physiology, performance nutrition, sports psychology, biomechanics, performance analysis, performance lifestyle, soft tissue therapy and talent identification. As can be imagined these specialised services are expensive and this demonstrates to some extent where UK Sport Lottery monies are distributed. The athletes' allowances, dependent upon their position within the World Class Performance Programme, will be utilised to develop a bespoke package based around some of these services. The organisation has its own independent board which is chaired by Steve Cram. The role of the Board is to interpret policy from UK Sport and to provide strategic direction to the three regions of the EIS: North, Central and South.

Learning Activity 5.3

Since the devolution of the UKSI at the end of the 1990s the home country institutes for sport have been established. Conduct some research in order to establish what the institutes do in Northern Ireland, Scotland and Wales.

The following websites will help:

Sports Institute Northern Ireland   http://www.sini.co.uk/
sportscotland Institute of Sport   http://www.sisport.com
Welsh Institute of Sport   http://www.welsh-institute-sport.co.uk/

Underpinning the World Class Programmes

Since 1997, SportsAid has focused on giving grants to young people aged 12 to 16, from 50 able-bodied and 25 disability sports. These athletes compete in national teams and these grants, generally worth £500, help with costs such as travel, training, accommodation, competition fees and equipment. Since its foundation in 1976, SportsAid has distributed around £20m and now gives 1,500 grants per year (SportsAid 2009a). Sport England has just provided over £0.5m of funding to SportsAid over the next two years to support 16 promising athletes who have the potential to be successful at the Rio de Janeiro Olympic Games in 2016 (Sport England 2009f). Athletes awarded funding by SportsAid are selected by their sport's national governing body in conjunction with the sport's performance staff. Previous recipients include Dame Tanni Grey-Thompson, Victoria Pendleton, Denise Lewis, Sir Steve Redgrave and Dame Kelly Holmes.

In a press release in October 2009, the Mayor of London, Boris Johnson, in partnership with SportsAid announced funding for 30 aspiring Olympians who each received £1,000 for their development because of their exceptional sporting talent (London.Gov 2009). He was joined by double Olympic gold medalist Dame Kelly Holmes (athletics) and bronze medalist Louis Smith (gymnastics). According to SportsAid (2009b) their athletes spend on average around £5,000 a year to support their development.

Reflection Point 5.1

Where else do you think young athletes could acquire money/support in order to continue their development in their chosen sport?

Talented Athlete Scholarship Scheme

The Talented Athlete Scholarship Scheme (TASS) is a government-funded programme which aims to support and fast track talented athletes in order to achieve success. It is a partnership between NGBs and educational establishments and in similarity to the UK Sport World Class Performance Programmes, athletes can acquire sporting services up to a certain value but there are no personal awards to athletes under this scheme. There are 50 sports involved in the programme and support is available up to a maximum of £3,000 normally, and up to £10,000 for those awarded a TASS 2012 Scholarship. The aim of these scholarships is to fast track the athletes into world class programmes. In order to be eligible, individuals must be undertaking a recognised education programme, not receiving funding via any of the world class programmes and be able to represent either the Great Britain or English representative team in their chosen sport. Individuals have to be nominated for an award by their sport.

Both SportsAid and TASS are reliant upon commercial sector sponsorship, alongside support from central government. At present, both funders receive sponsorship from Deloitte and between them they have a number of sponsors including Asda, Lloyds TSB, JPMorgan and Fitness First.

Local authority grants

In addition to the TASS and SportsAid, funding can sometimes be obtained by individuals from their local authority. In some instances, local authorities will have a grants scheme that recognises and provides financial support to young people representing their sport at a county, regional or national level. These grants will be based upon local criteria and eligibility will be determined by the local authority. In Preston the city council are supported by the Preston Sports Forum. They consider funding applications for up to £100 from people who are performing at county standard. Funding can be obtained for items such as purchase of equipment, training and educational opportunities and events.

This figure summarises the progressive funding possibilities available to some performers in their sport. At the bottom there are local authority grants of around £100 (county/regional). At the next level, successful performers (national) can perhaps secure as much as £3,000–£10,000 via SportsAid and TASS funding. And finally, those within their NGBs world class programme (talent/development/podium) have the potential to secure up to £27,000 per annum and support services worth over £50,000. Figure 5.1 demonstrates this as a progressive pyramid.

Figure 5.1 Talent development funding

The British Olympic Association Olympic Coaching Programme

The role of the British Olympic Association (BOA) will be discussed in more detail in Chapter 7. For the purposes of this chapter you need to be aware that their role is to:

> *prepare and lead our nation's finest athletes at the Olympic Games and the BOA has the responsibility for developing the Olympic Movement throughout the UK. In addition, the BOA delivers extensive support services to Britain's Olympic athletes and their national governing bodies throughout each Olympic cycle to assist them in their preparations for, and performances at the Games.*

(BOA 2009b)

In September 2006 Sir Clive Woodward, the former world cup winning England rugby union coach, was appointed as the BOA's Performance Director. His role was originally intended to oversee the work of the performance directors in each of the Olympic sports. He was expected to work closely with UK Sport in order to develop an infrastructure to ensure success at the 2008 and 2012 Olympic Games and his role and responsibilities have expanded to overseeing the preparation camps for the Olympic Games. Woodward and the BOA announced in 2007 a £20m plan to develop 25 top British athletes into Olympic champions in London 2012. At the time UK Sport expressed concern about duplication with their own Mission 2012 programme. Based on a 12-month pilot scheme with 20-year-old golfer Melissa Reid, Woodward developed a supposed advanced coaching system which he aimed to transfer to the development of Olympic performers. A review of his impact in his first year by the BBC (Slater 2007) unearthed some interesting findings. BBC Sport spoke to 28 of the 35 representatives of Olympic sports and while some responses were positive, 18 said he had made no impact so far.

Feedback included:

> *In the past the BOA have perhaps been glorified travel agents but Clive has already sharpened their thinking.*

(Dave Brailsford, British Cycling's Performance Director)

I don't see how he can help – is he just a figurehead.

(A national performance director)

He's dedicated to elite performance, has fresh ideas and believes that no compromise means no compromise.

(Colin McIver, British Judo's Performance Director)

Is Clive's model adaptable? How is it funded? How does it sit alongside the UK Sport system? But had this come along seven years ago . . . who knows?

(A senior performance director with a leading sport)

The system appears confusing not only from the outside but also for some of those operating within it. More recently, Scott (2009) reported that Woodward's role was to change and that he would now focus on developing sports and consequently athletes who had had their funding cut by UK Sport. He has been asked to devise a strategy that fits around and beneath that of the World Class Performance Programme. Upon reviewing further articles and literature it still appears confusing as to how this role complements the work of UK Sport and the performance directors. What is without question is that in 2008 Team Great Britain experienced its most successful Olympic Games to date, achieving fourth place on the medals table and surpassing all expectations. In one sense they are four years ahead of their targets with London 2012 being identified as the Games to achieve the target of fourth place on the medals table.

World class coaching

The development of a successful performer rarely occurs without the services of an effective coach. Across the UK there are an estimated 1.11m individuals undertaking a coaching-related role at least 12 times a year (sports coach UK 2009a: 54). SkillsActive (2009) indicate that this figure is slightly higher at 1.2m, but go on to state that 81 per cent of these are volunteers. In the recently produced Coaching Workforce Plan for Coaching across the UK for 2009–16, sports coach UK suggest that out of the 1.11m coaches just over half hold some form of qualification. Only 12 per cent are qualified at levels 4 and 5 with 69 per cent having obtained a level 1 or 2. In order to improve the quality and standard of coaching across the UK measures are being taken.

Coaching Task Force 2002

In 2002 the government established the Coaching Task Force (CTF) to consider the proposals that they had made for the improvement of coaching. The CTF reviewed the coaching system and structures across the UK and conducted a benchmarking exercise with other countries to identify good practice. The CTF recommended the implementation of a National Coaching Certificate at five levels. This has evolved into the UK Coaching Certificate (UKCC) which currently underpins the way in which many sports deliver their coach education programmes.

There are four recognised coaching levels within the programme:

Level 1: assisting a more qualified coach in planning and delivering aspects of a session, under supervision;

Level 2: preparing, delivering and reviewing a coaching session on your own;

Level 3:   planning, delivering and evaluating an annual programme of coaching;

Level 4:   this is currently under review and is concerned with professional coaching and innovative coaching methods.

The UKCC has been integrated into the National Occupational Standards and the Scottish Credit and Qualifications Framework. The certificate is recognised and transferable across the UK. The overall aim is to advance coach education programmes in order to enable coaches to develop participants and performers, to support the development of coaching as a profession in the UK and to offer continuous professional development for coaches. Sports have to submit their coach education literature to sports coach UK at each of the levels in order for it to be endorsed under the UKCC. At present, 23 sports have UKCC Level 1 accreditation, 20 have Level 2, and 15 have Level 3. Currently, there are no sports that have specific level 4 accreditation; however, some educational establishments have developed courses endorsed by UKCC at level 4 (sports coach UK 2009c).

The University of Central Lancashire and the Pentagon Group

The UKCC Level 4 Postgraduate Diploma in Elite Coaching Practice is a new programme designed to share best practice and integrate cross-sport learning. Competing against other universities from across the country, the University of Central Lancashire was chosen by five key governing bodies to lead the programme. The programme has been organised by the Pentagon Group of sports, which is made up of representatives from the national governing bodies of five sports – rugby league, basketball, table tennis, squash and hockey. The Pentagon Group Level 4 is the first to achieve full endorsement through the UK Coaching Centre of Excellence based at Leeds Metropolitan University.

The first course has been attended by top level rugby league coaches including John Kear and Steve McCormack as well as national coaches from hockey, table tennis, squash and basketball.

Vision and outcomes of the UK Coaching Framework

The vision of the UK Coaching Framework according to (sports coach UK 2009c) is to:

- create a cohesive, ethical, inclusive and valued coaching system where skilled coaches support children, players and athletes at all stages of their development in sport;
- become world number one by 2016.

The UK Coaching Framework will:

- enhance the quality of coaching at all stages;
- Provide active, skilled and qualified coaches to meet demand.

This will lead to:

- sustained and increased participation;
- improved performances in sport underpinned by clear career structures for coaches within.

These recent developments support and bring to life some of the ambitions in the UK Coaching Framework (UKCF). The UKCF builds upon the recommendations from the CTF and is an attempt from the sporting partners across the UK to develop a world-leading coaching system by 2016.

sports coach UK and their partners will attempt to achieve these ambitions by adopting a phased approach. The diagram below, taken from the UKCF, summarises this approach.

In addition to these developments UK Sport in 2000 devised an elite coaching programme designed as a three year coaching course for the best coaches in the UK who have the ability to develop the best athletes. They are nominated to take part in the programme by their sports and they are provided with a bespoke coach education programme which serves as further professional development. There are plans to evolve this programme by sports coach UK and they are currently having discussions with UK Sport and the EIS about developing a coaching and practitioner apprenticeship programme. A consultation process is due to take place between the relevant partners and individual sports to shape the development of this elite coaching qualification. It would appear to make sense if this is somehow incorporated into the UKCC.

If we are to continually strive for sporting success then we must have a successful and efficient coaching system. The steps taken to transform the coaching system in order to be a world leader are the signs that the UK is serious about developing excellence in sport, whether it be supporting the individual performers, successful teams, governing bodies of sport or coaches.

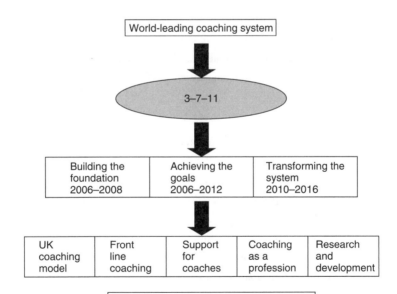

Figure 5.2 The UK Coaching Framework

Chapter Review

The aim of this chapter was to develop your understanding of the support systems in place for elite sports development. This chapter explores and describes the work of national agencies such as UK Sport and attempts to bring this to life with a profile of sports-specific work and individual athletes. The chapter provides some information about the funding and finance that is invested into elite sports development by the public sector and again relates this to the impact that it can have on individual athletes. The world of elite sport in the UK is complex and varied and we have not even begun to consider the approaches adopted by sports such as rugby, football, cricket and tennis. Chapter 14 will consider the more commercialised approach that is operated within football.

Before you read Chapter 14, consider this fictitious scenario:

> Football is no longer reliant upon commercial sponsorship, TV rights and spectator income. Clubs continue to operate but receive a large proportion of their finances from the government and the National Lottery. The 22 players striding out at Wembley, representing England and Wales, are receiving personal athlete awards from UK Sport to supplement their training. They do not get paid the high wages that are regularly reported in the press but generate income similar to that of a long jumper who is successful on the world stage.
>
> The question is this:
> Should individual sports be as reliant on government funding in order to pay their competitors or should sports strive to operate more commercially like football does? What is the motivation for those sports that are currently obtaining significant funding from the government to operate more commercially?

With London 2012 just around the corner it is difficult to see the momentum within elite sport subsiding and it appears that there is a collective ambition from the government, relevant sporting organisations and the public at large to strive for success and to develop a successful team to represent Great Britain at the London 2012 Olympic Games. Beijing was the Games that surpassed expectations when it came to performance. What will London 2012 be remembered for? Finally, what is the longer term future for those sports currently producing success, but reliant on funding from public sources? Will sports become more reliant upon technology as in the case of Formula 1? Will sports therefore need to operate in a manner that generates revenue sources outside public support? British Cycling and its sponsorship deal with Sky appears to be moving in this direction.

Further Reading

Historical policy changes within elite sport:
- Green, M. and Houlihan, B. (2005) *Elite Sport Development*: *Policy Learning and Political Priorities*. London: Routledge.

- Houlihan, B. and Green, M. (2009). *Modernisation and Sport: The Reform of Sport England*. Loughborough: PSA.

Elite sport development in other countries:

- Hill, M. (2007) *In Pursuit of Excellence*. London: Routledge.
- Houlihan, B. and Green, M. (eds) (2009). *Comparative Elite Sports Development: Systems, Structures and Public Policy*. London: Butterworth-Heinemann.

The following websites will develop your understanding further:

- http://www.uksport.gov.uk
- http://www.sportsaid.org.uk
- http://www.sportscoachuk.org
- http://www.eis2win.co.uk
- http://www.olympics.org.uk
- http://www.britishcycling.org.uk

Chapter 6
A review of the UK sporting landscape

Learning Objectives

This chapter is designed to help you:

- bring together all the information from Parts 1 and 2 to give an overall understanding of the sporting infrastructure in the UK;
- review how the delivery agencies support and develop sport across school, community and elite areas to provide opportunities for development from playground to podium;
- understand the sporting landscape through the development of a model.

Physical activity by its very nature is a cross-cutting government responsibility and a range of delivery agencies are leading in the creation of more opportunities to get physically active across the UK. Their visions and reforms are set against the backdrop of the drive to raise levels of physical activity and for the UK to become a more active nation.

Participation

Increasing participation is the fundamental reason why many individuals and organisations get involved in the development of sport and physical activities. The challenges faced when trying to increase participation in sport and physical activity across the country are varied and well established. Despite participation levels rising slowly over the last decade there are still significant deficiencies in getting sections of society involved in participating in sport and physical activity. Since the 1970s, 'target groups' have been identified as needing specification to encourage their activity and those target groups are still relevant today. All of the home nations' strategies for the next 5, 10 and 20 years acknowledge that increasing the target groups' participation levels is fundamental to achieving participation targets. The target groups are women and girls, people with disabilities and people from ethnic minority backgrounds.

Reflection Point 6.1

In England what do you consider to be the key agencies driving forward the actions to achieving targets in community sport, school sport and elite sport?

The delivery framework

There are many commonalities within the visions and objectives of all the governments and delivery agencies in all four of the home nations. The key features are that:

- There is a commitment both in philosophy and funding to developing key pillars of the sporting infrastructure including: participation, elite performance, school sport, competition, fit-for-purpose delivery agencies and coaching.
- Partnerships are an essential component of achieving targets. A co-ordinated approach to delivery by a variety of agencies is needed and everyone needs to know the role they play in the delivery framework.
- Historically mass participation and elite success have been joint objectives of successive governments. There is continued commitment to these joint objectives despite the mass–elite dichotomy has that proved so challenging over the years.
- In the modern era, characterised by rising obesity levels and a potential UK obesity epidemic, with people storing health problems for the future and putting huge pressures on the NHS, there is a necessity to educate and encourage the whole nation to adopt a healthier lifestyle.

Schools

A logical place to begin when exploring the UK sporting landscape is the philosophy and delivery of sport and physical activity in the school setting. As discussed in Chapter 3, one of the key objectives of the delivery agencies involved at this level is getting young people started in sport and physical activity. Across all of the UK, school is seen as being a vital component in getting young people on the right path in terms of healthy living and an active lifestyle. School is one of the first places that young people will experience and explore a range of sports and physical activities through the physical education curriculum.

> Reflection Point 6.2
>
> Think back to your early experiences of the range of activities you tried at school. Explain what those experiences were like (good, bad, fun, exciting, boring, etc.). How do your experiences compare to other people? How do you think your experiences were influenced by:
> the school you went to, its location and the teachers?

The Youth Sport Trust works with all the home nations to educate teachers, develop programmes for school children of all ages, to support gifted and talented young people and maximise on the legacy of the Olympic and Paralympic Games. Targets in this setting centre on participation levels and specifically the number of young people achieving the five hour offer. Success in this setting will be measured by the number of young people participating in school sport, the number of gifted and talented athletes, increased standards in PE, teaching and CPD programmes for teachers. In Scotland, the Active Schools network is a cornerstone of life in the vast majority of schools. It is referenced throughout national and local plans for sport, including

Scotland's National Strategy for Sport, *Reaching Higher* and **sport**scotland's Corporate Plan 2007–2011. The fundamental aim is to offer all children and young people the opportunities and motivation to adopt active, healthy lifestyles, now and into adulthood. Funding for the network has now been secured until the Scottish government's next spending review which is planned for 2011 (**sport**scotland 2009c).

Communities

The next area of the UK sporting landscape to consider is the philosophy and delivery of sport and physical activity in the community setting. As discussed in Chapter 3, one of the key objectives of the delivery agencies involved at this level is keeping young people involved in sport and physical activity by ensuring that there are strong links between schools and clubs. It is also essential within this setting that families are encouraged to take part in activities together, as research has shown that parental influence is a significant factor when determining participation of young people. In England, the active community's projects are well established and an excellent example of the development work taking place in this setting. Sport England has invested £213m in 2009/10 towards funding sport in the community. Targets in the community setting centre on participation levels of the general public and those doing 3 × 30 minutes of moderate activity per week. It also focuses on building up school–club links, strengthening communities through sport and breaking down barriers to ensure community sport is more equitable.

Learning Activity 6.1

Consider your current activity levels and record your participation levels in an average week. Are you achieving the recommended 3 × 30 minutes of moderate activity in a week? Look at your activities and identify which of them take place within a college or university setting and which take place in the community setting? What can you conclude about your participation trends?

Success in this setting will be measured by achieving mass participation figures set by the various home nation governments and if improvements are made in the participation figures of the various target groups. In Wales, the well-established Dragon Sport programme epitomises the philosophy of sport and physical activity development in the community setting. The initiative is funded by the National Lottery and is designed to offer 7–11 year olds fun and enjoyable sporting opportunities outside the school curriculum and in the community. Dragon Sport is promoted and delivered through a network of full-time Dragon Sport Co-ordinators, based in each of the 22 local authorities in Wales (Sports Council Wales 2007d, 2007a). Community sports development programmes are still reliant at the delivery end on the local authority sports development teams. A case study of Preston has been provided and demonstrated a snapshot of the work they that do. The voluntary sports sector continues to play a major role in the provision of sporting opportunities within local communities. A wide range of sports-specific and multi-sport clubs operate at a local level led by an army of volunteers. They are often referred to as the lifeblood of British sport and it would seem impossible for sport in the UK to continue to operate without their support, drive and passion.

Elite sport

The other significant area of the UK sporting landscape is the philosophy and delivery of sport and physical activity in the elite setting. It is obvious that in this setting that sport takes priority over increasing participation levels because of the need to achieve success at the highest level. As discussed in Chapter 5, a renewed focus has been placed upon this area of sports development with the securing of the Olympic Games in London in 2012. Already we have begun to see a re-emergence of resources and finances flowing into this area. The successes of Team GB in the Beijing Olympics in 2008 have provided the UK with a level of achievement which will take some beating at the next Olympics in 2012. The overall responsibility for developing Team GB at the Games falls under the remit of the British Olympic Association. However, as has been discussed in Chapter 5, UK Sport plays a pivotal role in supporting the talented athletes across the UK. They work in partnership with national governing bodies and the Institutes of Sport in order to develop a bespoke programme of development and training for these athletes. UK Sport has developed the World Class Performance Programme alongside a 'no compromise' approach. The elite sports development partners faced a target for London 2012 of achieving fourth place on the medals table (DCMS 2002). However, this was obviously achieved in Beijing and it now appears that the aim for London is to consolidate the success. Sports such as cycling and swimming are enjoying a great deal of success and the systems and structures that they have implemented are beginning to prove fruitful. There appears to be a pathway in place for talented athletes. They are heavily reliant upon their national governing body in order to progress through their performance pathway, but are able to do so with support from funding programmes such as SportsAid and TASS. By innovation, forward thinking, or possibly chance, it also appears that the run up to the Olympics will engender an added step within the performance pathway with the inception of the BOA Olympic Coaching Programme. This seems to be dependent upon funding in order to make it a success. Although this area of development is gaining momentum, there is little doubt that the government will neglect the policy of utilising sport in order to contribute towards wider societal issues.

Equity in the delivery framework

Fundamental to the infrastructure jigsaw and the work of the key delivery agencies is trying to ensure that sport and physical activity becomes more equitable across the UK. All of the home nations' sports councils have outlined their commitment to equality, for example, the Scottish government stated that

> *The* National Strategy for Sport in Scotland, *requires all of us involved in resourcing, delivering and promoting sport in Scotland to achieve the vision of Scotland as a country where sport is more widely available to all, where sporting talent is recognised and nurtured, and where world class performances in sport are achieved and sustained. By 2020, 60 per cent of adults in Scotland should take part in sport once a week.*
>
> (The Scottish Executive 2007: 16)

In Wales, The National Assembly for Wales stated that, 'All Climbing Higher deliverers must include equality plans and appropriate levels of investment to support the required action to redress known imbalances in sports participation' (Welsh Assembly Government 2006: 4).

Coaching

These ambitions of providing equitable sporting practices across community and elite settings are reliant upon a workforce of coaches who are able to engage and develop people in sport, whether that is in order to retain their interest, to keep people active or to enhance performance. sports coach UK have made inroads into rolling out the UK Coaching Framework and sports are buying into the concept of the UK Coaching Certificate. An agreed framework for coach development is seemingly in place and steps have been taken to develop a truly world class coaching system.

The UK sporting landscape – a model

Record levels of investment from Exchequer and Lottery monies are being channelled into the sporting landscape. This brings added pressure on those responsible for ensuring targets are set and outcomes achieved. National governing bodies of sport are being utilised by the government and national sporting partners perhaps more than ever before. In England, 46 sports are now more accountable through the Whole Sport Planning process and have clear ambitions for their sports. With this comes the added pressure of ensuring that they deliver.

The sporting landscape is complex and varied. It is ever-changing and heavily influenced by government policy. Some structures remain constant and others appear to evolve on a regular basis. The names may stay the same but their priorities will shift. The organisations are the actors: some are ever present and others come and go. Some of the actors change their role(s) and some appear content to continue their part over a longer period. The next section of the chapter will attempt to draw together the main organisations and demonstrate their role within the sporting landscape. Like any film or play, the actors appear in some scenes

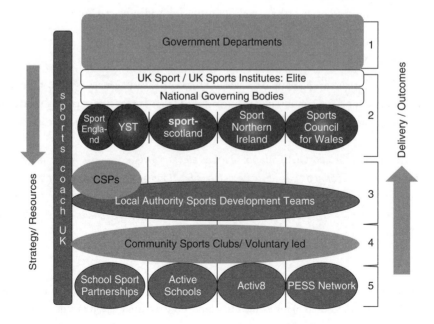

Figure 6.1 The UK sporting landscape

and not in others. They work with fellow actors for a period of time and then move on to the next scene or script. They are ever-changing in order to meet the desires and needs of the audience. Sport is not dissimilar and we shall explore that now.

Figure 6.1 above attempts to provide an overview of the key sporting organisations that aim to increase participation in sport, develop talent or support elite performers. The model appears to adopt a hierarchical approach but this is not the intention. It is a model that highlights some of the key sporting agencies across the UK and groups them by number based upon their similarities. It does attempt to demonstrate the direction of strategy, resources, delivery and outcomes. However, this does not apply in every instance, especially when local projects are delivered to meet local needs.

Group 1

The top tier of the model relates to key government departments across the UK that have a vested interest in sport. Examples of this would be the Department of Culture, Media and Sport and the Department of Culture, Arts and Leisure in Northern Ireland. As discussed in Chapter 1, the respective UK governments provide direction in the way of sporting policy and strategy. They shape the direction of the key sporting organisations in Group 2 through such documents as the DCMS sporting strategy, *Playing to Win: A New Era for Sport* (2008), and the sport strategy in Scotland which was published in 2007, *Reaching Higher – Building on the Success of Sport 21.*

Group 2

At the top of Group 2 are UK Sport and the UK Sports Institutes. Their role is specifically geared around the development of elite performers (and this has been considered in Chapter 5). The national governing bodies of sport provide direction for their own sporting stakeholders and develop opportunity throughout the sports development pathway. They are included in this model as they are responsible in their respective sports for increasing participation levels and the development of talent. Some of the sports, at the elite end of the scale, rely upon finance and support from UK Sport. Both the national governing bodies and UK Sport rely upon the delivery of sports participants from Groups 3, 4 and 5. These organisations operate at arm's length from the government departments. UK Sport and the home country sports councils are referred to as non-departmental public bodies. An NDPB has traditionally been referred to as an organisation which supports the government but is not a government department, and which accordingly operates at arm's length from ministers. The Youth Sport Trust is a charity and the governing bodies of sport are independent organisations. What they all have in common is the financial support that they receive from the government. They all utilise Exchequer funding and money from the National Lottery but none of the organisations are fully accountable to the government.

Each country in the UK operates with a home sports council but the system in England is slightly different to the others. Up until 1994 the English Sports Council (now rebranded as Sport England), through the Active School programme, was responsible for developing and co-ordinating sports development opportunities in English schools. In 1994 the Youth Sport Trust was established and took on the role of enhancing physical education and sporting opportunities in schools. Sport England now has a more focused remit to develop sporting opportunities within communities. Sport England is also supported by nine regional teams, but their role has diminished since the dissolution of the Regional Sports Boards and the centralisation of their grants programme. The other UK Sports Councils have a dual responsibility for community and school sport.

Group 3

This group relates to organisations at the delivery end of the sporting landscape. This group differs from the next group as they are led by and contain professional sports employees. County sports partnerships operate across England, after initially being put into place to deliver the Active Sports Programme and to bridge the gap between regional Sport England Offices/Regional Sports Boards and local authority initiatives. Chapter 4 provides an overview of the work of these partners. The model shows strategic direction and resources as coming down the system from the national organisations to local bodies. The case studies in Chapter 4 demonstrate this, but it must be treated with caution. Certainly at local authority level, sports development teams are more influenced by local priorities and may be more likely to ensure that work meet targets in their community or cultural strategy, rather than a government sporting strategy. These will vary depending upon the finances that they have secured from organisations such as Sport England.

Group 4

This group includes the army of voluntary-led, community sports clubs. They are an integral part of the sporting landscape and collectively have a workforce that surpasses most sports organisations. According to SkillsActive (2009a) there are approximately 1.2m coaches in the UK, 81 per cent of whom are volunteers. Most of these will ply their trade in community sports clubs. The Active People Survey 3 commissioned by Sport England recorded that 4.6 per cent of the adult population of England, which equates to 1,947,600 people, are doing at least one hour a week of volunteering in sport. Despite this being a slight decrease from the 2007/08 survey it still represents a significant contribution by the voluntary sector workforce that is at the very heart of UK sport (Sport England 2009a). It is estimated that volunteers contribute 1.8m hours of unpaid support every week of the year, which equates to over 54,000 full time jobs (Volresource 2009). This army of volunteers – coaches, administrators, officials and parents – represents the heart and soul of the UK sporting landscape, and without their valuable contribution the system would come crashing down. The value and significance of the voluntary sector is discussed further in Chapter 13.

Group 5

This group draws together the schools' PE and sports development programmes that are led by government departments and resourced nationally. The actual programmes and initiatives are led locally but are heavily influenced by the home country sports council or, in the case of England, the Youth Sport Trust. Examples of this include the work strand within the PESSYP Strategy in England and the Active School Programme in Scotland.

Running alongside the groups is the work of sports coach UK. As previously explained, the UK Coaching Framework supports coaches from across all stages of the sporting landscape.

The model is illustrated to show how policy, strategy and resources filter down through the sporting landscape and how the organisations in Groups 3, 4 and 5 support this by delivering 'on the ground' and providing actual results or outcomes. The success of all of this work is dependent upon a partnership approach and there is deliberate crossover in some of the work of the key agencies. In some instances, this crossover and partnership work is not always as effective as it could be. The complexity of the sporting landscape perhaps part way explains why this might be.

Chapter Review

The aim of this chapter has been to draw together the key information from Chapters 1–5 and to contextualise this information in relation to a wider sporting landscape. This has been attempted by providing a summary of the work that occurs in school settings, local communities and within the elite end of the sporting pathway. It has been recognised that the sporting landscape is complex and ever-changing. The chapter reviews how the key delivery agencies support this development of sport in the UK and draws this together in the sporting landscape model. Not all sporting organisations are represented in the model as it would be an impossible task. Hopefully you will now have a clearer understanding about the role and priorities of these agencies.

After reading this chapter and attempting the learning activities you should now be able to answer the following questions:

1 What are the three main components of the UK sporting landscape?
2 What role do the following play in the UK sporting landscape?
   - the respective UK governments
   - sport coach UK
   - volunteers
3 Give an example of how a number of the different agencies would work in partnership to achieve shared targets within the UK sporting landscape.

Further Reading

For school sport and government policy:
   - Houlihan, B. and Green, M. (2006) The changing status of school sport and physical education: explaining policy change. *Sport, Education and Society,* 11(1): 73–92.

For sport in the community setting:
   - Sport England (2008) *Sport England Strategy 2008–2011.* London: Sport England.

For sport in the elite setting:
   - Green, M. (2004) Changing policy priorities for sport in England: the emergence of elite sport development as a key policy concern. *Leisure Studies,* 23 (4): 365–385.

Chapter 7
London 2012: issues and controversies

This chapter is designed to help you:

- understand the role of the key agencies whose role it is to plan and deliver the Games in London in 2012;
- develop an awareness of the proposed legacy benefits;
- develop a critical awareness of the issues relating to the impacts of the Olympic Games and events across the UK.

As seen in Chapter 1, the government continues to play an important role in the development of sport and physical activity in the UK, despite the fact that, as Houlihan (2001: 92) suggests, historically much of its involvement has been haphazard and reactive rather than strategic. Sport has never been higher on the government's agenda because of the potential opportunities of London 2012. As a result of London hosting the Games, the investment in sport from central government has reached unprecedented levels. Winning the right to host the Games was not an easy path: years of preparation and hard work by individuals and organisations went into delivering the Games to London. Staging a successful event that will live up to the potential that was recognised in the bid by the International Olympic Committee will require a concerted effort by the key agencies that are tasked with such a challenge. After the Games have been held in London we will have all had very different experiences and levels of involvement. We cannot foresee what impact it will have on us as individuals in the years that follow.

Introduction: funding the Games

In March 2007, the government announced a £9.325bn budget for the 2012 Olympic and Paralympic Games, funded through central government (£5.975bn), the National Lottery (£2.175bn) and London (£1.175bn). As part of this funding package, the 2007 Comprehensive Spending Review (CSR) confirmed the first phase of central government investment of £3.623bn over the first three years to deliver the foundations for a successful 2012 Games (HM Treasury 2007).

The London 2012 Games are delivered by two key organisations: the London Organising Committee of the Olympic Games and Paralympic Games (LOCOG) and the Olympic Delivery Authority (London 2012, 2008a). It could be argued that it is difficult to distinguish between the two, with shared offices and a shared sense of focus. However, they both have very different roles in the staging and delivery of the

London 2012 Games. The Olympic Delivery Authority (ODA) is the public sector body responsible for the delivery of the new venues and infrastructure required for the London 2012 Games. The ODA budget is drawn entirely from the public sector. The ODA is funded by the Department for Culture, Media and Sport (DCMS), the Greater London Authority, the London Development Agency and the Olympic Lottery Distributor. LOCOG is the private sector company responsible for staging and hosting the 2012 Games. It has a £2bn budget, with almost all of it to be raised from the private sector. This commercial revenue will come from several sources, with LOCOG receiving income from the International Olympic Committee (IOC) as well as generating its own income from sales of tickets, merchandise and a domestic sponsorship programme.

Learning Activity 7.1

What kind of legacy will the Games create? Write down a list of five things that the Games in London will impact upon and then rank them from 1 to 5 (1 being the highest), based upon which will have the greater impact.

The government Olympic Executive in the Department for Culture, Media and Sport (DCMS) is responsible for the delivery of the London 2012 Olympic Games and Paralympic Games. It reports to Tessa Jowell, the Olympics Minister (based in the Cabinet Office). In this role, she has direct responsibility for delivery of the government's overall Olympic programme and reports to the Prime Minister (Cabinet Office 2008). The DCMS is responsible for managing central government funding for the Games and wider regeneration costs. In addition, the DCMS is also responsible for bringing together the legacy benefits brought by all the wider sporting, cultural, environmental, educational and business enterprise initiatives that will take place all over the country as a result of the Games before, during and after 2012 (London 2012 2008b).

In order to make sense of all this, an Olympic Board was established which provides oversight, strategic coordination and monitoring of the entire 2012 Games project, ensuring the delivery of the commitments made to the International Olympic Committee when the Games were awarded to London, and a sustainable legacy from the staging of the Games. The Olympic Board is made up of Olympics Minister Tessa Jowell, Mayor of London Boris Johnson, British Olympic Association Chairman Colin Moynihan and London 2012 Organising Committee Chair Sebastian Coe (London 2012 2008b). Team GB is then selected by the British Olympic Authority. They define their role as follows:

> The BOA is not funded or controlled by government, has no political interests and is completely dependent upon commercial sponsorship and fundraising income. The BOA is the strong, independent voice for British Olympic Sport. The BOA's role is to lead and prepare our nation's finest athletes at the Olympic Games and has the responsibility for developing the Olympic Movement throughout the UK.

(British Olympic Association 2008)

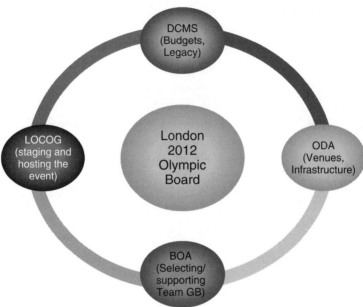

Figure 7.1 London 2012 organisational priorities

Figure 7.1 attempts to summarise the roles of the organisations and how they work in partnership to deliver this exciting opportunity.

Learning Activity 7.2

The budget for the Olympic Games has increased significantly from the pre-Games estimate of £2.4bn to £9.35bn (BBC 2007).

1   What would you consider to be the main contributing factors to the budget increases?
2   What are the likely impacts on clubs and small organisations of increasing Lottery funding to £2.2bn?
3   To what extent do you think the Olympics offers 'value for money'?
4   Consider what impact the London 2012 Olympics will have across the UK and what the main impact in the way of a legacy should be.

The legacy of London 2012

Winning the right to stage the Games in London was made possible not just by suggesting that London could actually stage the event, but by instilling confidence in the voting members that London could provide a legacy that would benefit the UK for years to come. The DCMS released an intial legacy plan titled *Our Promise* in June 2007, and then followed this up with a revised legacy action plan in 2008 titled: *Before, During and After: Making the Most of the London 2012 Games.*

Learning Activity 7.3

Visit the website of the DCMS: www.culture.gov.uk/images/publications/2012LegacyActionPlan. pdf and download a copy of the Legacy Action Plan. See page 10 for a breakdown of people's priorities for the 2012 legacy. As you look at the data, be aware that it has to be treated with some caution, as it appears that the views have been ascertained by asking people if they care a lot or a little about these legacy themes. If respondents stated that they cared a little then it would be recorded as a positive response.

Consider the following:

1   Do any of these priorities feature on your list from Learning Activity 7.1?
2   Which of these priorities are important to you and why?
3   Which of these would be the easiest and most difficult to achieve?

Research conducted by the British Market Research Bureau (BMRB) intended to inform the action plan found that people's priorities for the legacy of the Games included creating more jobs, seeing an increased take-up in sports, and opportunities for business. After the extensive research by BMRB, the government prioritised five areas for the legacy of the Games. These are now based around five key promises:

1   Make the UK a world-leading sporting nation.
2   Transform the heart of East London.
3   Inspire a generation of young people.
4   Make the Olympic Park a blueprint for sustainable living.
5   Demonstrate that the UK is a creative, inclusive and welcoming place to live in, visit and for business.

Past Games and legacy issues

When considering whether or not these promises and ambitions can be achieved we can evaluate past Olympic Games to establish the impact of this global event upon the host city and nation. Shipway (2007) explains that most host cities tend to view legacy in economic terms but suggests that there is growing emphasis on the other forms of legacy. These other forms of legacy would include inspiring young people through sport and getting people active. The next section of this chapter will briefly consider some of the literature around the participation and economic legacy issues at previous Games.

Impact on sporting participation

Promise one includes the ambition to get more people active. Wang and Theodorald (2007) suggest that little attention has been paid to the impact the Olympic Games can have on mass participation levels in sport. This is supported by Cashman who states that:

> There has been inadequate attention paid to planning for the post-Games period and the legacy of an Olympic Games. Bid cities focus to such a large extent on winning the bid, planning for the Games and staging a successful Games that the post-Games period has been neglected.

(2002: 12)

Wang and Theodorald (2007), when researching participation levels in Qingdao in China, host to the sailing regatta for the Beijing Games, found that interventions directly linked to the staging of the Games did demonstrate increased levels of sports participation. The increases in this particular geographical area accounted for a 4 per cent increase in participation levels from 2004 to 2006. However, if these interventions were linked to the Games then it is probable that increased funding was invested in this area. It could well be the case that the increases would have occurred anyway with the increased amount of funding. Coalter (2004) reviewed a range of literature and considered the impact of past Olympic Games on sports participation levels. His findings suggest that the impact was limited and in some cases participation declined.

Impact on volunteering

The Games in London will rely upon the recruitment of over 70,000 volunteers (London 2012, 2008c). Individuals are currently being encouraged to register for information with applications being invited early on in 2010. A wide range of roles will be required in order to service the event. You can register your interest by visiting the following website: https://www.london2012.com/settings/login.php?reason=volunteering.

Lessons have been learnt from the successes that the organisers of the 2002 Manchester Commonwealth Games had. Their recruitment campaign, *Count Me In,* was very successful and recruited 10,500 volunteers from over 20,000 applicants to support the event. This was the biggest volunteer recruitment drive in peace time (UK Sport, 2002). In a qualitative study following the Games in Manchester (UK Sport 2002), 698 volunteers completed a survey outlining their experiences and views on volunteering at the event. Generally the feedback was positive but some negative views included poor training, supervision, communication, food and refreshments provided, and long shifts. These responses represented a small amount of the survey, but nonetheless, they are issues that will help those recruiting and retaining volunteers for London 2012.

Impact on the economy

Baade and Matheson (2002) state that it was probably only after the 1984 Los Angeles Games that the Games were seen as an opportunity for a city or host nation to improve its economy, and that a properly run Games generated billions of pounds of profit. The 1976 Games in Montreal and the 1980 Games in

Moscow both operated at a loss. Baade and Matheson (2002) state that, in part, cities and countries invest in the Olympics because of the prestige and the opportunity to make a political statement, but it is arguable that the primary motivation for hosting the Games is economic. They go on to point out that by having only one bid city, as in Los Angeles in 1984, the IOC's monopoly was broken. The Los Angeles organising committee refused to sign the contract with the IOC and were exempt from the infamous IOC rule 4, which requires the host city to assume financial liability for the Games. Since 1992 there have been at least four other candidate cities bidding for each Games.

Atlanta's hosting of the 1996 Summer Olympics was tainted by scandal, and it is alleged that they simply 'outbid the competition' in violation of Olympic principles and US federal laws (Baade and Matheson 2002). Hotchkiss et al. (2003) established that Atlanta won the rights to host the 1996 Summer Olympics and despite the $2.5bn price tag, the benefits derived from hosting the Games were expected to outweigh costs. Hotchkiss et al. (2003) conducted a study to measure the effects they had on the economy, comparing the effects the Games had on employment with the projected employment rates if the Games had never come to town. They found that the Games boosted employment by 17 per cent in the counties of Georgia affiliated with and close to the Olympic activity, compared to non-venue counties not within close proximity. They did, however, deduce that the impact on wages was weak and that the jobs were transitory – in other words, there for the Games and gone once the Games left town.

Kasimati (2003), referring to pre-Games studies that estimate the potential economic growth, increased tourism and additional employment, states that ambitious claims of the benefits of the Games were never confirmed by post-Games analysis and asks whether the money could be better used elsewhere to provide similar if not greater benefits. Kasimati concludes that 'the high expectations released by most of them could be considered to be potentially biased, because the ambition of those commissioning the studies is to favour the hosting of the games' (2003: 442).

Impacts of Olympic Games and other major events

Since the summer Olympic Games of Montreal in 1976 and Los Angeles in 1984, the Olympic Games have been the subject of attention from within the political and academic arenas: the attention from these two areas are not necessary unrelated. Much of the attention has generally been to do with whether the Olympic Games are worth the amount of public expenditure. It is not only the Olympics that attract such inquiries. The Olympic Games to some extent represent the pinnacle of major hallmark sports events and therefore attract attention from a vast array of commentators. Other major events that also generate such interest include the FIFA World Cup football championships, UEFA's European Football Championship and the IRB Rugby World Cup in rugby union. Other events of note but not to the same scale include the IAAF World Athletics Championship and the world championships of many other sports.

The scrutiny that is now commonplace when assessing the impact of major sports events like the Olympic Games is perhaps just. After all, an enormous amount of public subsidy goes into the staging of the event. For events like the Olympic Games, the costs of staging the events include the building of sports facilities, improvements in transport infrastructure, the building of the Olympic village to accommodate the athletes and, for modern day events, the cost of safety and security. These are just some of the expenditures that have to be met during the preparation phase. There are also costs incurred during and after the event too. Such is the huge cost of staging the Olympic Games, many have questioned whether the benefits of staging the Games outweigh the cost of doing so. Put another way, is the overall impact of staging the Olympic Games positive?

Since the staging of most contemporary Olympic Games, public officials have had to provide rationales for their decisions to bid for and host the event. These rationales have to some extent remained consistent over the past years and have been the subject of research in the academic literature. The extents to which these rationales are themselves justifiable are debatable. In the remainder of this section, some of the rationales that are commonly put forward are discussed in the general context of major sports events and the specific context of the London 2012 Olympic Games.

Job creation

Often the motivation and rationale for staging sports events is based on the number of jobs that will be created. In fact the very mention of job creation stirs up emotion. After all, not many will argue against public money being used to stage a sports event which in turn will generate sustainable jobs for families and members within the community. The theory and logic behind this assertion seems appropriate, but does the evidence and practice reflect the theory? It is true that the staging of major sports events creates jobs but some of the critical questions that need to be addressed relate to: the number of jobs that are created; their sustainability and how long they last for; and their value.

For major sports events like the Olympic Games, the demand for new sports and sports-related infrastructure means that jobs are created during the pre-Games phase. The stadiums, arena and other venues, along with new and updated transport links, mean that many of these jobs are in the construction sector of the economy. And while these jobs are of value, their sustainability is limited as once the construction projects are completed and the Games do start, there are no further requirements for these jobs and their respective roles.

During the event itself, there is likely to be a substantial supply of jobs. Many of these jobs are associated with the running of the Games. Some will involve working with the various national Olympic teams and many will involve working with the organising committee at events ensuring that the events run smoothly and to plan. One of the most remarkable effects of the Olympic Games and other major sporting events is their ability to galvanise communities. Such is this effect that armies of volunteers often emerge, providing the organising committees with a host of skills and labour. The value of community cohesion often goes unreported but the benefits that accrue to the volunteers should not be understated. After all, if there was no benefit to offering the skills and labour, many of them would simply not volunteer. Precisely for this reason, many of the 'jobs' created around major events like the Olympic Games are performed by volunteers at zero cost to the event organisers. This is good news for the volunteers who clearly benefit from being involved, and it is also good news for the event organiser who faces much lower labour costs. However, these jobs and roles are short term and not sustainable beyond the period of the Games itself. Hence, the level of job creation during the Games is likely to be limited.

And now, in accordance with tradition, I declare the Games of the XXIX Olympiad closed, and I call upon the youth of the world to assemble four years from now in London to celebrate the Games of the XXX Olympiad.

The above is an extract from the closing speech of Jacques Rogge, the President of the International Olympic Committee, during the closing ceremony of the Olympic Games in Beijing in 2008. The speech is part of the tradition of the Olympic Games and marks the conclusion of the current Games and the advent of the forthcoming one. Similar remarks will no doubt be offered at the closing ceremony of London 2012 and at that point, the Games will officially move to the post-Games phase. The phase of the Games is just as important as the preceding two phases. However, unlike the other two phases, there is no definitive end point and in theory this phase goes on and on. At various points, matters of an Olympic nature will diminish somewhat. However, this period is technically indefinite. It is in the period that the notion of sustainable jobs created by the Olympic Games becomes more critical. Have jobs been created by the Games only for the post-Games period and how long will these job be sustained for are often the critical questions.

A key legacy of the Olympic Games is the facilities that remain for the communities after the Games have moved on. The sports and sports-related infrastructure will create jobs but the number of jobs is often a key issue. Jobs in areas of sports development, facilities management, coaching and other sports-related jobs will have been created but not in the numbers that compare with the headline expenditure of staging the Olympic Games.

The notion of job creation applies not only to those jobs created by the Games but also to jobs created in various sectors of the economy; jobs that would not have been created if it were not for the Olympic Games. The staging of an Olympic Games will inevitably create wealth among owners of business and enterprise within the economy, be it in the city where the Games is being staged or in the wider geographical regions. The impacts of staging major events on job creation within the economy can be learnt by researching and investigating what happens in other events. Crompton (2001) noted that the analysis of job creation needs to be treated with care and caution. In a survey of studies that have considered the impact of events on job creation, Crompton noted that employers were more likely to respond to additional consumer demand at the time of sports events by making greater utilisation of the existing labour force and 'that it is unlikely that that business would hire additional employees as a result of a sport event, because the extra demand only lasts for a short period of time' (p 20). Thus the full-time jobs anticipated to be created by events often do not materialise, as any further demand is met by temporary staff.

The creation of jobs is not the only motivation for staging major sports events and should therefore not be the only criterion on which to judge an event's success. However, as one of the many motivations proffered by event organisers, there are limitations to what sports events, even those on the scale of the Olympic Games, can deliver by way of jobs.

Tourism expenditure and income

As with jobs, one of the visible and tangible benefits of staging mega-events like the Olympic Games is the 'new' tourism and associated income it generates. The critical emphasis here is the term 'new'. London, like many previous cities which have staged the Olympic Games, is a major city and tourism is a significant part of its economy. The value of tourism to the London economy can be measured in a number of ways including tourist receipts, the number of tourists or the number of bed nights. For example, there were 15.6m overnight visits to London by non-domestic tourists in 2006. This figure fell to 15.3m in 2007 and to 14.8m in 2008 (Office of National Statistics 2009).

When London does host the Olympic Games, what impact will the Games have on tourism? In addressing this question, every effort must be made to identify those tourists who have specifically travelled to London for the Games. Those tourists who engage with the Games but who would have been in London anyway should not form part of the analysis as they would still have made the expenditures, and therefore the Olympic Games should not be credited for generating this. Major events such as the Olympic Games are also likely to displace regular tourism. Without the Olympic Games, tourism in London can be measured by the number of overnight visits, which, as we have seen above, stands at around 15m overnight visitors from the rest of the world, and around 24m from other parts of the UK (VisitBritain 2009). A significant proportion of these regular tourist visits may not materialise during the Games because of the likely increase in levels of congestion in and around London during the event. Hence the staging of the Games to some (large or small) extent may cause a fall in regular tourism.

Another intriguing issue surrounding Olympic Games is the deadweight expenditure. Residents within London and farther afield will enthusiastically engage with the Games, financially and emotionally. Studies (e.g. Crompton 1995, 2001) have argued that when assessing the impact of major events, efforts must be made to identify and quantify expenditures by residents and these should not be classed as income generated by the event. This is what is commonly referred to as deadweight expenditure. With or without the Games, it is argued that residents are likely to make these expenditures. However, the presence of the Games only serves to divert resources from other sectors of the economy to the newly-created *Olympic sector*. Hence no new income is generated from residents for the local economy as existing resources are simply being diverted from pre-existing sectors. The notion of deadweight expenditure also links with the concepts of *time-switchers* or *casuals*. Time-switchers and casuals are those who would have visited without the event and therefore would have spent money within the area.

The treatment of tourism and income when assessing the impact of major events like the Olympic Games is complex. Without accurate and precise treatment of tourism and income, the reported impacts are likely to be erroneous. Researchers and public officials involved in assessing such impacts need to accurately report them noting all the aforementioned issues of tourism and income. As a result, surveys amongst visitors to events should distinguish between those who are residents and those who are tourists. In identifying tourists, further efforts should also be made to identify time-switchers and casuals. Only expenditure by those tourists who have made purposeful and dedicated visits to the Olympic city for solely for the Olympic Games should be credited to the Olympic Games as additional impacts over and above what previously was present.

Sports facilities and sports participation

Amongst the mega-events, the Olympic Games stand out as requiring substantial investment in a sports infrastructure. The facility demand necessary to host the Games is significant given the number of sports events taking place during the two-week period. The vast array of sports events that will be on show means that it is unlikely that any city selected to host the Games will have in place the necessary facilities. Cities therefore face the challenge of building and installing many new facilities. What will become of these once the Olympic Games moves on?

One of the perceived benefits of hosting major events, particularly multi-sports events, is that the local community will have access to sports facilities that were previously absent. This benefit is particularly welcome, especially since significant portions of the costs of staging Olympic Games are met by the cities' residents. If the presence of these new facilities is a benefit, a major challenge that faces those responsible is how to make sure that the benefits are distributed across the community in a fair and equitable manner. To explore this point further, consider the following hypothetical case study.

Case Study
The (fictional) case of local community sports facilities

The residents within the local community have recently witnessed the conclusion of a successful multi-sports event and while the cost of staging the event was partly met by central government, large sums of local community resources and local taxes were also used. Consequently, there are other worthwhile projects within the community that can no longer be funded, an opportunity cost to the local community. One of the facilities to emerge as a direct consequence of the Games is the tennis arena. The arena boasts 12 tennis courts, 5 of which are indoor courts. Many of the courts have spacious surrounds and therefore have space for temporary stands for spectators during major tournaments. The arena is certainly a welcome addition to the portfolio of tennis provisions within the community. Although there was an entry charge, this was not too prohibitive given that public subsidies were provided to the arena's management, which were intended for and used to encourage mass participation.

Prior to the Games, the public tennis facilities within the community were unassuming and basic in quality. Collectively there were some 32 of these courts geographically distributed across the wider community. While there are private tennis clubs with numerous indoor and outdoor tennis courts, these unpretentious public tennis facilities were all that were available to the local community. In fact significant benefits were derived from the humble public facilities. First their geographical distribution across the community served to provide wider access to tennis courts. Many local residents can access the courts within a short walk or drive. Second, their unassuming character meant that there was no direct charge. Tennis players, young and old, wealthy and poor, came and went, playing tennis for free. In fact survey data by the local council showed that the majority of the users were from socio-economic groups C2, D and E. These courts were essentially public goods from which no members of the community were excluded. These long-standing tennis courts along with those of the new tennis arena provided the community with an enriched tennis environment.

Two years after staging the event which brought the community the tennis arena, spending cuts were made in sport and leisure services. Firstly, the modest amounts that were used to maintain the 32 tennis courts in parks across the community were cut. The result was that many of these courts became disused and derelict. Second, the tennis arena also faced cuts to its subsidies and consequently entry charges had to increase and in some cases to prohibitive levels. The council justified the cuts in finance to the 32 public courts on the grounds that those who used these could and should now divert their demand to what they called the 'world class' tennis arena, which after all is a community facility of the 'highest standard' and available to all. With regard to the cuts to the subsidy that the arena received, the council's response was that all local public services had to make 'efficiency savings' and the sport and leisure division and its constituent parts were no exception.

So what does this mean for tennis enthusiasts in the community? First, their taxes were used to stage a major event at the expense of other arguably worthwhile projects. Second, their 32 unassuming modest local tennis courts became disused and derelict. Third, without the 32 local courts, tennis players now have to travel lengthy distances to the tennis arena, incurring substantial travel costs along the way. Fourth, the increased entry charge is prohibitive for many participants. Even without the increase in entry charge, those players who previously used the tennis courts at the local parks were facing an increase in cost. Interestingly enough, much of the demand that is realised within the tennis arena is by those who belonging predominantly to socio-economic groups B and C1. What is the reason for their disproportionate access? The entry charge is below the average charged by those private tennis clubs.

On many levels, the hosting of the event has disadvantaged those who should be benefiting most. Furthermore, the benefits of staging the event that do remain are, inadvertently or otherwise, being disproportionately allocated to those who need it least.

Sports facilities and urban regeneration

A rationale that has often been used to justify major sports events is the development of the urban and physical environment. In theory as well as practice, this is a worthwhile objective. However, hurdles lie in the pre-event and planning phases. If badly planned, using major events and the accompanying sports facilities to regenerate the urban and physical environment may not necessarily meet the needs of the local community. The installation of new sports facilities often has the biggest impact on the urban and physical landscape and while these facilities may be attractive and boast the latest in technology and architectural designs, they generally exceed the needs of the community they are meant to serve.

Taking the main Olympic stadium as an example, very rarely do communities have the need for so big a stadium. Without careful strategic planning at the pre-Games phase, there is the danger that large scale sports facilities end up being under utilised and overwhelming for the community. The City of Manchester Stadium, which is now home to Manchester City Football Club, is a very good example of good strategic planning. It had always been intended that after the 2002 Commonwealth Games the stadium would be converted from a track and field stadium to a football stadium, and these issues were no doubt considered in the original design of the stadium.

Not all stadiums or facilities that have been designed for mega-events have incorporated the needs of end users. The Don Valley Stadium in Sheffield is an example. This stadium was designed for athletics during the World Student Games in 1991. In the immediate aftermath of the Games, it hosted a number of IAAF athletics meetings. However, the stadium's ability to accommodate other sports besides athletics is compromised. For sports like football and both codes of rugby the separation of the crowd from play by an athletics track means that the atmosphere, which professional teams in England value highly, is missing. While athletic tracks in football stadiums are common across Europe, this is an unfamiliar and less welcome practice in England.

The Don Valley Stadium has been the home ground to Sheffield Eagles Rugby League Football Club since 1991. However, as of 2010, they will move from this stadium to Bramhall Lane, to share with Sheffield United Football Club. Given that most stadiums in England are used by professional sports teams, if the hosting of a professional sports team was an objective from the outset, their needs should have been part of the design; just as it was in the case of the City of Manchester Stadium.

At present, Rotherham United Football Club will use the Don Valley Stadium on a temporary basis until its new stadium is ready. In the absence of a permanent professional sports team, the Don Valley Stadium is likely to be used predominantly for one-off events such as concerts. The only frequent and regular use of the stadium is by the City of Sheffield Athletic Club. Most will agree that a 25,000-seater stadium is overwhelming for a local athletic club. So while new sports facilities do contribute to urban regeneration, it is important that they are used as community facilities or as prudent commercial enterprises. Having expensive unused facilities is perhaps only marginally better than having disused or derelict ones.

Learning Activity 7.4

Consider the cases of previous Olympic cities: Beijing in 2008, Athens in 2004, Sydney in 2000, Atlanta in 1996 and Barcelona in 1992. With regard to developing the physical environments and improving the images of the cities, how has the staging of summer Olympic Games benefited these places? What evidence is there to support your assertions?

Chapter Review

This chapter has examined issues relating to the forthcoming Olympic Games in London. The Olympic Games, when they are staged in 2012, will be the biggest sporting event to be staged in the UK. The pre-Games phase had mobilised various agencies and resources to ensure that the Games prove to be successful. The level of government commitment is evident by the cabinet representation and the appointment of an Olympics Minister. Other agencies involved in delivering the Games are London Organising Committee of the Olympic Games and Paralympic Games (LOCOG) and the Olympic Delivery Authority (ODA), just to mention a few. This shows the level of importance attached to London 2012 and the staging of a successful event.

Judging the success of the Olympic Games, however, is a complex undertaking. The difficulties that emerge are that whilst the Olympic Games is a major sporting event, many of the criteria for judging success combine sport and non-sport related factors. Often these factors form the basis of what is generally known as (economic) impact assessments. The main attention of such studies tends to focus on issues such as job creation, tourism measures, urban regeneration, infrastructure development and sports participation, to name a few.

Some of these criteria were discussed and for each of them, a series of issues and controversies were noted and in some instances, evidence and lessons from previous hosting of major sports events were presented. The challenges that face the organising agencies of the Olympic Games in London are to maximise the overall positive impacts of the Games and to ensure that the benefits that emerge are long-lasting and widely distributed, so that as many people as possible benefit from the Games.

After reading this chapter and attempting the learning activities you should now be able to answer the following questions:

1   Who are the key agencies responsible for ensuring the successful staging of the Olympic Games in London and what are their principal roles?
2   The government prioritised five areas for the legacy of the Games. What evidence would suggest that these promises have been kept?
3   What are the main benefits of staging a major event such as the Olympic Games?
4   What are the pitfalls of staging major sports events and how might these be minimised?
5   As a result of staging major sports events, Manchester and Sheffield have a diverse range of sports facilities. How are these facilities being used and do they benefit the community at large?

Further Reading

- Crompton, J.L. (1995) Economic impact analysis of sports facilities and events: eleven sources of misapplication, *Journal of Sport Management*, 9: 14–35.
- Gratton, C. and Henry, I. (2001) *Sport in the City: The Role of Sport in Economic and Social Regeneration*. London: Routledge.
- Gratton, C., Shibli, S., and Dobson, N. (2000) The economic importance of major sports events, *Managing Leisure*, 5: 17–28.
- Lee, C. and Taylor, T. (2005) Critical reflections on the economic impact assessment of a mega-event: the case of 2002 FIFA World Cup, *Tourism Management*, 26: 595–603.
- Siegfried, J. and Zimbalist, A. (2000) The economics of sports facilities and their communities, *Journal of Economic Perspectives*, 14: 95–114.
- Szymanski, S (2009) *Playbooks and Checkbooks: An Introduction to the Economics of Modern Sports*, Princeton: Princeton University Press.

Part Three

The commercial sector

Chapter 8
Sports sponsorship

Learning Objectives

This chapter is designed to help you:

- understand the concept and fundamental issues of sports sponsorship;
- understand the relationship between sport and sponsorship;
- examine the impact of sponsorship on sport;
- examine the objectives of the various parties involved in sports sponsorship;
- identify sources of conflict and problems associated with sports sponsorship.

Just like the symbiotic relationship that has developed between sport and television, sport and sponsorship are inseparable. Sponsorship is now a dominant feature of professional sports and those who are in charge of sport often extract as much as is possible from the sponsorship market. As a result of sports sponsorship, there are now new protocols that have to be followed by all those involved in sports, be they competitors, managers, coaches or members of the media. In Formula 1, the top-placed drivers are obliged to give interviews to media representatives and be the subject of press conferences. It is a modern-day custom for these drivers to wear caps crowded with the logos of various sponsors, so that the millions of television viewers and newspaper readers are exposed to the brands which support the drivers and their teams. In team sports such as football, the manager and coaches of the teams are obliged to give post-match interviews and these generally take place in front of a board displaying the brand names and logos of those who sponsor the team and the league.

The issues noted above are not limited to team sports, but also feature in individual sports and major tournaments. The reach of sports sponsorship has also been extended: traditional influences of television are now complemented by those of new media; sponsorship is not just what happening in sports arenas but outside them. These issues and many more are the subject of this chapter.

Introduction

Sponsorship and sport are inextricably linked but it is also a relationship that is hard to quantify. Gratton and Taylor (2001) present the values of sports sponsorships as reported in a number of studies from 1971 to 1983 and while there have been studies of sports sponsorship in the UK dating as far back as 1971 (Sport Council Working Party on sports sponsorship), The Howell Report in 1983 was one of the first major reports on the subject. Mintel produced more contemporary information on the value of sports sponsorship, however, given the pace of change in the market, reports do not always precisely present the value of sports sponsorships.

Another difficulty in measuring the value of sports sponsorship is that the sponsorship contract between the sponsor and the sponsored does not always involved the exchange of money. In many instances, the exchange itself could be of services. A telecommunications company may find it more beneficial to provide services and this also might be more beneficial to the sponsored. Notwithstanding the difficulties of estimating the value of sponsorship to the UK, Mintel in 2006 produced a series of annual estimates, forecast and projections (see Table 8.1). Based on these, the value of sports sponsorship in the UK is projected to be worth over £1bn. Given these significant amounts, sports leagues, sports organisations and other sports entities have to engage with the sports sponsorship market effectively as the potential amounts of revenue from sponsorship can be substantial.

Year	Current prices (in millions of pounds)
2001	782
2002	793
2003	797
2004	818
2005 (estimated)	846
2006*	871
2007**	906
2008**	952
2009**	1,005
2010**	1,062
2011**	1,118

Table 8.1: Annual values of sponsorship in the UK
(and ** indicate forecast and projections respectively)*
Source: Mintel (2006)

The relationship between sponsorship and sport is complex. This complexity influences the practices that have now become customary in sport. During a normal weekend in which Manchester United host one of their rivals in the Premier League, viewers are normally exposed to the names and brands of those companies who sponsor either Manchester United or the Premier League. In the case of the former, these firms include Audi (automobiles), Budweiser (beer) and AIG (insurance). In the case of the latter, the sponsors include Barclays (banking), who are the official sponsors, and Budweiser (beer), who are the official website partners rather than sponsors of the actual league. But why does Budweiser not sponsor the league even in the capacity of a secondary sponsor with the tagline 'official beer supplier to the Premier League'? This sort of relationship induces problems. Some Premier League teams are sponsored by beer companies either in a large or small capacity: Liverpool and Carlsberg (who are the team's main shirt sponsor); Everton and Chang Beer (who also sponsor the team's shirt); and Sunderland who are sponsored by Scottish and Newcastle (whose portfolio of beer includes Foster, Heineken, John Smiths and Kronenbourg). And these clubs would not welcome advertising boards and messages from a rival of one of their own sponsors. This is one of the features of free-riding and ambush marketing which we will consider in this chapter.

Within the international sports market, sponsorship is also key too. There are many factors that are likely to influence the relationship between a sponsor and a sponsored. For example, national football teams, when participating in FIFA and UEFA sanctioned tournaments, are not allowed to have sponsors on their shirts. It makes sense for FIFA and UEFA to prevent this so that their own principal sponsors, which currently include Coca-Cola, Emirates, Hyundai-Kia Motors, Sony and Visa, do not face competition in the sports sponsorship market. By doing so, FIFA and UEFA are able to extract larger sums from these sponsorship partners by, to some extent, providing them with exclusive communication channels to football fans.

Sponsorship arrangements involving individual athletes are just as complex as those of sports federations or event organisers. A significant part of the sponsorship market is the relationship between sponsors and individual athletes. Athletes are quick to repay their loyalty to sponsor by ensuring that their sponsors' logos are visible on television broadcasts and that they mention them in television and radio interviews. The relationships between athletes and sponsors are likely to depend not just on how good athletes are but also how well they are able and willing to promote the sponsors' name and brand. Measures of this loyalty include interruptions to athletes' competition schedules to appear at and promote sponsors' events. In some instances, this may include participating in an event sanctioned by a sponsor over and above other events.

The remainder of the chapter is organised as follows. The next section examines the concept of sports sponsorship. This is followed by an analysis of the different types of sports sponsorship. We then look at a series of cases demonstrating the growing phenomena of free-riding and ambush marketing in sport.

The concept and objectives of sponsorship

Sponsorship is a sophisticated tool for communicating with audiences and while it shares some common features with advertising and promotion, the approaches used in sponsorship are somewhat different. As with advertising and promotion, the objectives of sponsorship can be to improve revenue from sales, increase consumer awareness of brands and products, and to generate a positive return on investment. However, unlike advertising and promotion, sponsorship normally involves partnership between two parties. Furthermore, sponsorship can cut through the *noise* and *clutter* that exist in the world of mass advertising. The principal–agent theory can be used to understand the dynamics of sponsorship. The principal, in this case the company looking to sponsor, provides a benefit to an agent, the party looking for sponsorship. While it is common for the principal to provide benefit in the form of money to the agent, this is not always the case. In some instances, the agreement between the two parties might be for the principal to provide services to the agent. In return the agent provides the sponsorship opportunities for the principal. For this relationship and agreement to work, the interests of the principal and the agent must be compatible and aligned with each other. This is the fundamental basis of sponsorship and is shown in Figure 8.1.

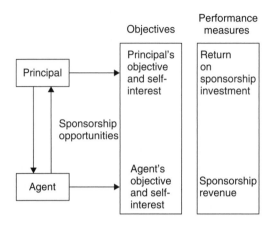

Objectives

Performance measures

Figure 8.1 The principal–agent theory and sponsorship

Sports sponsorship can be analysed using the principal–agent theory with particular attention placed on the objectives of the two parties. For the principal, some return on sponsorship investment is sought. This return could be measured in a variety of ways. For some companies, this may be as explicit as to increase profit or increase sales. For others it may be brand awareness and exposure. As sport is able to attract large audiences, be it live or accessing content in newspapers or online, it provides the ideal opportunities that sponsors are looking for. For the most part, sponsors are seeking communications channels and access, to audiences. The greater the audiences they can access, combined with exclusive control of the means of access, the more they are willing to pay.

For the agent being sponsored, the objectives vary depending on the party. For example, the objectives of athletes in the sponsorship market are likely to be different from the objectives of event organisers or, say, sports leagues. For athletes, objectives may include maximising their earnings – although while this may be the dominant objective, there are likely to be other important objectives too. For some athletes, sponsorship is also an opportunity to develop an association with the sponsoring party, and this association may be valued by the athlete enough to forgo some earnings. The objectives of the athlete are likely to depend on a number of factors including how well he or she is established in the sport. In Chapter 14, you will find some discussion of the salary-endorsement ratio for different athletes. For some sports, salary earnings from playing are substantial enough to make sponsorship and endorsement less important.

For event organisers, the objectives are often to maximise revenues that can be generated from sponsorship by offering an array of sponsorship opportunities. This is also the case for leagues, governing bodies, teams and clubs.

Case Study
It's not about the money

Andre Agassi has had a long relationship with Nike since he turned professional in 1986. Their relationship was epitomised by the Challenge Court range, a line of clothing and footwear developed for the player during the late 1980s/early 1990s; the majority of the other players in the Nike tennis stable used the Supreme Court line. The move to Adidas in 2005 after 17 years with Nike baffled many sports sponsorship experts. This is because Agassi's symbiotic connection with the brand was of a stature similar to and comparable with the likes of Tiger Woods in golf, Michael Jordan in basketball and Lance Armstrong in cycling, all of whom have had long-term sponsorship deals with by Nike (Rovell 2005). One of the reasons why Agassi opted for Adidas over Nike was that the former was willing to support his charitable foundation. Erich Stamminger, member of the Executive Board of Adidas-Salomon AG responsible for Global Marketing, said:

> *Andre is indisputably one of the biggest athletes of the 21st century and we are excited to support Andre not only with the best product on court, but also through his foundation.*
>
> (Adidas 2009)

In this instance, the objective of the athlete is not just to maximise earnings from the sponsorship market but to work with a company that is willing to support his children's charity.

For the sponsored, the rationale for seeking sponsorship is often to further maximise the earnings that could be generated. However, there are costs associated with sponsorship. For the sponsor, the association and relationship with the sponsored may change and may not align with its values. For example. during the semi-final of the 2009 US Open Tennis Championships, Serena Williams launched a tirade of abuse at a line official. Her behaviour resulted in a point penalty on match point, ending her defence of the title. She was at first unrepentant over her behaviour and initially failed to apologise. While sponsors of athletes derive benefits from being associated with the athlete, there are limits to the extent to which they can exert control over athletes' behaviours and, in some instances, those behaviours may be damaging to the sponsor. In these instances, the sponsors have to minimise any damages and costs. So while sponsors benefit from athletes promoting and endorsing their products and services, they have to bear the cost of negative associations when things go wrong.

Another cost and risk that sponsors face is when they sponsor young athletes. The rivalry by sponsors to recruit athletes to their stables means that companies are signing athletes at a young age. However, there is the risk that some of these athletes will not make it to the professional ranks of their sports, or that performances are below expectations when they do get there. Another risk associated with sponsorship of athletes is seeing them promoting rival brands. This is now common in team sport and has been known to cause problems for sponsors. There were allegations that Nike had interfered in the Brazilian national football team's selection of Ronaldo and other players contracted by the company during the run up to and including the 1998 FIFA World Cup in France. This culminated in a court case in Brazil in which the player and representatives from the Brazilian Football Confederation were amongst those who had to give evidence. In the case study on page 181 (Chapter 14), you will find the case of David Beckham, Pepsi and Coca-Cola; another example is Christiano Ronaldo (sponsored by Nike) playing at Real Madrid, sponsored by Adidas.

Types of sponsorship relationships

Over the past 20 years, the nature of sponsorship and the relationship between the sponsor and the sponsored has changed and various developments have seen more sophisticated approaches used. In part, the reason for these developments is that being a *sponsor* has not always been associated with positive experiences. Masterman (2007) notes the variety of categories of sponsorship rights: title; presentation; naming; sector; and supplier. These categories and approaches are particularly evident when examining the sponsoring of sports federations and sports leagues.

Title rights allow the sponsor the opportunity to have its name or brand incorporated into the title. For example, Barclays Premier League and Barclays ATP (Association of Tennis Professionals) World Tour Finals. In these instances, the sponsors usually have the rights to use the graphics of their brand logo with those of the sponsored. Furthermore, being the title sponsor has its advantages as these are often acknowledged in the media: television, print and electronic. For example, broadcasters who are covering the Tennis Masters Cup will refer to it as the *Barclays ATP World Tour Finals*.

Presentation rights are similar to title rights but rather than being incorporated in the title, the sponsor's name appears alongside it. For example, the FA Cup is sponsored by E.ON. Again the logo and graphics of the sponsor will appear and careful management of the media is necessary as the sponsor's name can be omitted.

Naming rights often refer to facilities and arenas. This is commonplace in North America and is a practice that is now being replicated in England and across Europe. Taking the example of English football clubs and other sports or sports-related venues, names such as Emirates Stadium, Reebok Stadium, Ricoh Arena and O2 Arena are becoming more common. This is particularly a contentious issue in English football. For some clubs, selling the naming rights of the stadiums to sponsors is a departure from more than 100 years of tradition. Aston Villa's stadium, Villa Park, has regularly featured in the news over naming rights. Officials at the club insist that they will not be departing from tradition.

Learning Activity 8.1

Compile an audit of the 44 stadiums in the English Premier League and the Championship division of the Football League. Of these clubs, how many of them have naming rights? What are the benefits to the sponsors of these stadiums?

Selling the naming rights of football stadiums is a trade-off between commercialism and traditions. Conduct a simple survey of both football fans and non-football fans, identifying whether they are for or against naming rights. Between the two groups, football fans and non-football fans, what proportion of each are for naming rights?

Sector rights refer to the exclusive territory that is allowed to sponsors. In offering these territorial rights, competitors from the sponsor's market are (proactively) excluded. Examples of territorial or sector rights are British Airways' partnership with the British Olympic Association (BOA); with BOA's air travel exclusive to the airline. Often sector rights are identifiable by the types of communications attached to the sponsorship vehicle. At the Wimbledon Tennis Championships, Blossom Hill is the official wine to the Championship. Similarly, Rolex, IBM and Robinsons are the official timekeeper, supplier of information technology, and official still soft drinks, respectively. The allocation of these sector rights to these sponsors mean that entry by or dealings with rival companies from these sectors are foreclosed.

Supplier rights are normally based on agreements to supply or sponsorship-in-kind in addition to sponsorship fees. The supply could be of products, services or expertise. Supplier rights and sector rights need not be mutually exclusive. The supply of sponsorship-in-kind can be more efficient than paying a sponsorship fee. The sponsor can normally offer sponsorship supplies below competitive market value or even at cost and therefore reduce the overall cost of acquiring the rights.

Sponsorship structures

Many sponsored parties normally have different sponsoring structures; Masterman (2007) notes three. The first of these involves one sponsor. This is very rare and such sponsorship vehicles are highly valuable. Another is a tiered structure with a number of levels, with those sponsoring at the highest levels having to pay a greater fee than those sponsoring at the lower levels. Sponsoring at the highest will involve benefits which are exclusive to these sponsors. This tiered structure is common. The Lawn Tennis Association has two tiers of sponsor partnership: lead sponsor and official supplier. Currently, the lead sponsor is AEGON, a pensions and investment company. The official suppliers are BNP Paribas, Highland Spring, Lucozade Sport and the InterContinental Hotel Group. The final sponsoring structure is a flat structure in which all sponsors have the same status, although the sponsoring fees and sponsoring rights may differ across the sponsors. Figure 8.2 illustrates these structures with examples using the cases of the International Amateur Athletics Federation (IAAF) and the 2010 Marathon De Paris. For the IAAF, besides an official supplier, the structure is flat with a series of partners. On the other hand the 2010 Marathon De Paris is tiered with various layers: major sponsors, institutional sponsors, official sponsors, official suppliers and media sponsors.

FIFA, the world governing body for football, refers to its sponsors as *partners*; while the International Olympic Committee (IOC) refers to its sponsors as The Olympic Partner (TOP) programme. These descriptions are designed to elevate sponsorship relationships and bestow privileges. For example, there has been a long-standing battle between Adidas and the other sportswear brands. Adidas has traditionally been sponsor of and associated with the Olympic Games and FIFA World Cups for many years. The complaint of the other sportswear brands, over many years, has been that Adidas is given an unfair advantage and greater prominence as it is allowed to place the three stripes along athletes' uniforms; this is in addition to its logo. For other companies like Nike, Puma and Reebok, the promotion of their brand is constrained by a rule limiting logo space to 20 square centimetres on athletic uniforms (Sports Business 2009). At the 2008 Beijing Olympic Games, and for the first time in the history of the Games, the uniforms of Adidas sponsored countries did not have the traditional three stripes. It remains to be seen as to whether FIFA and UEFA will bow to the same pressures. The last editions of UEFA's European Championships hosted by Poland and Ukraine in 2008 and the FIFA World Cup hosted by Germany in 2006 featured the prominent three stripes on the team jerseys of countries sponsored by Adidas, noticeably Germany, France, Spain and Greece to name a few. While history and tradition has seen the famous three stripes on team uniforms in the Olympic Games and international football tournaments, its presence in today's sports branded market confers a competitive advantage to Adidas over its rivals and the reluctance of the sponsored or partners, in this case

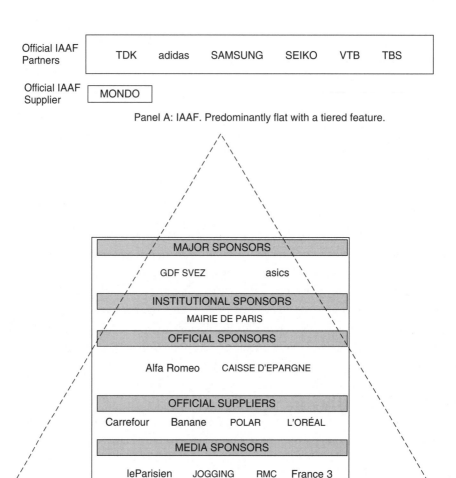

Panel A: IAAF. Predominantly flat with a tiered feature.

Panel B: 2010 Marathon De Paris. Tiered structure

Figure 8.2 Different models of sponsorship structures

UEFA and FIFA, to eliminate this advantage is in all likelihood because of the sponsorship arrangement between the parties.

Learning Activity 8.2

Identify five incidents across different sports in which the behaviour of athletes has (potentially) caused embarrassment to or damaged the relationships they have with their sponsors. What was the response of the sponsors to the various situations?

Free-riding and ambush marketing

As noted in the preceding sections, the sponsorship relationship is one that exists between a principal and an agent. The benefits that accrue from the sponsorship transaction are internalised so that only the two main parties benefit. The two main parties will endeavour to make sure that third parties are not able to benefit or free-ride. Free-riding occurs when third parties outside the sponsorship relationship use unauthorised approaches to benefit from the sponsorship vehicle. The practice of free-riding has become so severe that terms like guerrilla marketing and ambush marketing are now commonly used to describe it. Events and event organisers are often the victims of this practice and have to be aware of the various strategies and approaches used by ambushers.

The two parties involved in sponsorship do their best to foreclose any free-riding opportunities to third parties looking to free-ride or ambush. This can be done through licensing and copyrighting. For the most part, the sponsoring party will be given permission and licensing to use the various names and logos of the sponsorship vehicle. In the case of the Olympics, these will be the word 'Olympic' and the five rings. However, this only goes so far and other approaches are necessary. During the 2002 Winter Olympics in Salt Lake City, Anheuser-Busch was the official beer to the Games, having paid a reported US$50m for the privilege. During the Games, a (very) small local company posted advertisements on its delivery lorries that read 'Wasutch Beers. The Unofficial Beer. 2002 Winter Games'. As the company had not used the word 'Olympics' or the five rings of the Games, the organisers of the Games and the official beer sponsor had no course for redress.

In the remainder of this section, the concept of free-riding and ambush marketing will be examined using a series of cases. The extent of free-riding and ambush marketing in some cases is quite blatant. However, in some cases, it could be argued that some degree of censorship or monopoly power is being exercised and in these instances, it could be further argued that consumer interests are at the very least being compromised.

Keep a close watch: Federer, Rolex and Maurice Lacroix

For those whose interest in tennis goes beyond admiring the quality of the players' games and takes in some of the esoteric happenings of the modern game, no doubt you will have noticed certain protocols and habits. One in particular happens frequently in the finals (of singles normally) soon after the umpires have concluded matches. On returning to their chairs, players reach into their bags and put on their wristwatches. In modern sport, where every centimetre of advertising space is highly valuable, even those small spaces on tennis players' wrists are highly sought after. It is not that these players are eager to know the time; after all most events will have a clock displayed somewhere on or next to the scoreboard. This is simply a form of advertising and marketing, or put another way, free-riding or ambush marketing.

Taking the case of the Wimbledon Championships, Roger Federer has contested the finals on seven occasions, winning every one since 2003 to 2009 inclusively (with the exception of the 2008 final, which he lost to Rafael Nadal in what has been widely acclaimed as one of the best, if not the best, matches in Wimbledon history). In 2004, Federer signed a five-year endorsement deal with Maurice Lacroix, a Swiss watch manufacturer. A significant part of endorsement and sponsorship deals of this sort will involve the player playing in events in regions in which sponsors wish to increase their exposure. Additionally, sponsors would also like to benefit from having their products *displayed*. For a watch manufacturer, one of the best ways of having its product displayed is on the wrist of the Wimbledon singles champion as he or she lifts the championship trophy aloft. This is in fact what Maurice Lacroix has been able to do courtesy of its relationship with Roger Federer. Interestingly enough, the official time-keeper of the Wimbledon Championships is Rolex, another Swiss watch manufacturer. The extent to which this is ambush marketing is one of debate. Players are allowed to have their own sponsors and without this professional tennis cannot function; the sponsorship of players to a large extent contributes to and allows the game to function. Nevertheless, Maurice Lacroix has been able to free-ride, inadvertently or otherwise.

Rolex's take on matter is in itself interesting. Having sponsored the Championship since 1978, the company is less likely to be pleased that another Swiss watch maker is able to free-ride using the Wimbledon Championship. Two years into the Roger Federer–Maurice Lacroix deal, a break-up fee was paid and the deal terminated. Roger Federer then signed a multi-year deal with Rolex and in his 2009 Wimbledon final victory over Andy Roddick, he raised the men's trophy wearing a 41mm Rolex Datejust II. Whatever the reason for the termination of the Roger Federer–Maurice Lacroix deal, the Wimbledon–Rolex partnership and the Federer–Rolex partnership is more harmonious, and given that he has won the singles title on six out of the last seven occasions, his regular appearances in finals at the All England Lawn Tennis and Croquet Club will certainly suit Rolex.

It's all in the suit: BOA, Adidas and Speedo

The Olympic Games is the biggest multi-sport event in the world and the relationships between the principal, the IOC who own the rights to the event, and the multiplicity of agents, which includes the organising committee of the host city, the national Olympic associations, the athletes, broadcasters and media, just to mention a few, are complex. Each of the agents' relationships with the principal, as well as with each other, has to be managed in such a way that it does not create conflicts.

During the 2000 Olympic Games in Sydney, a row broke out between the British Olympic Association (BOA) and Speedo, the swimwear company and supplier of the FastSkin suit. The source of the row was the conflict of relationships. One of the BOA's partners is Adidas, the sportswear company, who provide the uniforms to the Great Britain and Northern Ireland Olympic Team. Speedo, however, sponsors many of the British swimmers and the swimmers therefore feel obliged to wear their sponsor's swimsuit rather than its competitor's. One of the BOA's arguments is that the swimsuit is part of the team uniform and since this is sponsored by Adidas, the swimmers' obligations lay with the BOA and they should therefore wear the Adidas swimsuit. After all, many, if not all, the Great Britain and Northern Ireland Olympic athletes will be wearing the uniform irrespective of who their personal sponsors are, for instance the track and field athletes, the rowers, and the cyclists. Track and field athletes, as an example, however, are allowed to wear running spikes made by companies other than Adidas. The reason for this is that running spikes are viewed as technical equipment and are therefore not classed as being part of the uniform. It was argued that the swimsuits should also be classed as technical equipment and should therefore be exempt just like the running spikes. The BOA, however, insisted that the swimsuits were not exempt and that Adidas had an equivalent suit for the swimmers.

Some agreement had been reached between the BOA and Speedo over colour; they agreed that the FastSkin could be supplied in Speedo's own blue as opposed to Adidas's blue, but they insisted that the suits be supplied unbranded in accordance with the BOA's contract with Adidas. Speedo refused to do so and the suits were supplied with Speedo's logo only for the BOA to arrange for this to be covered with the Union Jack.

So are swimsuits to swimmers what running spikes are to track runners, or tennis racquets to tennis players? Whatever the answer, there certainly was a free-riding opportunity available to Speedo, like many of the sport and non-sports companies who sponsor representatives of the Great Britain and Northern Ireland team. It is unclear as to whether Speedo intended to free-ride or not, however, the publicity generated from the row itself provided Speedo with *free* advertising and marketing (*The Independent*, 2000). This *free* advertising and marketing is after all in part what free-riding and ambush marketing is all about.

A new ball game: Champions' League, partners and advertisers

The UEFA Champions' League, like the English Premier League, is one of the most lucrative football tournaments. The major source of the vast sums of revenue generated by UEFA is television and broadcasting. The total prize fund for the competition in 2007–8 was €585.6m (Deloitte 2009). For example, FC Porto, a league club from Portugal, defeated AS Monaco in the 2004 final. AS Monaco received a total of €26.3m while FC Porto on the other hand only received €19.7m for its efforts; under normal tournament and competition conditions, the winner normally receives more than the losing finalist. This imbalance was not limited to the final. Chelsea, in reaching the semi final, received €28.9m. Arsenal, who reached the quarter final, received €28.4m, while Manchester United, who *only* reached the last 16, received €27.9m (Deloitte 2005). The imbalance is due to the size of the various national domestic markets. As the English broadcast market generated more income for the UEFA Champions' League, the English clubs' participation in the tournament received a greater share of the prize fund. Effectively, controlling for other influences such as the stage reached in the competition, the resources are diverted to the most profitable entrants and these are English clubs. Notwithstanding the lucrative value of the competition, the UEFA Champions' League is an event subject to free-riding and ambush marketing.

Attempts to prevent ambush marketing are causing interesting transformations to football stadiums. The top English Premier League clubs will normally have matches scheduled on Saturdays or Sundays, if the following week is a designated week for European club matches. For any of these top English clubs playing at home, their sponsors would have enjoyed exposure on television either as a result of live broadcast or a secondary highlights programme. If hosting a Champions' League match the following Tuesday or Wednesday, their stadium must undergo a significant transformation. All advertising boards and hoardings bearing the sponsorship logos and brands of those whom are not partners of the UEFA Champions' League competition must come down. Consequently, these clubs face (decoration and refurbishment) costs each time they play a Champions' League match at home. This is a concerted effort by the principal and agent to foreclose ambushing opportunities to third parties, even if these third parties are sponsors of the agent.

There are, however, other avenues to free-riding and ambushing. The Partners to the UEFA Champions' League are UniCredit, Ford, Sony, MasterCard, PlayStation and Heineken. The domestic broadcaster, however, provides each of the competition's partners with the opportunity to be the sponsor of the television programme. In fact, at the end of each half's play, audiences see a short commercial advertisement 'messages' from the sponsors of the programme. However, this does not entirely eliminate free-riding. No sooner have audiences seen the preferential message or advertisement by a competition partner, there are advertisements in the commercial break by the partner's competitor. For example, other financial, automobile, electronics, games console and beer companies are able to advertise during this period. A common practice by many companies is to purchase advertising space many years in advance in the knowledge that these free-riding opportunities will arise. This is particularly common for the Olympic Games and FIFA World Cup events. In New York, the NYC2012 secured 95 per cent of the outdoor advertising space – billboards, transport, street signs, etc. – prior to actually bidding for the event. This was a serious attempt to prevent ambush marketing (Masterman 2007).

Learning Activity 8.3

The wars between Adidas and Nike, Pepsi and Coca-Cola, Visa and American Express, and other rival companies are notorious in sports. Analysing events like the FIFA World Cup, the Olympic Games, Grand Slam tennis tournaments and English test cricket, identify:

1　The sponsor
2　The free-rider or ambusher
3　The practices of the event organiser to prevent free-riding and ambushing
4　The practices of the sponsor to prevent free-riding and ambushing
5　The practices of the ambushers

Making a judgement and ruling, should any of these free-riding and ambushing practices continue or should they be prevented? What is the rationale for your justification?

Eliminating free-riders

Is free-riding and ambushing an acceptable practice in sports sponsorship? Imagine that you and your colleagues have just completed a group assignment only you were the only person who worked on the assignment. Having presented your assignment, your colleagues were not shy in coming forward to share in the credit. No doubt your immediate thoughts are that matters are unfair. This is the view of sponsors, as they believe those who have not paid for the rights to sponsor should not be allowed to make devious attempts to create associations with the event or sponsorship vehicle. On the one hand, sponsors undoubtedly work hard to position themselves strategically in the market and contribute to the enhancement of the sponsorship vehicle, be it an event, an athlete or a sports governing body. On the other hand, ambush marketing is not illegal and in a free market, competition is highly valued, irrespective of whether some parties are official sponsors or not. Furthermore, branding ambushers as scourges of the sponsorship and branding market might be considered unfair. After all, why should any company monopolise the channels of communication with consumers. Monopolies are after all against consumer interests and competition in this part of the sports sponsorship market, the ability and freedom to communicate with sport consumers, will benefit consumers and improve their overall welfare.

Most sports federations and other principals within the sponsorship relationship are quick to condemn this practice. One of their beliefs is that these third parties are extracting benefits from the sports without contributing to the sports' development. This is an interesting point but also one that is complex. Take, for example, the FIFA World Cup. The revenue that is generated from events is used in a variety of ways including the development of football in countries and territories that are lacking resources. On this and similar grounds free-riding should be eliminated. However, the popularity and attractiveness of the FIFA World Cup is to a large extent a result of the quality of the competing national teams. For the most part, much of the free-riders' and ambushers' resources have been used in developing these teams. So one argument is they have contributed to the game and therefore their practices are justified. The argument could even be extended to suggest that FIFA itself is free-riding, using the resources of national teams to generate vast sums of revenue without adequately compensating the teams and players.

Whether one champions the cause of the ambusher or the two parties involved in the sponsorship arrangement, every effort to eliminate free-riding and ambush marketing is being taken. Perhaps the most significant step so far is the Olympics Bill. The Bill has been introduced as a result of the London 2012 Olympic Games. The main motivation of the Bill is to protect the Games' official sponsors and in doing so, prevent ambushers from benefiting from the Games. In what is a first by any country hosting the Games, the Bill outlaws the use of words, phrases and logos such as 'Olympic', 'Olympiad' and 'Olympian', the Olympic rings, Team GB and British Olympic Association logo, 'London 2012', London's bid logo and derivatives of London2012.com, the 2012 Games logo and mascots, Olympic motto 'citius, altius, fortius' (faster, higher, stronger), and the British Paralympic Association and team logos. Other banned words include games, medals, gold, silver, bronze, 2012, sponsor, summer (Fraser 2005). The Bill has received criticism from the Institute of Practitioners in Advertising, who say the Bill goes too far in protecting official sponsors and that a balance is needed.

As to whose position is more tenable, this is a matter for detailed empirical analysis. But as to who will prevail, the sponsor with the support of the sponsoring or the free-riders and ambushers, it is difficult to say. However, the battle lines have been drawn and the sponsors and those being sponsored have an upper hand in the sports sponsorship arena.

Chapter Review

The relationships that exist between sport and sponsorship have developed in such a manner that it is difficult to conceive one being able to exist without the other. For sport, the revenues from sponsorship are so great that without it, modern sport will certainly not be able to function in the ways that we have become accustomed to. For the sponsors that provide the vast sums of revenue, be they sports or non-sports companies, their ability to use sport as a vehicle to communicate with large audiences will be severely compromised.

The relationships that have emerged between sport and sponsorship have dramatically changed over the years and so have the various issues that surround sport and sponsorship, and the manner in which these issues need to be managed. To a large extent, sponsorship is influencing and changing sport, be it clubs, league, events or even athletes. Sport's special relationship with sponsorship is such that new protocols have to be observed and managed. No longer can athletes just focus on performing and exhibiting their athletic skills, special attention has to be given to serving sponsors and in many instances, this dictates and influences many aspects of their professional lives including their schedule. For teams, events and governing agencies of sports, protecting sponsors' interest have become a priority.

This chapter has considered a series of issues that reflects and encapsulates the modern sports sponsorship market. However, the vast nature of sponsorship is such that it is not possible to comprehensively deal with all the issues. For example, how do sponsors evaluate the return from sports sponsorship? Can sports sponsorship be evaluated on the same basis as more traditional marketing approaches such as advertising and promotion? These questions are important but the lack of space means we cannot consider them here. Notwithstanding these, this chapter has considered a wide range of sponsorship issues including various concepts, the relationships between those sponsoring and those being sponsored and their underlying objectives, some of the impacts of sponsorship, and the conflicts associated with sports sponsorship.

After reading this chapter and attempting the learning activities you should now be able to answer the following questions:

1   What are the underlying motives and objectives of the parties involved in sports sponsorship? Given the different principals and agents involved in sponsorship, are the objectives of the various parties mutually compatible? Where compatibility issues exist, what compromises do the various parties have to make?

2   Meeting the obligations of sponsors is critical in managing the relationships within sport sponsorship. Has this compromise the core functions and integrity of sports? Have the changes to sport which have come about as a result of sports sponsorship been beneficial to consumers?

3   To what extent is ambush marketing a form of competition within the sports marketing?

4   Considering the theoretical issues of government intervention, are there justifications for government intervention in the form of an Olympics Bill to combat free-riding and ambush marketing?

Further Reading

- Amis, J. and Cornwell, T.B. (2005) *Global Sport Sponsorship*. Oxford: Berg.
- Andreff, W. and Szymanski, S. (eds) *Handbook on the Economics of Sport*. Cheltenham: Edward Elgar.
- Gratton, C. and Taylor, P. (2001) *Economics of Sport and Recreation*. London: Routledge.
- Lagae, W. (2005) *Sports Sponsorship and Marketing Communications: A European Perspective*. Harlow: Prentice Hall.
- Mastermann, G. (2007) *Sponsorship for a Return on Investment*. London: Butterworth-Heinemann.

Chapter 9
The commercial sector and sports participation

Learning Objectives

This chapter is designed to help you:

- describe the range of activities that make up the commercial sector;
- understand why people choose to participate in sport and physical activities delivered by privately-owned sports clubs and facilities;
- understand how and why the commercial sector is used to help deliver the UK's sports participation and physical activity policy objectives;
- demonstrate how the commercial sector works in partnership to affect the UK's wider health and well-being indicators;
- describe some of the future challenges and issues that will impact upon the commercial sector's delivery of sport and physical activity.

The preceding chapter has introduced the commercial sector and focused upon the sponsorship, marketing and branding elements of private companies' operations. In this chapter the importance of the commercial sector will be discussed in relation to the public's participation in sport and physical activity. First, the sector's component parts will be described and a historical reference made to the sector's developing role. How consumers differentiate and select the commercial sector's offer will then be explored with examples which demonstrate how the sector works in partnership to complement the sport and leisure provision in the public and voluntary sectors. Particular reference will be made to the health and fitness industry, golf, and the activities of professional and private sports clubs. Finally the future role and scope of the commercial sector's sport and physical activity provision will be discussed in light of the current economic downturn.

The commercial sporting sector

The commercial sector in sport is becoming increasingly important, as industries such as heath and fitness continue to grow and commercial sports clubs increase their levels of economic activity. Since the 1970s, the number of private operators of sport and leisure facilities has increased massively. This has enabled the commercial sector to become the most dominant sector of sport (Gratton and Taylor 2000).

When considering what the commercial sporting sector contains we can first break it down into its component parts of either sporting goods, or sporting services. For the purposes of this book it is the services that we are most interested in – these include spectator events, commercial services, business services, media, and sponsorship. We have already covered some of these elements in detail, so our focus here is directed primarily to the commercial services, which for clarity can be subdivided into the categories of health and fitness, golf, and other private sports clubs. Each of these will be covered in detail within this chapter.

One important point to note is that the commercial sector does not compete for business throughout the sports market. Commercial sector businesses are only concerned in making a profit for their shareholders or owners and will only enter into competition where they can provide a similar product at higher quality and a higher price, e.g. fitness centres, country clubs, golf clubs, etc. Commercial companies aim to grow their business by increasing their user base. They often focus on creating a national brand and a network of similar sports facilities; this establishes them as a mark of quality which can in turn be marketed to increase their numbers yet further (Gratton and Taylor 2000).

Historical perspective

Since the 1970s there has been a considerable increase in private companies wishing to establish themselves as providers within the sport and leisure industry. Lifestyle changes and the increase in disposable income have created greater demand for the sport and leisure offer. Private companies have entered the traditional public service market to provide a service more tailored to the individual's needs. New facilities have been created, whilst significant numbers of local public sports facilities are now operated by commercial companies, which is a result of the introduction of CCT in the 1990s and more recently of Best Value. There has also been a growth in partnerships between commercial operators and public or other bodies, such as educational establishments and national governing bodies of sport (Audit Commission 2006).

Learning Activity 9.1

Investigate your local sport and leisure facilities – how do they influence sport and physical activity in your area?

1　Audit the range of sport and leisure facilities available in your local area. Are they privately owned or run, a charity, or a public body? How do prices or ease of access vary between the providers?

2　Go along to your nearest public sports facility. When was it built? What sort of activities are provided? How affordable are the services to the local population?

3　Visit a privately-owned facility in your area and compare its image, facilities and pricing structure with those of the public facility above.

Think about your own use / consumption of sport facilities / clubs. Are they publicly or privately owned and run? What first impression did they create when you first visited or joined? What factors were an influence on your choice?

Why do consumers choose to use commercial leisure services?

Many believe that sport and leisure participation is merely determined by economic factors. In this scenario different sports and activities appeal to the consumer dependent upon cost alone. If this is the case, however, why do people choose to pay for a commercial service to satisfy their need for sport when there may be a publicly provided and often cheaper alternative available? Obviously other issues are important in the decision-making process, such as the availability, location, access to transport, time constraints, family unit and peer pressures. Indeed the selection and purchase of these commercial services can provide the consumer with a whole range of personal and social functions. At first they may serve to satisfy needs, wants or desires but they may also be used to symbolise success or power. They can be used to communicate social distinctions or reinforce relationships of superiority and inferiority between individuals or groups. They can also be used to communicate specific messages from one person to another such as status, attitudes or states of mind. Finally they may be used as an instrument to create or confirm an individual's sense of self or personal identity (Campbell 1975). We may in fact be socialised into this leisure and lifestyle choice by a number of external factors such as our social class expectations, family role models and educational background (Bourdieu 1984). The choice of more bespoke sport and leisure options traditionally offered by the commercial sector may be based on individuals' desire to separate themselves from the masses and identify with subsets of people who have the same interests and social background as themselves (Clark and Clegg 1998). In response to this need the commercial sector has promoted niche based markets and developed specialist facilities and clubs to cater and sustain these sources of identity.

Consumers may also choose to join or visit private sports clubs due to the status this infers. This belief is based upon wealth being associated with success in our society. Exclusive sports clubs and facilities reaffirm this belief and reinforce the idea that class privileges enjoyed by powerful and wealthy people are well deserved. The clubs are therefore seen as sites for establishing relationships which will then perpetuate the users' status (Coakley and Pike 2009).

In summary, the decision to choose the commercial sector for sport and fitness provision is made on many levels. The sector has reacted quickly and positioned itself to deliver the activities that consumers want, at a high quality, in easily accessible facilities, which meet the social environment expectations that their users demand ...

How does the commercial sector help increase the UK's level of participation?

This potential role of the commercial sector has been recognised by successive governments in their development of national sport strategies. Indeed within the DCMS (2002) strategy, *Game Plan: A Strategy for Delivering the Government's Sport and Physical Activity Objectives*, the delivery framework with which to achieve participation and performance targets included active partnering of public, voluntary and private organisations.

This document set highly optimistic participation targets for the UK of getting 70 per cent of the population physically active for 30 minutes at least three times a week. Game Plan was a benchmark government policy which used sport and physical activity proactively for the first time. The proposed increased activity rates aimed at improving the health of the nation, reducing the burden on the National Health Service, improving the nation's self image, and stimulating economic activity whilst also reducing crime and anti-social behaviour. Despite the Game Plan target ultimately being recognised as too difficult to achieve, the focus of increased participation has continued within future government sport strategy. The most recent strategy, *Playing to Win: A New Era for Sport*, presented a target of getting 2m people physically active, with a recognition that this target is only achievable through engaging not only the public and voluntary sectors but the commercial sector also (DCMS 2008a).

Government targets for increasing participation are also being helped by the commercial sector's desire to tap into new markets and provide attractive and more inclusive activity opportunities. The links between sports such as golf, tennis, squash, badminton and fitness centres have also helped to maintain participation in the sport, despite the costs of memberships. Other commercial sports such as football, rugby and cricket also help to contribute to the economic and social impact of sport through the activities of their professional teams.

The commercial sector helps increase the UK's sport and physical activity levels, and complements the public and voluntary sectors in a number of ways. These range from working directly with local authorities to deliver against centrally set targets, to providing funding for capital and community projects. In each instance the commercial sector's drive, however, is to build its market share and reputation which will lead to long-term benefits for its shareholders or owners.

According to Mintel (2009), the value of the overall UK sports participation market is estimated to be approximately £4.4bn. Private enterprise is expected to play a significant role in expanding this market, in everything from sponsorship and marketing partnership to facility development and operation. Much public grant aid is in fact conditional on being match-funded by equivalent sums committed by business. The National Sports Foundation (NSF) is a government-led organisation that works to encourage this type of business–community partnership, committing £14.5m of its own funding in 2006–7 for projects to set against an equivalent sum provided by commercial partners including Sainsbury's, Tesco, EDF Energy, npower, BSkyB, Norwich Union and Kellogg's.

According to government statistics, more than 27m adults in England alone are not getting enough exercise, while obesity is responsible for 9,000 premature deaths each year. The Department of Health puts the cost of physical inactivity to the NHS at £1.8bn a year and to the wider economy (primarily through sickness absence) at potentially £8.3bn. This linking of health to activity has increasingly brought sport into government health policy, most recently in the Be Active, Be Healthy strategy launched in February 2009, in which the key elements that the commercial sector could impact upon included: developing 'learn to swim' programmes; creating a new national Physical Activity Alliance to pool voluntary and private sector resources (ranging from leisure centres to grass-roots clubs, and supporting many participation initiatives); and encouraging GPs to advise patients exercise referrals at health and fitness clubs.

New Labour's national PSA targets (Public Service Agreement), introduced in 1998 in order to assess the quality, effectiveness and efficiency of government services, also provide an opportunity for the commercial sector. There are now 30 PSAs against which local government authorities (LAs) can be assessed in a Comprehensive Area Assessment. The targets in which LAs most often engage the help of the commercial sector are PSA 21 (increase the proportion of adults taking part in sport), and PSA 12 (achieve a reduction in childhood obesity) (HM Treasury 2009). The commercial sector may impact on these targets directly by increasing the numbers using their own clubs and facilities, or those which they manage on behalf of the local authority. Indeed from the late 1980s onwards the introduction of Compulsory Competitive Tendering led many publicly-owned facilities to franchise out the management function to private companies to reduce costs. The more recent Best Value drive and the government's Comprehensive Spending Review in which each local authority must reduce its overall expenditure by 10 per cent have increased the involvement of the private sector yet further in the management and delivery of the public sport and physical activity offer (Tomlinson 2007).

Many other examples of private and public partnerships exist to promote and increase the access to sport and physical activity. These include the Change4Life healthy living campaign, free swim initiatives, GP exercise referrals, after-school sport club activities, Building Schools for the Future (BSF) initiatives, a range of partnerships with individual national governing bodies and UK Sport, as well as the Olympic 2012 legacy plan which engages private companies to develop facilities and affect long-term participation improvements – not just through their sponsorship money but also by providing their own facilities and services.

Learning Activity 9.2

Take one of the above partnerships and investigate which commercial companies are involved and what specifically does their involvement entail? Is it the donation of funds, resources and time, or is there a greater commitment?

Reflection Point 9.2

What do you consider to be the overall motives for private companies to get involved in the partnership activities above? Is it philanthropic, purely commercial or a combination of these?

Change4Life

Change4Life is a nationwide movement designed to help people make changes to their lifestyles, so that they can eat well, move more and live longer. It is a government-sponsored initiative delivered through the National Health Service but utilising a range of volunteers and commercial partners. It is a reaction to the evolution of 'modern life' which has meant that many people are a lot less active. With the opportunities to watch so much TV or play computer games, and with convenience and fast food available, it is argued that people do not move about as much, or eat as well as they used to. This in turn has led to the increase in childhood and adult obesity which can cause life-threatening diseases like cancer, type 2 diabetes and heart disease (Change4Life 2009)

The Change4Life initiative asks partners to promote the Change4Life message through their own activities in order to help families make positive changes to their lives. Many private companies are involved in the partnership already such as Aviva, Nestlé, Nickelodeon, Nintendo, Sky, JJB, Halfords and many others. Some examples of the Change4 Life partnerships in action include:

- Lean East – A glowing success from the north east of England, Lean East has established a programme called 'Match Fit' by working in partnership with Newcastle United FC, using players and coaches to visit schools and community centres promoting the message of healthy eating and exercise.
- ASDA Sporting Chance is a community sports initiative that gives children access to free sports sessions during the school holidays.
- Kellogg offers support through Breakfast4Life and Swim4Life to help individuals make simple changes to their lifestyle. Kellogg has provided British Swimming with £3m to fund free swimming sessions for children with weight issues and for family swim sessions.

Learning Activity 9.3

Access the Change4Life website, www.nhs.com/Change4Life. Choose any three of the funding partners and follow the links to their sites. List the activities they offer as part of the partnership and assess what impact they will have on their target audience.

Professional and private sport clubs and sports development

Professional sports teams, such as those in football, rugby or cricket are commercially run but often have an obligation to improve the lives of those in their local area through sport and physical activity. Many professional football teams in particular create charitable trusts focused entirely on helping their communities. One such example is Everton Football Club, whose aim is to generate and maintain an unbreakable link with their local community.

Case Study
Everton FC – 'the people's club'

In 1988 Everton Football Club launched an independent, co-ordinated community programme under the name of Everton in the Community (EITC), a registered charity. With Everton Football Club as the main sponsor, EITC has instigated a range of engaging sports-related activities, programmes and initiatives with the aim of making a difference to the lives of people on Merseyside. EITC use football and sport-based programmes to engage all members of the community, regardless of their age, sex, ability or background. On 16 May 2009, EITC was officially relaunched as the Everton Foundation.

The foundation now runs a wide range of football-based courses to affect social change. The flagship programme is Creating Chances – Places for Players. *This is a high profile initiative that utilises Premier League players' support to highlight the diversity and quantity of community and good cause work being carried out by Everton Football Club.*

Some of the other headline initiatives operated by the foundation include the largest and most respected disability football programme in the world, with over 10,000 football opportunities for disabled children and adults delivered each year.

The Everton Foundation operates a range of soccer and fitness schools throughout the year which aims to help children achieve their five hours of exercise a week.

A social inclusion programme has also been developed with the aim of providing more opportunities for young people through the provision of combined sports and educational activities. In doing this, the foundation hopes to develop self-esteem and confidence through self-expression and practical performance of all those who take part (Everton Foundation 2009).

Learning Activity 9.4

Access the website of your local professional sports team. Do they have a community or education section, a charitable trust, or foundation? What activities do they get involved with in the community to promote health and physical activity?

Continuing to use football as the example even here the private sports clubs and companies are increasingly involved in the sector to satisfy the demand for facilities and coaching.

Case Study
Powerleague 5-a-side

Powerleague is the market-leading operator of indoor and outdoor five-a-side football centres in the UK. There are 44 centres throughout the UK with more than 450 floodlit pitches and an average of 130,000 players each week.

Powerleague offers its customers the option of competitive league matches, corporate tournaments or social play within an environment of excellent service and first-class facilities.

The English Football Association has reported that the number of adults playing small-sided football in England has experienced rapid growth, increasing from 4.4m players in 2002 to 6m players in 2004.

This situation has continued with small-sided football now played by more adults than the 11-a-side game. Users are drawn to this form of the game by its time and location convenience, its non-weather dependence, the ease of finding enough players for a team, the quality playing surface, and the inclusive social environment.

Powerleague believes that there is a significant opportunity to develop a further 100 centres in the UK where either currently none exist or in areas where the size of population can accommodate more than one commercial operator. If this vision is achieved then the major provider of grassroots football throughout the UK may become the commercial sector (Powerleague 2009).

Health and fitness industry

According to the Fitness Industry Association's (FIA) state of the industry report the health and fitness industry in the UK is estimated to be worth £3.6bn based on membership fees and subscriptions. There are 3,117 private clubs and a further 2,597 gyms in public sports centres, many of these privately managed. Since 2006, 232 new facilities have been built and there are over 7m members of a private or public health facility. As mentioned previously in this chapter this represents a very significant figure for the government given the importance of their PSA targets in participation and obesity. The FIA estimates that about 7 per cent of the UK population is a member of a private club, which also indicates that there is enormous potential for growth in this sector, as it still represents a very small proportion of the total UK population. Presently the largest single provider to the industry is the David Lloyd Leisure Group. Other major players in the industry include Fitness First, Virgin Active, LA Fitness, Bannatyne Health Club, DW Sport, Esporta and Nuffield Health Fitness and Wellbeing.

The UK situation is a reflection of what is happening internationally with health and fitness providers engaging with the wider social health and well being issues. Within Europe the industry has a massive impact. It generates revenue of more than €20bn annually, provides employment to 370,000 people and has more than 40m affiliates across Europe in members in public and private health and fitness clubs. The European Health and Fitness Association has the task of representing the industry within the European Union, the international Olympic Committee, and within the World Health Organisation forums and is committed to supporting the healthy living agenda. Its mission mirrors that of the UK's Fitness Industry Association to get 'more people, more active, more often' in order to improve the quality of life for citizens in Europe (EHFA 2009).

Case Study
David Lloyd Leisure

The David Lloyd Leisure Group operates 78 clubs in the UK. It offers an extensive portfolio of family-orientated clubs with unrivalled facilities and service levels for their members. It provides tennis, squash, badminton, gym, spas, steam rooms and saunas, restaurants and cafés, dance and weight loss classes. The company also provides personal training for rehabilitation, boxing and swimming. In addition it offers activity programmes, crèches, family events, children's activities, children's parties, outdoor activities, prenatal or postnatal, and water activities.

The group has over 450,000 members and employs some 6,000 people, including an expert health and fitness team of over 750 and more than 350 tennis professionals. Across all clubs, David Lloyd Leisure has 12,500 exercise machines, over 150 swimming pools (of which half are indoor) and offers over 10,000 exercise classes per week. With regard to the racquet facilities the group provides 700 tennis courts (over half of which are indoor), as well as 180 badminton courts and 140 squash courts. Additional facilities include health and beauty spas, club lounges with free internet access, crèches, nurseries and specialist sports.

The David Lloyd Group has built its customer base by specialising in a family-based multi-sport offer primarily developed around tennis. Indeed nearly three-quarters of their members join as couples or on a family membership, and more than 9,000 children and young people take part in their tennis programme. David Lloyd clubs aim to be the family's home from home. They pride themselves on being open, friendly places for all the family to relax and join in their extensive range of family activities. Parents are able to workout while their children have fun and are entertained. All the children's activities are supervised by qualified and well-trained staff. David Lloyd clubs aspire to provide activities for children that mean the family can learn and have fun together in a safe environment and be Fit for Life (David Lloyd 2009).

What will the health and fitness sector look like in the future?

In the UK half of men and a third of women are overweight whilst there is also the ongoing battle against childhood obesity. Despite the economic downturn the sector is still well positioned to cater for the continued need to make physical activity an attractive proposition. Although growth in private sector new-builds will be limited, the public stock owned by local authorities is increasingly in need of modernisation and replacement. Government ideology and funding would not seem to provide the resources necessary due to the scope and scale of the problem. Further public–private partnerships would therefore seem the most likely means of satisfying the demand for sport and physical activity.

The slowdown in the rate of economic growth and the 2009 banking crisis have impacted not only on club operators' expansion programmes but also on consumer attitudes towards how much they are prepared to spend on health club membership. Although many are interested in joining and using a gym, they cannot afford, or do not want to pay, the prices charged by many clubs. This has created the perfect conditions for the emergence of a budget health club concept in the UK such as Easy-Gym, Fitspace, and Pure Gym. In addition the potential threat from the world of gaming for consumers' precious leisure time is being utilised by the sector to promote the health and fitness offer through such platforms as the Nintendo WiiFit (Mintel 2009).

Learning Activity 9.5

Choose two of the health and fitness companies listed above. Visit their websites and list the type of activities they offer. Compare the two companies listing any similarities and differences in their offer, marketing, etc.

Golf

Golf is the second most popular ball sport and the fourth most played sport in the UK (Active People Survey 2008). Over 4m people play golf with around one and a quarter million being members of the 2,700 predominantly private clubs. The remaining two and three-quarter million golfers choose to play at pay-and-play courses, driving ranges, and academies. With club membership numbers declining, however, the sport has had to reassess its position, modernise its operation and grow its appeal. Golf has done this by working in partnership with the game's governing bodies. This has resulted in initiatives such as the Scottish Golf Union's Clubgolf, Golf Development Wales's d3 strategy, Junior Golf Ireland and those operated by the England Golf Partnership. Despite these efforts, clubs have found it hard to translate this into regular playing and memberships. To counter this, the industry has developed various projects to boost interest in the game.

Golf has traditionally been seen as an exclusive reserve of the rich and elderly. The commonly-held stereotype of golf was that it was a 'game for old men in bad trousers'. Many perceive golf as still having many barriers to participation. The most quoted views expressed are that golf is still too expensive for many to play and that the feeling of exclusivity still persists that can intimidate those considering taking up the sport. Golf is also too time-consuming and very frustrating for many people, who seek the instant gratification which is easily available in other competing leisure activities.

The sport is, however, reacting to these concerns. Each of the home nations' golf unions has adopted a range of measures aimed at alleviating some of these concerns. In England, the largest golf playing nation with over 70 per cent of the UK's golfers, the England Golf Partnership has been created to promote and grow the game.

Case Study
England Golf Partnership (EPG)

The England Golf Partnership is comprised of the English Golf Union, English Women's Golf Association and the Professional Golfers' Association, with the support of the Golf Foundation and Sport England.

Its aim, through the implementation of its Whole Sport Plan (WSP), is to increase and widen the participation levels in golf and achieve a vision of being 'the Leading Golf Nation in the World by 2020', from grassroots right through to elite level (English Golf Union 2009).

The way in which the EGP is growing the game is through working with clubs, schools and community projects. It has implemented a range of initiatives to target each of the 18 areas highlighted in its Whole Sport Plan. These range from offering scaled-down forms of the game to children, such as Tri-golf, and Xtreme golf at clubs and schools, to community-based projects in non-traditional golfing areas such as the Roots project targeting inner city areas. They have also offered free taster sessions and a junior National Skills Challenge, and have actively sought partnerships with schools, clubs, driving ranges, and short course academies to increase the ease of access to the sport.

These projects have been extremely successful. So much so that Sport England has actually increased the funding to the partnership from £8.75m to £12.85m for the second phase of the Whole Sport Planning 2009–2013 (EGU 2009).

Internationally, the England Golf Partnership is leading the way. Other golf associations and federations are adopting many of the EGP's strategies to 'grow the game' in their country. In partnership with the Royal and Ancient Golf Club of St Andrew's, hundreds of initiatives are being delivered throughout the world and having a real impact on participation (R & A 2009).

What does the future hold for golf?

Golf has been accepted into the 2016 Olympic Games, which should stimulate further interest in the sport from individuals and corporate sponsors. Despite golf reacting to the current situation, it still has a long way to go for it to be fully inclusive. Golf must become more accessible. Prospective players still state how intimidated they are by the sport, so many would like the opportunity to try before they buy and to play with like-minded people of the same ability. Golf clubs could make equipment available to prospective users and offer shortened versions of the game and indoor golf simulators on which to learn. Innovative games such as Urban Golf and PowerPlay, should be encouraged and ultimately the amount charged to play should be reduced. Golf still needs to become more family friendly. Clubs need to look at broadening their offer to incorporate a more family-friendly environment offering family memberships, child care services, and children's multi-sport activities such as in the business strategy adopted by the David Lloyd centres with tennis.

Learning Activity 9.6

Access the Golf England Impact Survey and analyse the 18 key targets and actions. Which actions to you think have had the greatest impact? What do you think should be the focus of the next golf WSP?

Learning Activity 9.7

Access WSPs from other sports, e.g. squash, tennis, swimming, badminton, etc. Analyse their participation targets and consider how the commercial sector could contribute to the sport achieving its targets.

Future challenges to the commercial sector

The current recession will no doubt impact upon the commercial sector's sport and leisure offer and its ability to affect the government's sport and physical activity targets.

Clubs may find it harder to keep their members as monthly subscriptions may be traded for pay-as-you-play fees at publicly-owned facilities. Indeed, the pay-as-you-play commercial operators are also vulnerable to reductions in frequency of participation and therefore revenue.

As a response clubs and private facilities may have to reduce their fees significantly and abolish 'minimum contract periods'. Many golf clubs have already reduced or removed their joining fees, and are offering many types of alternative memberships as well as payment holidays. Facilities offering pay-as-you-play must continue to look at discounting block bookings as a means of tackling their users' urge to play less when times are hard. This has already proved to be a successful strategy for many indoor soccer leagues which have implemented this policy through the summer in order to maintain their usage rates.

The London Olympics 2012 will also provide a positive influence on the industry. The experience of the Beijing Olympics indicates that Games-based participation initiatives can succeed by using the profile of the Olympic movement in the build-up. London 2012 must also capitalise upon the 'feel-good factor' following the games. Multi-sport membership clubs could capitalise pre-2012 on interest in Olympic sports, having the facilities, a suitably disposed customer base and elements that appeal to non-members interested in trying sports featured in the Games (Mintel 2009).

The 2012 London Olympics has been discussed in more detail in Chapter 7, however, with particular reference to the commercial sector, the important role of the London Organising Committee of the Olympic Games and Paralympic Games (LOCOG) in achieving the wide-reaching sporting participation legacy must not be underestimated. The LOCOG is the private-sector company responsible for shaping and hosting the 2012 Games. It is tasked with using its £2bn budget, which is all raised from the private sector, to deliver against the Games' five legacy outcomes (DCMS 2008a).

With regard to sponsorship, the current crisis in the financial sector may shrink the overall pool of money available to sport, but this could also help participation initiatives to increase their share as companies move away from expensive naming rights and brand awareness propositions, towards lower-cost, more socially responsible activities such as those offered by the Change4Life initiative. Community participation projects may seem more attractive, and the commercial sector could help fund programmes identified within NGB Whole Sport Plans to expand coaching provision, offer free or subsidised admission fees or improve the stock of facilities.

Finally, school sport may also be an area that could benefit from the commercial sector's increasing influence. Successive governments' sport policy has targeted this area as a means of increasing participation in the short and long term. Most recently the 'five hour offer' and the 'Sport Unlimited' programmes present the commercial sector with opportunities to get involved in sport and physical activity and deliver the provision of facilities through linking school sport to their clubs.

Other countries too are seeking greater input from the commercial sector. In Australia the government's total sport and fitness budgets are underfunded by approximately $60m per year. Here the Australian Sports Commission are actively working with Sports Industry Australia to try to meet this shortfall (Bloomfield 2004).

In Europe the archetypal private 'multi-sport' clubs have long served as a means to encourage more adults and young people to participate in sport and physical activity. These clubs are often given patronage by a high profile professional team in order to attract users to their facilities. One of these clubs with the highest profile is FC Barcelona. Named after the famous football team the sports club offers football, basketball, handball, athletics, ice skating and many other activities to its members. It has also created a FC Barcelona Foundation to support international sport development projects (FC Barcelona 2009). Within the UK therefore there may well be scope for our professional teams to attract more participants into a wider range of sports and activities. Indeed many football teams are already engaged in this process through the 'Premier league 4 sport' initiative where clubs introduce youngsters to a range of less popular Olympic sports in the run up to 2012.

Chapter Review

In this chapter we have looked at how the commercial sector has grown in the UK to become a vital and invaluable contributor to the government's drive to increase sport and physical activity. We have broken the sector down and focused primarily on the commercial leisure services it provides through the vast array of privately-owned or managed health and fitness, golf, and other sporting clubs. The chapter has briefly described some of the issues surrounding consumer behaviour and how these determine the user's choice in selecting the commercial offering. Despite the sector's overwhelming mission to create profit, working in partnership the commercial sector can have a real and noticeable impact on the public's health and well-being. Case studies have highlighted many of these issues above, reflecting how the commercial sector has reacted to the changing social and political environment to become a central pillar in the sport and physical activity delivery network. Finally, future considerations for the continued role and scope of the commercial sector's involvement in sport participation provision have been presented. The findings suggest that despite the current economic downturn the alarming predictions of the future health of the nation, coupled with central and local government spending cuts and the forthcoming London 2012 Olympic Games, will ensure that the commercial sector remains a pivotal influence on the UK's sport participation levels.

Now that you have read the chapter you should be able to answer the following questions:

- What activities and services make up the commercial sector?
- Why do people choose to participate in sport and physical activity delivered by privately-owned sports clubs and facilities?
- How does the commercial sector contribute to increasing the UK's participation targets?
- How does the commercial sector work in partnership to affect the wider health and well-being agenda in the UK?
- What will be the commercial sector's future involvement in promoting sport and physical activity?

Further Reading

- Coakley, J. and Pike, E. (2009) *Sports in Society: Issues and Controversies*. London: McGraw-Hill. Chapter 4 introduces sport and socialisation – how and why people choose to play or take part in physical activity. Chapter 11 describes sport and the economy, the growth of the commercial sector and the characteristics of commercial sport.
- Gratton, C. and Taylor, P. (2000) *The Economics of Sport and Leisure*. London: Routledge. This book describes the economic importance of sport. Chapter 8, Commercial Sector and Sport, offers definitions and breakdowns of the commercial sector n sport. It provides supply side information on the scope and range of the sector.

Websites

- Fitness Industry Association – trade organisation of the industry. The 'community engagement' tag on the home page is useful in linking to the range of initiatives supported by this sector. www.fia.org.uk
- English Golf Union – national governing body for men's amateur golf. The site links to the English Golf Partnership and also provides the game's whole sport plan, and impact survey information. www.egu.org
- Sport England – the website is useful to access the Active People Survey data which describes the sport and physical activity trends across the nation. www.sportengland.org

- Mintel – this site offers up to date market intelligence reports about the sport and fitness sectors. www.mintel.org
- Sports Business – up-to-date news about the sector and archive material available www.sportbusiness.com

Journals

Sports Management – articles focusing on funding, policy, and development updates. Case studies describing and debating the implication to sports managers.

Sports Business International – case studies, international business features and commercial reports.

Chapter 10
Professional sports leagues: the case of English league football

Learning Objectives

This chapter is designed to help you:

- appraise the importance of professional league sports by focusing on specific issues within the English Premier League;
- understand the structure of professional leagues and the objectives of the major stakeholders within league sports;
- understand critically gate attendance in sport and the factors that contribute to attendance demand;
- explore the market of television audiences in league sport and evaluate some of the factors that affect this market.

No textbook on sport in the UK would be complete without an examination or discussion of English league football, which is the focus of this chapter. From a social and economic viewpoint, English football has made substantive social and economic contributions to sport and wider society, not just in the UK but also worldwide. The origins of league football are very well documented (see Russell 1997) and what started out as a league of eight founder members has grown to become the world's biggest organised sports league with 92 clubs organised into four divisions: the Premier League, the Championship, League 1 and League 2 as they are currently marketed and promoted.

Those with a more advanced knowledge would be quick to note that the Premier League is a separate entity and technically a different league. However, a counter argument is that the promotion and relegation links that exist between the Premier League and the Championship suggest that issues of revenue sharing aside, the Premier League is part of English league football. Even if the Premier League was treated as a separate league, the remaining 72 clubs that constitute the Football League make it by far one of the biggest in the world. For example, the National Football League (NFL) by comparison has just 32 American football teams divided across two conferences: American Football Conference and National Football Conference. In the National Basketball Association (NBA), there are 30 teams making up the Western and Eastern conferences. Similarly in Major League Baseball (MLB), in which each team plays 162 games in the regular season, there are just 30 teams in the American and National Leagues combined. The only other sports leagues that are comparable or bigger are some of the football leagues in South America such as in Mexico and Brazil. However, the combination of size and economic value make the English football league system arguably the biggest in the world. For this reason, the importance of the English football league to UK sport should not be understated and much of this chapter is dedicated to exploring and analysing issues within English league football.

Introduction

The professional echelons of English league football are organised as four hierarchical divisions (Premier League, Championship, League 1 and League 2 respectively) which, amongst other things, are linked through a promotion and relegation system. The best performing teams from the lower division gain entry into the higher divisions and the worst performing teams in the divisions are demoted to the lower divisions. In the highest division, the English Premier League, the best performing teams, often the top four, gain entry into the financially lucrative Champions' League. Furthermore, another two teams usually gain entry into a less lucrative European club competition, the Europa League (formerly the UEFA Cup). The worst performing teams in the lowest of the four divisions normally face demotion out of the professional ranks of English club football and are replaced by the best teams from semi-professional feeder leagues.

The four noted divisions in English football are technically two leagues. The first of these is the Premier League which comprises of 20 teams. The other league is the Football League and this comprises the other three divisions, which are each made up of 24 teams. Prior to the establishment of the Premier League, all 92 teams were members of the Football League. However, differences between the top five teams at the time (Arsenal, Everton, Liverpool, Manchester United and Tottenham Hotspur) with the rest over the distribution of broadcast revenue resulted in a breakaway league and the start of the Premier League in the 1992–3 season. The disquiet over revenue sharing of broadcast rights had been going on for some time. Prior to the breakaway, the rest of the clubs in the Football League had agreed for the teams in the highest of the four divisions to keep 50 per cent of broadcast revenue while the remaining three divisions, Divisions 1, 2 and 3, took 25 per cent, 12.5 per cent and 12.5 per cent respectively (Dobson and Goddard 2001). Further concessions were made, and at one point the teams in Division 1 shared as much as 75 per cent of broadcast revenue. However, these concessions only prolonged the inevitable and the big five resigned from the league and were joined by 17 others for the inaugural season of the Premier League.

The cause of the split within the Football League is complex. The issue was not just that the big teams objected to the sharing of broadcast revenue and cross-subsidisation of other less financially prudent clubs; their objections were also over the manner in which the Football League as a body were dealing with the broadcast market. Prior to 1992, the volume of televised league football was limited (see Table 11.2 on page 145). The Football League was cautious of the potential negative impact televising league games would have on match day attendances. For this reason, only limited access had been provided to the broadcasters during the 1980s. The big five on the other hand felt that the Football League was overly cautious and that the overall impact of live broadcasting would be positive. The balance of power in this matter lay with the big five clubs rather than the league and the result, the breakaway, is what has been referred to as *regulatory capture* (Morrow 1999).

An understanding of the above and many other issues that underlie English league football and, more generally, professional team sports, can be advanced by analysing the objectives of the various stakeholders in football. This is the subject of the next section. The rest of this chapter is further divided into several sections. The analysis of the objectives of stakeholders is followed by an analysis of match day attendance in English league football. This next section presents an analysis of the various roles of broadcasters and the impact that they have had on the game to date. The final section provides an analysis of consumer demand for televised football.

Football's stakeholders and their objectives

The complexities within English league football to some extent result from the array of different interest groups. There is a large number of stakeholders in English league football. Some of them along with their objectives are the focus of this section.

Governing bodies of football

Governing bodies play an important role in football both within the domestic and international arena. In England, the bodies which have a major role in the governance of football are the Football Association (FA), the English Premier League and the Football League. Strictly speaking, the governance roles of the Premier League and the Football League are limited and they are membership organisations. However, they make significant and important contributions to football's governances within the UK.

The FA is responsible for many aspects of football including the England national teams, the FA Cup and various other competitions, aspects at grassroots and issues relating to disciplinary procedures, rules and regulations. The FA has a multitude of objectives given its portfolio and remit. One of its objectives is (no doubt) to maximise profits from its various activities, i.e. income from Wembley National Stadium Limited, income from matches involving the England national team and contracts with commercial sponsors such as Carlsberg, McDonald's, Nationwide, Tesco and Umbro. In addition to this commercial objective, the FA also exhibit objectives similar to those of the public sector in that they provide a public good. Public goods are those which are non-rival and non-excludable (Gratton and Taylor 2001; Downward et al. 2009). These characteristics mean that the public at large are able to consume the provisions of the FA and in doing so do not have to compete for its consumption and no one is excluded; in many cases, public consumption is desirable and encouraged. Examples of the public goods and opportunities provided by the FA include the provisions of grassroots football (although much of this is in conjunction with other agencies, e.g. local authorities and voluntary organisations), and the provision of the national football team. Interestingly, some aspects of consumption of the national football team are very much private goods that consumers have to pay to consume, i.e. games televised by pay television broadcasters. The above serves to highlight some of the FA's objectives and their complexities in balancing what is a combination of commercially driven and broader consumer welfare motives.

The leagues

Within the English domestic football arena are the Premier League and the Football League. Unlike the FA, these bodies are membership organisations. These leagues' principal role is to operate and manage their respective competitions. The success of these competitions could be measured using a set of criteria. First, the financial successes of the leagues are paramount. Hence, maximising revenues from sources such as broadcasting and sponsorship is important. As a result the leagues are able to enter into commercial contracts on behalf of their members. Second, maximising overall attendances across the entire league is also important and this is based on the collective success of all member clubs. Third, positive media exposure is also a key criterion and measures such as the total number of television audiences across televised matches and positive coverage in the wider media are vital. Fourth, the commercial success and financial stability of the member clubs are essential. Without this, the integrity of the leagues is sometimes called into question. In March 2004 Leeds United went into administration, having incurred large debts which were unserviceable (Gerrard 2006). The financial crisis that blighted the club at one point raised questions as to what would happen to the results of the league if the remainder of their fixtures could not be fulfilled. Even well-managed clubs need other clubs to be well managed; they are financially dependent on one another (see Buraimo et al. (2006) for a review of the financial crisis in English football). Therefore leagues have an interest in the financial health of their members. For this reason, the Football League deducts points from clubs that enter into administration. This is meant to act as a disincentive. Finally, leagues have a fundamental objective and duty to ensure that competitions amongst their members are balanced and sporting outcomes are uncertain. This is often referred to as the 'uncertainty of outcome' hypothesis (Borland and Macdonald 2003; Szymanski 2003). These five criteria are by no means exhaustive but cover some of the key objectives of leagues.

The clubs

Another group of stakeholders are the clubs. Sloane's (1971) seminal paper, *The Economics of Professional Football: The Football Club as a Utility Maximiser*, has been a significant precursor for research on the objectives of football clubs. Sloane suggested that the universal application of profit maximising may not apply to football clubs. Indeed the situation then and now is that many more clubs actually declare losses than profits. Slone argued that there are several quantifiable objectives that football clubs may pursue and these objectives need not be mutually exclusive. The pursuit of these objectives to different degrees is how clubs maximise their utility. Sloane's utility function comprised a number of objectives: playing success; average attendance; health of the league; and financial constraint (not necessarily profit, in many cases this is a minimum acceptable loss). Maximising these various objectives with differing degrees and different levels of priority enables clubs of different sizes and structures to maximise their utility.

Applying Sloane's utility function to today's clubs, Chelsea, for example, would be an example of a club that places higher priority on playing success over average attendance and financial constraints. The evidence for this is the substantial investment that the club has made in its staff over the past seasons. In 2006–7, it spent £132m on wages and salaries. The following season, this increased to £172m. During this period, its operating loss of £16m worsened to £31m (Deloitte 1999). Chelsea finished second in both seasons behind Manchester United. Clearly, Chelsea's priority is playing success and this dominates other objectives within the utility function. For this reason, Chelsea's accumulation of playing talent is very high, in both absolute and relative terms. By comparison, Manchester United, who came first in these two seasons, spent £92m in 2006–7 and £121m in 2007–8, an increase of £29m compared with Chelsea's increase in wage of £40m.

The health of the league is important to clubs as without a reasonably healthy league even the well-managed clubs stand to suffer. This is one of the reasons why the Premier League has favoured the collective selling of television rights over clubs being allocated their own television rights to sell on an individual basis. Theoretically, smaller clubs generate more revenue from collective selling than they would from individual selling.

Other empirical evidence also helps in assessing the varied objectives of football clubs. For example, Tottenham Hotspur, unlike the majority of English football clubs, is publicly owned and shares in the club are traded on the London Stock Exchange. In contrast with Chelsea, the investors and shareholders of the club are likely to place greater priority on the financial aspect of the utility function. Wages for Tottenham in 2006–7 and 2007–8 were £44m and £53m respectively. Over these two seasons, they declared profits of £30m (in 2008) and £27m (in 2007). Without further empirical research, it is not possible to assess whether profit maximisation is Tottenham Hotspur's objective. However, its *modus operandi* suggests that it needs to report profits given that the club is predominantly owned by investors and shareholders. Another interesting dimension to note is that there is a growing number of football clubs in which significant portions of the club are owned by the supporters and fans: supporters' trusts. Examples include Exeter City, Stockport County and Notts County. Clubs of this ownership structure are likely to behave differently from others. They might place less emphasis on playing success and more on attendance and the club's financial health.

Case Study
Club versus country

The training and development of players is important if football clubs are to fulfil their varied objectives. Some clubs spend significant resources on searching for players and subsequently on training them in the football academies and centres of excellence. The training and development of young players can take time and for this reason, clubs engage in the acquisition of players by buying their registrations on the so-called transfer market. However clubs go about acquiring their players, the resources needed to do so are very high. In addition, salary and wage costs further increase clubs' expenditure on players. The rationale for this high expenditure on players, through transfer acquisition or wages, is understandable. Clubs need players to fulfil their main function of hosting football matches.

The FA, like football clubs, also hosts matches and needs players to do so; particularly matches involving the national football team(s). However, unlike the clubs, the FA has no requirement or necessity to use its resources to acquire players or develop players. The England national team is assembled based on the quality of talent developed by the clubs. This has given rise to the club versus country debate.

The clubs have some objections. One objection is that the FA uses the clubs' playing resources to fulfil unimportant fixtures such as friendly matches. For clubs, this is ineffective particularly given the number of matches that elite players are expected to play during the course of a season. Another objection is that the FA enters into sponsorship and endorsement contracts which make use of these players. The FA is able to generate sponsorship and endorsement earnings using clubs' players. For the clubs, their playing resources are being used by the FA to generate earnings and they are not being compensated. In some instances, this can create marketing conflicts. The FA and *the national team have in the past been sponsored by Coca-Cola. However, some of the players are sponsored by Pepsi-Cola, a rival firm. In 2002 the BBC reported:*

> *England football captain David Beckham is at the centre of a 'cola war' between the world's leading manufacturers of the soft drink, it has been reported. The Manchester United midfielder has been made the star of Coca-Cola's World Cup advertising campaign. But he is also featuring in a World Cup-based campaign for rival Pepsi – who pay him an estimated £1m a year to advertise their product. Coca-Cola is able to use the 26-year-old footballer, despite his contract to market Pepsi, because of its multi-million pound sponsorship of the England football team.*

(BBC 2009)

Sloane's and subsequent analyses of the objectives of football clubs (Kesenne 2007; Dobson and Goddard 2001) provide invaluable insights into the operations and decision-making of clubs. In some respects the objectives of football clubs may not always be compatible with those of other stakeholders. The regulatory capture of the big five that led to the breakaway of the Premier League is a good example. The big five wanted to end the extensive distribution of broadcast revenue across all the 92 clubs; a policy which the league felt was necessary to maintain a healthy league.

In this section, the objectives of only some of the major stakeholders in English football have been considered. However, there are other important stakeholders and their objectives and motives are equally important and have shaped English football. Some of these include: broadcasters; competition authorities; consumers; managers and coaches; officials; players; and sponsors.

Learning Activity 10.1

Broadcasters, competition authorities and players are just some of the major stakeholders in English football. For each of these groups of stakeholders, consider the following questions.
1   What are their principal objectives and how do they go about achieving them?
2   What empirical evidence is there to support your answers?

Gate attendance demand

The level of interest in English league football has varied over the past decades. During the post-war era, demand for football increased to a record high of 41m, an average of 22,000 spectators per match across all four divisions of the Football League. English league football has never been able to match its former popularity and demand since the late 1940s has been in decline. The fall in demand has been consistent, albeit punctuated with small increases along the way. One of these was during the mid-1960s when England was triumphant in the FIFA World Cup. The positive impacts of the England win were only temporary and match day attendances continued to fall. The fall in demand during the latter parts of the 1970s and the first half of the 1980s can be attributed to a number of factors. English football was blighted by hooliganism during this period; the Football League and football clubs were found wanting when it came to issues of safety and security. Hooliganism, lack of effective crowd management and poor stadium accommodation resulted in fatalities.

Attendance reached a record low in 1985 with an annual attendance of 16m spectators, an average of 7,900 per game. The need for major structural changes in football was evident. Gratton (2000) notes three structural changes in English football during the second half of the 1980s and the early 1990s. The first of these was the impact of the Taylor Report, an inquiry commissioned by the government following the Hillsborough disaster. One of the Report's recommendations was for all stadiums in the top division of English league football to become all-seater by the start of the 1994–5 season. Another structural change was the breakaway of the top teams to form the Premier League. The creation of the Premier League combined with record revenues from the broadcast sector effectively created a new type of football. The revenues from the broadcasters meant that football clubs were able to spend significantly more than they were used to on acquiring players. Many of these players were from foreign leagues and this marked the start of the influx of foreign football superstars. A third change noted by Gratton was the change in status of a small but significant number of clubs. Clubs issued public share offers and became public limited companies floated on stock markets. This shift in ownership model from limited companies to public limited companies was (in theory) accompanied by a shift in objectives. These clubs would now have to operate on commercial ground and be accountable to shareholders and investors. Tottenham Hotspur was the first to make this change in 1983, and was followed by Millwall in 1989 and Manchester United in 1991. Another 16 clubs floated some or all of their equity on the market between October 1995 and October 1997 (Buraimo et al. 2006). Football's move into commercial markets, like broadcasting, brought additional resources to the game and clubs were able to use these to further enhance their playing squads.

Learning Activity 10.2

Figure 10.1 shows aggregated attendances for English league football from the post-war era to 2006–7. Compiling data from *Sky Sports Football Yearbook* or other equally reliable sources, construct graphical illustrations of annual attendances for the Premier League and the three divisions of the Football League from 1992–3 to the most recent and complete season. How might the changes in annual attendances in your graphs be explained?

Many of the structural changes noted occurred during the latter part of the 1980s and during the 1990s after the fall in attendances had halted. It is therefore not possible to attribute the change in demand to these factors. Nonetheless, the subsequent rise in the late 1980s and onwards can be credited to these changes. The rise depicted in Figure 10.1 should actually be greater. Nowadays, as much as 47 per cent of matches played in the Premier League are in front of capacity crowds. The capacities of many of the stadiums mean that attendances are in fact constrained. Without this constraint, reported attendances would be much

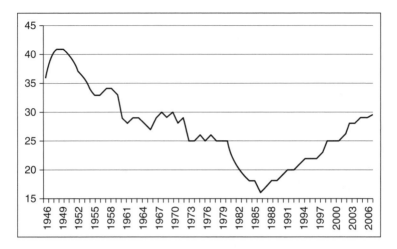

Figure 10.1 Annual match day attendance in English league football from 1946–7 to 2006–7.
Source: data from various editions of the Sky Sports Football Yearbook

higher. Within Europe, the Premier League is unique with respect to capacity constraints. In other European major leagues, such as the Bundesliga in Germany, the Primera Liga in Spain and Serie A in Italy, capacity constraint is not as big a problem league-wide although clubs like Real Madrid, Barcelona and Bayern Munich often play in front of capacity crowds.

As noted, broadcasting has had a major impact on English league football and Chapter 11 considers many of the issues involved from the perspective of the market and its structure. The following sections consider broadcasting from the perspective of the consumer and analyses television audience ratings for English league football.

Television audience ratings

One of the most dramatic changes that has occurred in English football is broadcasting. Prior to broadcasting, consumers were limited to attending games at stadiums. Outside of this, consumption was limited to radio, newspaper coverage and highlights on television. By limiting live consumption of football to stadium attendances, a constraint on spectator demand was effectively being imposed. Within the spectator market, there are limits to the number of people who could actually attend football games. The factors that determine these limits are the capacities of stadiums, the cost of travel to games, the size of city and town populations in which clubs are located and the demographic characteristics of these populations. These factors and others combine to determine and limit the number of people that could conceivably attend football games.

The broadcasting of live football by BBC and ITV in the mid-1980s and subsequently by BSkyB in the early 1990s effectively expanded the viewing market. Consumers now had the option of attending games in the stadiums or watching them live on television. Prior to the emergence of the Premier League, the Football League resisted the televising of live games. The League's view was that televising games would have an adverse effect on attendances in the stadiums. Since the formation of the Premier League, the impact of televised games on match-day attendance has been of interest to researchers. Baimbridge et al.'s (1996) study was the first to assess the impact of televised games on attendance in the Premier League. They found that for games televised on Sundays there was no significant effect on attendance. However, for those televised on Mondays, attendances on average fell by 15 per cent. Other studies which have investigated the impact of televised games on attendance in the Premier League are Forrest et al. (2004) and Buraimo and Simmons (2008). In the latter study, the impact of televising games on Sundays and Mondays was found to be significant, causing falls in attendance of 5 per cent and 10 per cent respectively.

The negative impact of televised games means that while attendance, and by implication revenue, falls by a substantial amount, a facility fee received by clubs more than compensates them for this fall in attendance. The facility fee is a feature of the Premier League's contract with the broadcaster. Unlike other European leagues where the broadcast rights are sold on an individual basis, the Premier League pools its rights and sells them collectively. The revenue received from the sale of the rights is divided into three parts: basic award, facility fees and merit award. The basic award is worth 50 per cent of the rights fee and the remaining 50 per cent is equally divided between the facility fees and merit award. Table 10.1 shows the

Club	Final league position	Basic award £k	Facility fees £k	Merit award £k	Overseas TV £k	Total £k	Proportion %
Arsenal	3	13,534	11,360	13,051	9,579	47,524	6.2
Aston Villa	6	13,534	8,731	10,876	9,579	42,720	5.6
Birmingham City	19	13,534	5,663	1,450	9,579	30,226	3.9
Blackburn Rovers	7	13,534	7,416	10,151	9,579	40,680	5.3
Bolton Wanderers	16	13,534	5,663	3,625	9,579	32,401	4.2
Chelsea	2	13,534	9,196	13,776	9,579	46,085	6.0
Derby County	20	13,534	5,663	725	9,579	29,501	3.8
Everton	5	13,534	7,854	11,601	9,579	42,568	5.6
Fulham	17	13,534	5,663	2,900	9,579	31,676	4.1
Liverpool	4	13,534	10,484	12,326	9,579	45,923	6.0
Manchester City	9	13,534	8,292	8,701	9,579	40,106	5.2
Manchester United	1	13,534	12,227	14,501	9,579	49,841	6.5
Middlesbrough	13	13,534	5,663	5,800	9,579	34,576	4.5
Newcastle	12	13,534	10,045	6,526	9,579	39,684	5.2
Portsmouth	8	13,534	8,292	9,426	9,579	40,831	5.3
Reading	18	13,534	5,663	2,175	9,579	30,951	4.0
Sunderland	15	13,534	6,539	4,350	9,579	34,002	4.4
Tottenham Hotspur	11	13,534	6,101	7,251	9,579	36,465	4.8
West Ham United	10	13,534	6,101	7,976	9,579	37,190	4.9
Wigan Athletic	14	13,534	5,663	5,075	9,579	33,851	4.4

Table 10.1: Payment to clubs from the sale of television broadcast rights in the 2007–8 season
Source: Deloitte (2009)

distribution of rights fees for the 2007–8 season. From the proportions noted in the table, it is clear that the less wealthy clubs in the Premier League extract significant amounts from the broadcast market, more than they would do if they were required to sell their rights on an individual basis. In fact, if all the available revenue from broadcasting was shared equally, each club would receive 5 per cent. Although direct empirical evidence from within the League to support this assertion is unavailable, indirect evidence from leagues like the Primera Liga in Spain provide adequate support. Under the current arrangement, the club with the smallest share received 3.8 per cent and the biggest share was 6.5 per cent, 1.2 per cent below and 1.5 per cent above the equal sharing threshold respectively. Put another way, the difference in percentages for the highest and lowest earning clubs is 2.7 per cent or £20.3m.

Since the early seasons of televised Premier League football, live viewing audiences on BSkyB's coverage of Premier League matches have been growing, although there has been some stagnation along the way. During the early part of the 1990s, there was a steady rise in television audiences, up to the mid-1990s. The novelty of live televised football and the absence of competition are the likely explanations for this rise. This was followed by a sharp decline during the latter part of that decade. The reasons for this are less obvious and areas of research should focus on issues such as the teams which made up the league during this period and scheduling. Since the halt in decline of audience viewing figures in the 1999–2000 season, total audience figures in the league have been consistently rising to a high of approximately 120m viewers per season (see Figure 10.2).

What Figure 10.2 suppresses is the volume of matches that were televised each season and the impact of the number of games. The period after the 1999–2000 season in Figure 10.2 shows an upward trend in television audience ratings. However, taking into account the number of games televised each season, the story is rather different. Figure 10.3 shows the mean audience ratings per match by season. What is evident from Figure 10.3 is that there is a declining trend during the later part. The principal reason for this is the increased number of televised matches.

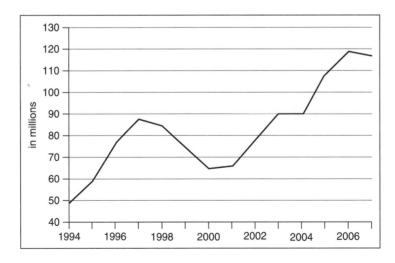

Figure 10.2 Total television viewing audiences for Premier League matches on BSkyB from 1993–4 to 2006–7

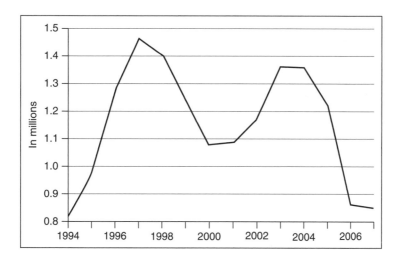

Figure 10.3 Mean television viewing audiences for Premier League matches on BSkyB from 1993–4 to 2006–7

During the earlier seasons, the Premier League and the BSkyB only televised 60 matches per season of the possible 380 matches available; there were even more matches available during the 1992–3 and 1993–4 seasons as the League comprised 22 teams. Televising 60 matches effectively limited broadcast output and in theory, this limits consumer choice and allows the suppliers to make abnormal profits, especially if there is no competition in the supply market as was the case. However, pressure from a number of key stakeholders, including competition authorities, forced changes.

The involvements of the competition authorities in the football broadcast market was unwelcome to the Premier League–BSkyB alliance. First, the investigation of the Monopolies and Mergers Commission into the proposed merger between BSkyB and Manchester United in 1998 concluded that it would not be in the public interest. Second, there was a court case involving the Office of Fair Trading and the Premier League over the collective selling of television rights. The League in its defence claimed that without collective selling, the it would be less competitive as the smaller clubs within the League would not be able to generate enough revenue. Claims of this nature are anti-competitive and are generally viewed as being anti-consumer. It is unlikely that in other industries this level of collusion would be allowed. For example, Virgin Airways and British Airways colluded in the pricing of transatlantic flights and consequently in 2007 competition authorities fined British Airways £121m; Virgin Airways escaped any fines as it whistle-blew and brought it to the attention of the authorities. The Restrictive Practices Court ruled in the Premier League's favour and collective selling was allowed to continue. Third, the European competition authority has been unhappy with BSkyB's monopoly in the market for live Premier League matches. In 2007, it ruled that no single broadcaster should be allowed to exclusively acquire all the live rights to Premier League matches. The practical implication of that ruling is that the rights have now been divided into six packages. For the period of 2007–8 to 2009–10, BSkyB acquired five of these, with the sixth going to a small broadcaster Setanta. The financial failings of Setanta resulted in the sixth package being acquired by ESPN.

Learning Activity 10.3

Consider the following interventions in the Premier League television rights market:

1 The proposed merger between BSkyB and Manchester United.
2 The European Court's ruling on the exclusive sale of Premier League television rights to BSkyB.

Had these interventions not taken place, what would the market for live Premier League matches be like and what would be the likely consequences for consumers?

As well as introducing competition, albeit very small, in the market for live Premier League matches, the pressure from the competition authorities has also increased the number of televised games. This restriction of output, in the case the number of televised games, can be viewed as being against the public interest. Rather than the 60 games that were previously broadcast by BSkyB during the earlier seasons, the broadcaster now televises 138 Premier League games per season. This in part is likely to explain why the mean number of viewers per game has declined. Consumers now have greater choice over which games to watch and these need not be games involving the bigger teams within the League. Games involving smaller teams will be more attractive to some consumers. In any case, the total audience for Premier League games is now spread across a greater number of matches.

Chapter Review

As noted in the opening section of this chapter, an assessment of the professional team sports market is important as its contribution to sport in the UK from both social and economic standpoints is substantial. The chapter has focused on a series of issues drawn from the Premier League and the Football League and, while these leagues have been the subject of the chapter's inquiry, the learning points are equally valid for other professional sport leagues in the UK and further afield. Although the impact of broadcasting on English football has formed a significant part of the chapter's analysis, similar impacts of broadcasting on league sports like rugby league can also be analysed. For example, rugby league was traditionally a winter sport in England. However, structural reforms as well as the lure of revenue from broadcasting saw the sport move from the winter months to those of summer.

The analysis has focused on the objectives of the various stakeholders in league football and while the list of stakeholders that formed the basis of the analysis is by no means exhaustive, it provides the foundation on which a more comprehensive stakeholder analysis could be conducted. Some of the features noted in the analysis include the conflict that arises from incompatible objectives and the different levels of power that some of these stakeholders are able to exert. Other areas that were considered in this chapter were the markets for gate attendance and television audiences. The complex relationship between attendances in the stadiums and television audiences was noted. Perhaps the fear of the Football League that televising matches would adversely affect gate attendance was justified. However, perhaps what they did not fully recognise was that revenue from the sale of television rights would more than compensate clubs for this adverse effect. The biggest five clubs in the Football League at the time exerted their collective power and instigated the birth of the Premier League in what Morrow (1999) termed regulatory capture.

The role of competition authorities in shaping the market has also been noted. Earlier in the chapter, their objectives in championing consumer interest were discussed. Later in this chapter, evidence of their impact on the market for live televised football games was presented. And while the market for televised football is not perfectly competitive, there has been a shift, albeit slight, away from the monopoly practices that have characterised the market. Finally, some of the discussions presented in this chapter compliment those presented in Chapter 11, The sports broadcast market, and both chapters provide a critical assessment of professional league sport within the UK.

After reading this chapter and attempting the learning activities you should now be able to answer the following questions:

1 Considering the objectives of the various stakeholders in English football, identify instances in which their objectives are incompatible and are likely to lead to conflict. What are the potential effects of these on consumers?
2 How might competition be further increased in the market for live televised games in the Premier League and what are the potential effects on key stakeholders?
3 To what extent are the issues that were noted in the Premier League replicated in other British Leagues such as the Football League and the Scottish Premier League?

Further Reading

- Andreff, W. and Szymanski, S. (2006) (eds), *Handbook on the Economics of Sport*, Cheltenham: Edward Elgar.
- Dobson, S. and Goddard, J. (2001) *The Economics of Football*, Cambridge: Cambridge University Press.
- Gratton, C. and Solberg, H.A. (2007) *The Economics of Sports Broadcasting*, London: Routledge.
- Monopolies and Mergers Commission (1999) *British Sky Broadcasting Group PLC and Manchester United Plc: A Report on the Proposed Merger*. London: The Stationery Office.
- Morrow, S. (1999) *The New Business of Football: Accountability and Finance in Football*, Basingstoke: Palgrave Macmillan.
- Morrow, S. (2003) *The People's Game: Football, Finance and Society*, Basingstoke: Palgrave Macmillan.
- Russell, D. (1997) *Football and the English: A Social History of Association Football in England, 1863–1995*. Preston: Carnegie Publishing.

Chapter 11
The sports broadcast market

Learning Objectives

This chapter is designed to help you:

- assess the developments within sports broadcasting;
- understand the structure of the UK sports broadcast market;
- understand the objectives within the sports broadcast market.

Sports broadcast markets over the past decades have emerged to become possibly the most important markets within sports. From the perspectives of different governing bodies for sports, major sports leagues and many sports rights owners, the revenue generated from the sale of sports rights generally dominates that generated from other sources. For example, sports leagues such as the Premier League in England and the National Football League in USA generate most of their revenue from the sale of television rights in their domestic and international markets. Similarly, the importance of sports broadcasting to international sports governing bodies cannot be overstated. Federations such as the International Olympic Committee (IOC) and Fédération Internationale de Football Association (FIFA) rely on sports broadcasting to meet both social and economic objectives. From the broadcasters' perspectives, many simply cannot afford not to have sports as part of their broadcast schedules, especially if they are to compete for television audiences in today's competitive broadcast market. The significance and importance of sports broadcasting has seen many broadcasters aggressively engage in auctions and bids to acquire broadcast rights for sports. As a result of these issues and many others that will be explored in this chapter, the broadcast landscape is constantly changing, and at a dramatic pace.

Introduction

Sport broadcasting has come to be recognised as one of the most important features of the sports sector in recent years. Even for minor sports, broadcasting remains significant to their economic and financial well-being. The significance of sports broadcasting can be analysed from a number of different perspectives. From an economic standpoint, sports broadcasting is important to the rights owners as it generates revenue over and above that generated from more traditional sources such as gate receipts, commercial activities inside stadiums and arenas, and sponsorship. Extending this economic viewpoint, the increase in revenue from sports broadcasting has provided wealth to these sports rights owners and in turn to sports men and women, who are among the principal agents of the sports. For example, the salaries and wages of professional football players across Europe and many parts of the world continue to grow to unprecedented levels. This growth is not unique to football or professional team sports: similar trends are noticeable in individual sports such as golf and tennis. One of the biggest single contributors to the increase in earnings by professional athletes is income from the broadcast market. For broadcasters, the economic value of sport is such that sport is an important feature of programme scheduling. In fact, across Europe, many broadcasters have channels dedicated to sports broadcasting and their business model is such that without sport, they would be less profitable.

Another important viewpoint is that of a social perspective – sports broadcasting also plays an important role within society. As many more people have access to sports through various media, particularly television, the impact of sports on society has become even more pronounced. Take, for example, success in international sporting competition. Studies (see Gratton and Taylor 2000) have examined and concluded that success in international sporting competition can benefit society at large. The benefits, it is often argued, accrue to a variety of people: sports fans and non-sports fans, active and passive consumers of sport. As more and more people access sports broadcasts, the potential for maximising these social benefits increases. The social significance of sports broadcasting is such that in some instances, it has been necessary for national governments to intervene to preserve the social benefits of sports broadcasts for society at large.

An important point to note for this chapter is what is meant by broadcasting and sports broadcasting in particular. The term broadcasting can normally be interpreted to cover a wide spectrum of media and formats. For example, the internet as a medium and the various sports content that can be found on it are examples of sports broadcasting. Likewise, handheld devices such as mobile phones and the ability to access sports content on them is another example. However, in this chapter, sports broadcasting refers principally, although not exclusively, to television broadcasts of sport. Many of the key learning points from the analysis of sports broadcasting on this medium can aid understanding of other forms of sports broadcast media.

The analyses of this chapter are for the most part based on the UK sports broadcast market. However, inferences can be made about other broadcast markets, particularly those in Europe and North America. The first of these sections focuses on developments of the UK sports broadcast market. This is followed by analyses of the structure of the UK sports broadcast market and the objectives of sports broadcasters. The chapter concludes with a review of the learning objectives.

Development of the sports broadcasting market

There have been significant changes over recent decades which have contributed to the structure of the UK's sports broadcast market. To understand the structure of the sports broadcast market, an understanding of the various advances in and impact of broadcast technology is necessary. During the 1980s, the UK broadcast market was dominated by a small number of *free-to-air* (FTA) broadcasters. The most dominant FTA broadcaster was the British Broadcasting Corporation (BBC). Other broadcasters were ITV, which was a network of independent regional broadcasters, Channel 4, a small broadcaster which at the time was government-owned but was managed and operated as an independent broadcaster. The BBC, who at the time operated two channels, was, and still remains, a public service broadcaster whose funding was through mandatory payment of a licence fee by all households with television sets. The other broadcasters, however, operated as commercial channels and were funded through the sale of commercial and advertising space around programming. During this period, the transmission of programmes was via an analogue signal which households received through television aerials.

The dominance of these broadcasters combined with the limited broadcast spectrum meant that sports broadcasting had to compete with other forms of programming such as soap operas, game shows and other forms of popular entertainment. For this reason, very few sports were televised. Broadcasters such as the BBC and ITV took an interest in major sports such as football, cricket and athletics and this formed a significant part of their sports programming. For Channel 4, its interests were less mainstream and more esoteric as it brought to the public sports such as American football from the NFL and Kabaddi, an Indian team sport. The competition for limited broadcast space meant that many sports did not feature at all, or did so very infrequently on television. Some only featured during the four-yearly cycle of Olympic coverage on the BBC and only then did the public have the opportunity to view these.

For broadcasters, and as a spectator sport, football had the strongest appeal. During the 1980s, it was a sport that attracted between 16 and 21m spectators per season to league matches played across the top four divisions. Given this appeal, televised football should generate audience interest and high ratings for the broadcasters. The relationship between the broadcasters and the football authorities, particularly the Football League, illustrates the dominance that the broadcasters, owners of the media, had over sports' governing bodies and rights owners, the owners of the content. The limited broadcast spectrum relative to the (potential) volume of sports content that could be broadcast meant that first, only a limited number of sports and sports events could be broadcast. Second, the balance of power lay with the broadcasters rather than with the sports rights owners (see case study BSkyB versus ITV in the battle for live football league rights).

Case Study
Broadcasters versus the Football League – the BBC–ITV cartel secure victory

During the early part of the mid-1980s, the Football League for the first time reached an agreement with the state broadcaster, the BBC, and the commercial broadcaster, ITV, to televise live football. The contract was for a period of two years from 1983 and was worth £5.7m per year. As a result, the broadcasters would televise 10 matches per season. As the contract was due to expire, the Football League and the broadcasters entered negotiations to renew the contract. The Football League looked to realise more revenue for its sports rights. However, as there was no competition to challenge the BBC–ITV cartel, this was not possible. In fact, no agreement could be reached for the start of the 1985–6 season. Consequently, no league matches were broadcast for the first half of the season. Eventually, the Football League and the cartel did reach an agreement worth £2.6m and this saw six matches broadcast during the second half of the season. In the two seasons that followed, the cartel was able to secure the rights for live football games, paying a price that was undoubtedly below what would have been realised in a competitive broadcast market. The BBC–ITV cartel was powerful enough to push the price of live football down in the absence of competition from other sports broadcasters.

The dominance of the FTA broadcasters came to an end in 1988 with the introduction of the then new *direct-to-home* (DTH) broadcast platform. This new platform for broadcasting meant that unlike traditional analogue broadcasting which all households with television aerials could receive, only those households with specific hardware, in this case a satellite receiver and decoder, could receive programmes.

As access to programmes was constrained by these hardware requirements, which could be controlled by the broadcaster, this paved the way for broadcasters to charge television viewers for content. The first of the DTH broadcasters was Sky Television. The emergence of Sky Television provided much-needed competition within the otherwise uncompetitive UK sports broadcast market. The dominance of the incumbent FTA broadcasters would now be challenged, particularly for sports rights. A year later, British Satellite Broadcasting, another satellite broadcaster, emerged. Competition within the broadcast market, although not perfect, was greater than before. The broadcast market now comprised the incumbent FTA broadcasters and the new satellite broadcasters.

Sky Television's business model was based on charging households for broadcast content through the payment of subscriptions. This approach proved unsuccessful at first: first, it faced competition from another pay-television operator, British Satellite Broadcasting; second, its ability to penetrate the market was very low given the limited number of households that were willing to subscribe to its service; third, there was very little that was distinct about its programming that provided it with a differential advantage over and above that provided by the FTA broadcasters. Sky Television adopted a number of strategies that would enhance its business model. In 1990, Sky Television and British Satellite Broadcasting merged to form British Sky Broadcasting (BSkyB). The merger effectively put an end to competition within the pay-television market and this part of the broadcasting market was served by the new monopolist, BSkyB. The other significant strategy by the broadcaster was to differentiate its programming: sport and film were to form the basis of this differentiation. In fact, BSkyB's owner, Rupert Murdoch, noted this would be his 'battering ram' approach to get BSkyB's programming into British households (Williams 1994). Consequently for sports rights owners such as sports leagues and organisers of major events who looked to have their events broadcast, there was now greater competition when selling their sports rights.

Advances in broadcast technology such as digital terrestrial transmission, digital satellite broadcasting and cable transmission have followed the above noted developments. The effects of all these are that there are now numerous broadcasters and wholesalers of channels, and consumers can access services in a variety of ways. For sports broadcasting this means, that (some of) the power that previously lay with the broadcasters has shifted to the sports rights owners, who are now able to demand and realise substantially greater amounts of broadcast revenue for their sports rights.

Structure of the UK sports broadcast market

The developments and the advances in broadcast technology have contributed to a complex sports broadcast market. An analysis of the structure of the sports broadcast market is helpful in understanding how the market operates. Prior to pay television, a sports rights owner would sell the television rights of a sport to a broadcaster, often on an exclusive basis. The broadcaster had the dual role of turning such rights into sports programmes, which were then distributed via its channel(s). This was then transmitted to households on the analogue terrestrial platform and viewers were able to receive these programmes through their television aerial. Figure 11.1 illustrates the structure of the supply chain prior to the arrival of pay television.

Advances in broadcast technology and increased competition have meant that the structure of the supply chain is now different. Furthermore, the sports broadcast market is fragmented and different agents perform different roles. For example, whereas before a broadcaster such as the BBC had the multiple

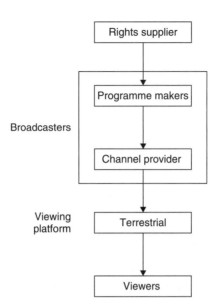

Figure 11.1 The television supply chain before the advent of pay television

role of programme making and providing channels on which programmes were distributed, nowadays, programme makers can be different from those who own the channel. In fact the channel providers may not necessary own the platform on which the channel is distributed. For example, BSkyB currently own the rights to broadcast live games from the English Premier League. Consumers wishing to subscribe to and watch these games need not do so by subscribing to BSkyB's service. Instead, they can access these games and programmes by subscribing to a different broadcaster and service altogether, i.e. Virgin Media. Figure 11.2 illustrates a more contemporary structure of the supply chain of the (sports) broadcast market, particularly with reference to pay television and BSkyB.

In this structure, the sports rights owners have a wider choice of to whom they sell their rights. There is more competition for sports rights acquisition at this stage of the market. For example, broadcasters such as the BBC, ITV, BSkyB, Channel 4, Channel 5, Virgin Media and ESPN all compete against one another to acquire sports rights. Once the rights have been acquired, the broadcasters then turn these sports rights into programmes. This process will typically involve recording the event live and turning this into a sports programme. In some instances, secondary non-live programmes may also be made, e.g. *Football Today* on the Sky Sports News channel or *Today at Wimbledon* on the BBC. Having turned the sports rights into programmes, these are then packaged into channels such as Sky Sports 1, Sky Sports 2, etc. It is these channels that are then transmitted on the various platforms which viewers are then able to access normally at a price. Viewers may access this directly from BSkyB on its (now digital) DTH platform. However, viewers can also receive this on different platforms too. The complexity of the supply chain is such that broadcasters like BSkyB will themselves buy sports programmes and channels produced and made by other broadcasters, e.g. television viewers can watch BBC's transmission of live tennis from the Wimbledon Championships on BSkyB's platform.

The advances in technology have not only seen changes to the pay television sector. The traditional terrestrial broadcasters have also taken advantage and provide a digital broadcasting service. The significance

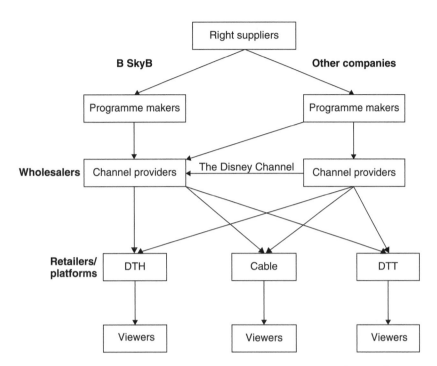

Figure 11.2 The pay television supply chain
Source: Monopoles and Mergers Commission (1999)

of digital terrestrial broadcasting (DTT) is that terrestrial broadcasters can take advantage of multi-channel broadcasting. Consequently they too, like the pay television operators, have many channels which need filling with content. Some broadcasters have taken advantage of technology and provided more enhanced coverage of sports. Examples include the BBC's coverage of the Wimbledon Tennis Championships in which viewers, through the interactive service, can choose which court's play to watch, and BSkyB's high definition (HD) broadcast which allows viewers to watch programmes transmitted in a higher resolution.

The greater numbers of broadcasters and channels mean greater competition in the market and, in theory, better value for consumers. The question therefore is, are sports consumers getting value for money when it comes to sports broadcasting? Put another way, are sports broadcasters making abnormal profits by over-charging their consumers? It is arguable that sports consumers are paying over and above what a competitive sports broadcast market would charge. The principal reason for this is that, while there are many broadcasters within the sports broadcaster market, the level and nature of competition between broadcasters is far from normal. The consequence and the evidence of this is the migration of sports rights to BSkyB. Furthermore, as channel distributors like Virgin Media rely on BSkyB for channels and content, they are unlikely to bid against it (BSkyB) given that if they do and then they lose, they will have to face a higher price than normal further down the supply chain.

The broadcast market has seen expansions in both the number of broadcasters and the number of channels being operated. The greater number of broadcasters has on the one had increased competition for sports rights. On the other hand, it has also created opportunities for collusions and cartels to operate. In fact, the European Broadcasting Union (EBU) is one such example. The EBU is an association of world national broadcasters and comprises many public service as well as commercial broadcasters. Whatever the stated aims and objectives of the union, the implications are that it is able to influence the manner in which sports rights are sold by acting as a cartel. For instance, the IOC often has to deal with the EBU when negotiating the sale of the television rights for the summer and winter Olympic Games. As a single entity, the EBU is able to negotiate terms and conditions which suit the collective interest of its members (see Gratton and Solberg 2007). This particular approach may not be in the interest of consumers at large.

In a more competitive market in which cartel members are prevented from colluding, competition is likely to improve the quality of transmission. Furthermore, the greater revenues from the sale of sports rights that are likely to be generated from a more competitive market could be used to improve sports. Cartels suppress the value of sports rights and this potentially has a knock-on effect throughout the sports broadcast market and sport itself.

Learning Activity 11.1

Taking the programme listings of a number of channels over a sample period, e.g. one month or longer, analyse the distribution of live sports programming across the channels and broadcasters. To what extent does the distribution of live sports programmes suggest a competitive sports broadcast market, or market dominance by a single broadcaster or a small number of large broadcasters?

Identifying the most valued sports rights for the UK for each of the following sports, which broadcasters currently hold the broadcast rights?

1   Men's and women's golf
2   Men's and women's tennis
3   Professional football
4   Rugby union
5   Rugby league
6   Track and field
7   Darts
8   The Commonwealth Games

Objectives of sports broadcasters

Another consideration when examining the structure of the sports broadcast market is to consider the objectives of the broadcasters within the market. By considering their objectives, the rationale behind their decision-making process and their role within the market becomes clearer. There are two broad objectives to consider when looking at the role of sports broadcasters: maximising consumer welfare and maximising profits. Although variations of these two broad objectives and other objectives exist, for the purpose of this chapter, these are sufficient. Most broadcasters' objectives are to maximise their profits. For example, broadcasters like BSkyB, ITV, ESPN are all profit-maximising broadcasters and the acquisition and broadcasting of sports rights is simply one of the many ways they try to achieve this.

For BSkyB, its ability to maximise profit from sports broadcasting has by and large been through the extensive acquisition of major sports rights. Irrespective of how the sports broadcast market is defined, whether as one large market that includes all televised sports or as a series of smaller markets based on reflecting different sports, BSkyB's share of the market is very high. For example, BSkyB's share of the rights for Premier League football in England from the period 2008–9 to 2010–11 is 83 per cent. In some previous seasons, its share has been as high as 100 per cent. Hence, some sports broadcast markets can be described as monopolies or complex monopolies in which a single firm dominates the supply of sports rights and sports programming. BSkyB's approach to fulfilling its profit-maximising objectives through the broadcast of sport has been through extensive acquisition of sports rights. This approach has contributed to the increase in subscriptions realised by BSkyB over the decades. In 2009, there were 9.4m subscribers to BSkyB's services; this compares with 7.8m in 2005 and 2.1m as far back as 1992 (BSkyB's annual reports, various years). Therefore monopolising sports rights and sports broadcasting is a means of maximising the number of subscribers. The number of subscribers itself is only part of the bigger picture. By being able to increase the number of subscribers, BSkyB is able to improve its revenue, principally, in two ways. The first is the revenue from subscriptions – the greater the number of subscribers the greater its subscription revenue. The second is from the sale of commercial advertising slots during sports programming. While there will always be firms willing to pay to advertise their brands and products around sports broadcasts, the amount they are willing to pay is likely to increase if the number of viewers watching the event is higher. Therefore, advertising revenue that accrues to BSkyB is dependent on the number of potential viewers, which itself is dependent on the number of subscribers. It is these revenues that determine the size of its profits. This approach to maximising profit is consistent with most pay television operators when it comes to sports broadcasting.

FTA commercial broadcasters like ITV are also commercial broadcasters with a profit-maximising objective. However, unlike the pay television broadcasters, consumers do not pay directly for programming. Instead, the broadcaster generates a significant proportion of its revenue from the sale of commercial and advertising space to firms willing to advertise during and around sports broadcasts. Hence, its revenue is predominantly from this single source. One of the main differences between FTA and pay television broadcasters is that FTA broadcasters are able to deliver greater audiences when televising sports and for this reason they are able to charge advertisers more.

The BBC is a public service broadcaster and a significant portion of its funding is through the payment of a mandatory television licence fee by all households with television sets. Unlike commercial broadcasters whose principal objective is to maximise profits, which in turn means maximising sports viewers, the BBC's objective is, in theory, not one that is commercially driven. Rather than maximise profits, its objective can be viewed as maximising the welfare of consumers or in this case, sports viewers. In practice, this does not necessarily mean maximising the number of sports viewers but a threshold audience rating must be achieved to justify public financial support. Given this, it is justifiable for the BBC to place as much importance on minority sports such as squash and hockey as it does on major ones like football and tennis. However, like all government agencies, it is faced with the challenge of allocative efficiency. How should the finite resources it has for sports broadcasting be allocated so that the benefits to the public are maximised? Simply broadcasting the most popular major sports does not achieve this aim, especially since many commercial broadcasters already do so even if consumers have to pay for access.

To maximise the welfare of all sports consumers, the BBC and other terrestrial broadcasters are advantaged by the legislation, particularly the Broadcasting Acts of 1990 and 1996. For sports broadcasting, the Acts mean that some sports rights, live and in some instances highlights (secondary coverage), cannot be acquired exclusively by pay television broadcasters as they are considered to be of national interest. The rights to which the Acts currently apply are noted in Table 11.1. The provisions of the Acts mean that the BBC, along with other terrestrial broadcasters like ITV and Channel 4, have an advantage in the broadcast market when competing for the broadcast rights of sports events. Furthermore, the Acts are recognition of the need to protect consumer interest when it comes to viewing sports on television. Given the dominance and wealth of the pay television sector, without the Broadcasting Acts many more sports rights would be likely to migrate to pay television.

Group A (full live coverage)	Group B (secondary coverage)
Olympic Games	Cricket Test Matches played in England
FIFA World Cup Tournament	Non-finals matches in the Wimbledon Tennis Championships
European Football Championship	All other matches in the Rugby World Cup Finals
FA Cup Final	Six Nations Rugby tournament matches involving home countries
Scottish FA Cup Final (in Scotland)	Commonwealth Games
The Grand National	World Athletics Championship
The Derby	Cricket World Cup
Wimbledon Tennis Championship finals	The Ryder Cup
Rugby League Challenge Cup Final	The Open Golf Championship
Rugby World Cup Final	

Table 11.1: Listed events protected by the Broadcasting Acts of 1990 and 1996

As can be seen the motives and incentives that drive broadcasters are different. However, their behaviour within the sports rights markets is similar; given their resources, they strive to acquire what they perceive to be the more popular sport rights for their programme schedule.

Case Study
BSkyB versus ITV in the battle for live football league rights

The dominance of BSkyB in the football rights market is one that has been very well established. Between 1992 and 2006, BSkyB acquired the exclusive rights to live games from the English Premier League. It also had the rights to live games from the lower tiers of English league football. Broadcasters like the BBC were not able to compete with BSkyB's might for the rights to live football league games and instead had to be content with highlights packages. Table 11.2 summarises the broadcasters' acquisition of live football rights in the English league from 1992 to 2013.

Year	Duration of contract (years)	Broadcaster	Matches per season
		The English Premier League	
1992	5	BSkyB	60
1997	4	BSkyB	60
2001	3	BSkyB	66
2004	3	BSkyB	138[1]
2007	3	BSkyB/Setanta[2]	138
2010	3	BSkyB/ESPN	138
		The Football League: all three divisions	
1993	4	ITV	
1997	4	BSkyB	55 during first season then 65
2001	4	ITV Digital[3]	80
2002	4	BSkyB	60
2006	3	BSkyB	70
2009	3	BSkyB/BBC	75

Table 11.2: Acquisition of live football rights from 1992 to 2013

1 Some of these games were broadcast on a pay-per-view basis, through which viewers had to pay per match over and above any subscription payments.

2 Setanta's rights package was transferred to ESPN after it went into bankruptcy.

3 Partway through the first season, ITV Digital, a subsidiary of ITV, went into bankruptcy and the contract between the broadcaster and league could not be fulfilled.

The absence of live domestic football on ITV undermined the broadcaster's efforts to be a premier sports broadcaster, particularly in a period when digital broadcasting technology had provided broadcasters with a greater broadcast spectrum and an increasing need to fill it with content. In 2000, ITV Digital, previously ON Digital and a subsidiary of ITV, acquired the live rights for games in the Football league for £315m. However, the rights turned out to be overvalued as matches attracted small numbers of viewers. The reason for the small number of viewers was that the ITV Digital platform at its highest had only 1.3m subscribers; this compares to BSkyB's subscription base of 10m at that time. ITV Digital's aggressive entry into the domestic football market with limited subscribers and inferior football to the Premier League saw it enter administration in March 2002 owing the Football League £178m.

Another broadcaster that followed a similar strategy to that of ITV Digital's was Setanta. Its entry into the live rights market for football and other sports was also aggressive. It too failed to attract the required number of subscribers to its pay television platform and, in June 2009, went into administration.

Chapter Review

This chapter has explored the various developments with the sports broadcast market, particularly the developments that have occurred from the 1980s to 2010. These developments have seen the transition from an analogue platform, in which sports broadcasts were dominated by a small number of broadcasters, to one in which there are multi-channel platforms with many broadcasters. However, while the number of broadcasters has increased, competition within sports broadcasting is far from perfect. There has been a consistent migration of sports rights to pay television operators and one in particular, BSkyB. It should be noted also that prior to the arrival of pay television and before technology expanded the broadcast spectrum, terrestrial broadcasters were not able to deliver sports broadcasting with the same level of abundance that has been realised in today's market.

The advances in broadcast technology have had a significant impact on the way the sports broadcast market operates. Consumers are able to access, albeit at a price in some instances, different sports broadcasts on different platforms and with enhanced features made possible by these advances in technology and more competition within the sports broadcast market. Although the scope of this chapter has been limited to television broadcasting, other forms of broadcasting should be considered, particularly as technology further advances. Such examples include viewing sports content on handheld devices.

The sports broadcast market and the roles played by many of its agents have also been examined. Whether the objectives are to maximise profits and revenue or to provide public service broadcasting, it seems that many broadcasters, in practice, look to achieve their objectives by acquiring, within financial constraints, the most attractive sports rights they can afford. The role of governments in this should not be overlooked. By legislating, the manner in which sports rights are distributed among broadcasters is significantly influenced. This therefore raises questions as to whether this form of intervention in the sports broadcast market is good for the public or not.

Further Reading

- Downward, P., Dawson, A. and Dejonghe, T. (2009) *Sports Economics: Theory, Evidence and Policy*. London: Butterworth-Heinemann.
- Gratton, C. and Solberg, H.A. (2007) *The Economics of Sport Broadcasting*. London: Routledge.
- Jeanrenaud, C. and Késenne, S. (2006) *The Economics of Sport and the Media*. Cheltenham: Edward Elgar.
- Monopolies and Mergers Commission (1999) *British Sky Broadcasting Group PLC and Manchester United PLC: A Report on the Proposed Merger*. London: The Stationery Office.
- Wenner, L.A. (ed.) (1998) *Mediasport*. London: Routledge.
- Wladimir, A. and Szymanski, S. (eds) (2006) *Handbook on the Economics of Sport*. Cheltenham: Edward Elgar.

Part Four
The sports labour market

Chapter 12
The sports labour market

Learning Objectives

This chapter is designed to help you:

- gain an overview of the growth and development of the sport labour market;
- explore how government policy influences the sport labour market;
- identify and understand the main occupational sectors in sport and the organisations associated with those occupations;
- explore the key issues facing the sport labour market.

Employment in sport in the UK has grown substantially over the last three decades, evidenced by an increase of 28 per cent in England between 1985 and 2003 (SIRC 2007). Alongside this growth, the structure of the sport labour market has also changed beyond recognition. It has become increasingly complex, both in terms of the types of jobs that are now available in sport, but also the nature of the issues faced in recruiting and developing an appropriate sport labour force.

The purpose of this chapter is to provide an overview of the sport labour market in the UK. It will begin with the statistics to indicate the current size of the market in England, Scotland, Wales and Northern Ireland. The chapter will then explore how the sport labour market has developed; analysis which is important as many of the issues it now faces can be traced back to its historical development. The latter part of the chapter will outline the current situation in the different occupational sectors of the sport labour market and will particularly highlight the influence of government policies on employment in sport.

Employment in sport

As has been discussed in the rest of this book, the sport industry is fragmented, with a myriad of organisations involved in its provision. This means that it is extremely difficult to accurately measure the actual size of its labour force. This difficulty is reflected by the following statement by **sport**scotland (2007: 4) and is supported by the Northern Ireland Assembly (2009).

> *Employment statistics should be viewed as indicative, in most cases figures for sport related employment in Scotland do not exist, and calculations have to be made on the basis of assumed employment generated by overall expenditure, often pro-rated from the available UK data.*

Table 12.1 provides the most recent measurement by the Sports Industry Research Centre (2008) for Sport England. This is followed by figures for Scotland, Wales and Northern Ireland which are all presented differently due to the different methods of collection.

	1985	2000	2003	2004	2005
Commercial sport	97	115	116	133	134
Commercial non-sport	144	175	192	202	197
Voluntary sector	31	38	46	47	52
Public sector	32	37	48	49	51
Total	304	365	401	431	434

Table 12.1: Sport related employment in England 2003 (thousands)
Commercial non-sport sector includes the production of sport-related goods and services by non-sports organisations. Source: Sport Industry Research Centre (SIRC) (2007).

	1995	1998	2001	2004
Commercial non-sport	16,500	16,120	16,520	19,800
Commercial sport	11,390	11,130	13,360	13,900
Local government	6,980	5,490	6,980	7,000
Voluntary sport	4,850	4,280	4,850	4,500
Central government	180	190	240	300
Total	39,890	37,210	41,950	45,500

Table 12.2: Employment in sport in Scotland
Source: **sport**scotland (2007)

	1998	2004
Commercial non-sport sector	8.9	11.1
Voluntary sport	2.0	2.0
Sport retailing	3.0	3.4
Spectator clubs	1.2	1.2
Sports facilities	1.8	2.4
Education	1.1	1.6
Other	1.4	1.5
Total	19.4	23.2

Table 12.3: Employment in sport in Wales (thousands)
Source: Sports Council Wales (2008)

Commercial sport:	
Spectator clubs	327
Participation clubs	394
Retailers	1,846
Voluntary sector	914
Central government:	
Teachers	925
Transport	35
Sports Council for Northern Ireland	36
Local government:	
Sports facilities	1,725
Commercial non-sport:	1,447
Total	7,649

Table 12.4: Employment in sport in Northern Ireland
Source: Northern Ireland Assembly (2009)

The tables indicate that the commercial sector is the dominant employer in the sport industry, but this sector also includes sports goods manufacturers, retailers, professional and participant sport; whilst the voluntary and public sectors focus on providing participant sport.

The increasing numbers of those employed in sport have meant that the UK government has recognised sport's increasing importance to the economy. This has led to greater government intervention in sport employment, leading to a greater emphasis being placed on upskilling the sport workforce. In order to discuss the current approach to workforce development in sport it is necessary to set the context through a brief analysis of how employment in sport has developed and changed over the last 100 years.

Historical development of employment in sport

The beginnings

Sport as an area of work can be traced back to the early 1900s with the establishment of the Institute of Baths and Recreation Management in 1921, and the Institute of Parks and Recreation Management in 1926. It was very much a technical occupation, reflected in the type of qualifications the two bodies provided in swimming pool technology and horticulture respectively.

This focus continued until the 1960s; up to this point little sports provision was made by local authorities as much of the direct provision of sports opportunities was left to the voluntary and, to a lesser extent, the private sector. During the 1960s the Wolfenden Report identified that there was a need for more effective and professional organisation and management of sport (Houlihan and White 2002). As will be seen, this is a theme that has continued in sport until the present day.

Growth

During the 1960s and 1970s, as the role of the public sector in sport increased, the management of sport came under greater scrutiny leading to the Sports Council's (1969) report *Professional Training for Recreation Management*. This reiterated the call for more highly skilled managers and, in particular, for them to consider how people used facilities, in terms of increasing opportunities for sports participation. Despite this, the need to upskill sports workers continued to be an issue resulting in the 1975 Government White Paper, *Sport and Recreation*, which proposed the setting up of a committee to investigate sport and recreation management training. The Committee's final report, commonly known as the Yates Report, was not published until 1984.

A key problem that the report identified was that the industry was staffed by technicians who were perceived as having low status and limited elementary or secondary education (Yates 1984). Consequently, one of the effects of the expansion of sport and recreation provision was the rapid promotion of staff from narrow specialist backgrounds to senior leisure officers. The managers themselves acknowledged to the Committee that they had difficulty in adapting their technical skills to being more concerned with the management of people and their leisure needs. Additionally, the expansion of facilities and the changing nature of sport management meant that there was an influx of people from other areas of work in the public sector, particularly teaching, youth and community work and the armed forces, attracted by the changes and expansion that were taking place (Henry 2001, Yates 1984, Veal and Saperstein 1977). A consequence of this influx was that in many cases people were appointed without appropriate qualifications (Yates 1984). Moreover, the Yates Report (1984) also identified that there was a lack of educational provision to provide appropriate qualifications for this growing workforce.

A result of the entry of new people from other professions was the acceleration of the claims for professionalisation of sport management in local authorities (Henry 1993). Bacon (1996) believes that this attempt to be recognised was to counteract people's perception of sport management being of low status, as professionalisation may confer status and power to an occupation. Thus, a key recommendation of Yates's interim report (1980) was the need to create one professional body, as sport workers were confused by the myriad of professional associations available to them. In response to this recommendation, the Institute of Leisure and Amenity Management (ILAM) was established in 1979 as a conglomeration of the majority of the professional bodies serving sport, recreation and leisure. However, a major issue for the professionalisation of sport and recreation was the refusal by the Institute of Baths and Recreation Management to merge and thus there was still not one overall professional body for the industry.

The impact of the Conservative government

In 1979 the election of the 'New Right' Conservative government was to create further changes in sport employment, particularly with the introduction of Compulsory Competitive Tendering (CCT) to local authority sport. Moreover, the Audit Commission (1989, 1990) published several reports that questioned the effectiveness of sports provision and its ability to achieve social objectives. This led to a perception of poor management within the sector (Stevens and Green 2002). Consequently, CCT introduced a very different culture that encouraged cost control and entrepreneurship (Henry 2001). It also led to the downsizing of the local authority sport workforce, the introduction of more flexible working practices and in some cases reduced pay and conditions (The Public Services Privatisation Unit 1992, Henry 2001, MacVicar and Ogden 2001).

Henry (2001) argues that the pressures on local authorities in the 1980s and 1990s meant the commercial sector began to become more significant for sport with new employment opportunities being created. Also, Roberts (2004) believes that this shift to market disciplined sports provision and consequently the need for more entrepreneurial staff was in conflict with the sport sector's aspiration to become a profession. On a more fundamental level, Coalter (1990) suggests that the Thatcher government saw professions as a threat to the core New Right tenet of individual freedom, particularly in sport and leisure where individuals were seen as the best judge of their needs. He maintains that professions were seen as being 'motivated by self-interest, lack of accountability and unresponse to consumer demands' (Coalter 1990: 110).

Despite this unfavourable environment, sport continued to make claims to be a profession in order to achieve, what Bacon (1996: 5) identified as, a 'sense of identity, focus and enhanced public respect'. However, the arguments he put forward, that ILAM should regulate and control the access to sports management with the intent to 'increase the market value of ILAM membership and consequently the strength of the institute', to some extent reinforced Thatcher's view of professions.

A key element of professionalisation is the educational requirements for entrance which enable it to legitimate its authority (Fleming 1996, Henry and Spink 1990). With regard to the level of education, Bacon (1990) argued that the status and identity of sports managers would be more likely to be enhanced if they were graduates. In contrast, research into the education and training needs of sports managers, commissioned by the Sports Council (Coalter and Potter 1990) in Greater London and the South East concluded that sports managers had relatively low levels of qualifications. They reported that 87 per cent of the respondents to their survey had some form of qualification; of those who had qualifications, 25 per cent had either a master's degree, bachelor's degree or a postgraduate qualification. They also found that the majority of those studying for future qualifications were following professional courses, such as ILAM and IBRM, rather than academic qualifications. Thus, there was no clear educational pathway leading to entrance into the sports profession.

The focus of this section has to a great extent been on sport and recreation management and sports facilities staff, as this was the main occupational area in sport up to the 1990s. It could be argued that another impact of the Thatcher government was that it facilitated the formation of the new occupation of sports development. In the early years of the Thatcher government sport was used to address specific social problems with emphasis on provision for the unemployed and inner city groups. Consequently, central government grant aid was given to the Sports Council to fund programmes such as Action Sport, which can be seen as a precursor to the establishment of sports development in local authorities. However, CCT also had significant negative impacts on sports development, leaving it marginalised within sports services where it was treated as a self-contained, time-constrained and project-specific activity (Houlihan and White 2002).

Houlihan and White (2002) identify that during the early 1990s sports development was beginning to produce distinct variations in approach. Local authorities continued to oversee the two different but overlapping approaches of the promotion of mass participation and the focusing of sports development on social problems, whilst national governing bodies concentrated on their own sports targeted at young people.

During this time the Sports Council also emphasised selectivity both in terms of funding for Olympic sports and also high performance athletes (Houlihan and White 2002). This was reinforced by the Major government's policy statement, *Sport: Raising the Game* (1995), which more specifically moved the Sports Council's focus to elite sport and the use of sports science and coaching to develop elite performers, increasing the role of higher education institutes in the process (Green 2004). The introduction of the National Lottery in 1996 also meant that many NGBs received substantial funding through World Class Performance Funding, creating opportunities for paid professional staff within these organisations and increased employment opportunities in sports science and coaching in general.

This expansion of the coaching labour force was problematic. A review of coaching in 1991, *Coaching Matters*, identified a number of issues with coaching as an occupation which, it could be argued, were exacerbated as coaching grew. A key problem was the lack of standards for the employment and deployment of coaches, particularly in relation to remuneration and terms and conditions. As with sports management, there were also no strategies in place for training, education, employment and deployment. Also highlighted was the lack of clarity on the moral and ethical responsibilities of coaches (*Coaching Matters* 1991). These issues are still relevant today and are only now being addressed as will be discussed in the next section.

New Labour

The election of the Labour government in 1997 meant that there were further changes for sports workers. They introduced Best Value which required fundamental service reviews, where services had to demonstrate their contribution to the cross-cutting, generic or corporate goals of the authority (Henry 2001). Henry suggests that this led to a more integrated planning approach to sport, which was a key difference from the New Right approach. However, he also argues that Best Value is characterised by tensions between the importance of managers of sport adopting an enabling role and partnership but also promoting competition and market testing.

With regard to New Labour's impact on local authority sports development, their re-emphasis on Sport for All has given it greater priority in sports policy (Houlihan and White 2002) through the development of Sport England's Active Programmes framework. This set up three programmes – Active Communities, Active Sports and Active Schools. The Active Community projects concentrate on addressing social issues such as community safety, crime, drug abuse, truancy, multicultural development and community health. Houlihan and White (2002) describe the approach as a move from development *of* sport to development *through* sport. A key aspect of the Labour government's strategy, 'A Sporting Future' (2000) was the recognition of the work of SDOs and the need to establish a national training scheme. The National Association for Sports Development (NASD) was set up in 2000, with part of its remit to develop a more effective framework for training and development for this area of work (DFES/DCMS 2002). However, unpublished research on local authority SDOs by Houlihan and King (1999), cited by Houlihan and White (2002), found that amongst SDOs who were in senior posts, many felt that there was not a clear career path and that their next career move would be away from sports development.

The establishment of NASD meant that there were three professional bodies for sport with overlapping and to some extent competing remits. In order to address this, the three main professional bodies (ISRM, ILAM and NASD) began working together in October 2004 to develop a new single professional institute for sport, culture and leisure (Sport England 2004a). This new professional body was established in 2006 under the title of the Institute of Sport, Parks and Leisure (ISPAL); however ISRM refused to amalgamate with the other professional bodies and continued as a competing professional body for sport management. Consequently, it would appear that this is a repeat of the same situation as 1984 when ILAM was formed and thus the claim for professional status by the industry continues to be undermined.

The chapter so far has focused on the public sector, primarily because this was the main sector providing jobs for those working in participant sport. Also, there has been very little research regarding sports employment in the commercial sector. However, at the start of the millennium the commercial sector expanded rapidly. Private health club membership grew by 28 per cent between 2002 and 2006 to reach 4.8m members (Mintel 2007), creating further opportunities for sports workers. The issues arising from the growth of the commercial sector labour force, and in particular health and fitness will be discussed in the next section.

As can be seen from the historical analysis, sport has rapidly developed as an occupational area with a number of new occupations emerging during the last two decades – sports development, coaching, exercise professionals and sports scientists.

Learning Activity 12.1

Carry out an interview with either a sports manager, sports coach or sports development officer who has worked in the occupation over a number of years. Ask them to reflect specifically on the changes they have seen during their working life in sport and how these have impacted on their career.

The contemporary sports labour market

This section will analyse the current situation with regard to the sports labour market. The historical analysis of the sports labour market demonstrated the huge influence of government on sports occupations and the first part of this section will show that this still continues to be the case. It will also outline the organisations that are currently trying to influence the sports workforce. The section will then go on to look more specifically at the different sports occupations and the key issues that they are facing.

As has been discussed, a major preoccupation of sports occupations has been the aspiration to be recognised as legitimate professions, with the aim of increasing their status and authority. Unlike in previous years, this aspiration, to some extent, corresponds with the policies of the current Labour government. Their focus is on improving human capital throughout the UK economy, consequently an aim is to establish minimum training standards for sports workers in the UK (Lloyd 2005). As a result, the government has been supportive of sport in developing and restructuring organisations to attain professionalisation with the objective of achieving a more highly skilled workforce.

In order to improve the skills in the UK economy the government established the Sector Skills Development Agency (SSDA), which in turn set up 25 Sector Skills Councils (SSCs), including one for sport and recreation, health and fitness, outdoors, playwork and the caravan sector – SkillsActive. The

SSDA and SSCs claim to be employer-led, independent organisations, however, Reid et al. (2004) point out that the SSDA itself is funded by the treasury and so does not have complete independence. SkillsActive have introduced a number of initiatives to upskill employees within the industry, some of which will be identified in this section. Its vision and objectives can be seen in the box below.

SkillsActive group vision and mission

SkillsActive's unique contribution is to lead the development of the expanding, skilled and qualified workforce of paid industry professionals and active volunteers needed to deliver the increases in active participation that will ensure the industry's ongoing success and continued growth.

SkillsActive group vision

More people, better skilled, better qualified.

SkillsActive group mission

Delivering the workforce for the nation's well-being.

Skills priorities for the industry

1 To improve recruitment and retention of the workforce.
2 To upskill and professionalise the existing workforce.
3 To match training supply to employer demand.
4 To redirect and secure new funding for training to meet employment needs.
5 To increase sector investment in our people.

A key influence of SkillsActive has been the establishment of regional workforce development plans for sport. The aim of these plans is to identify the key strategic priorities for the workforce; to map the current situation within regions with regard to recruitment and retention of staff and their training needs; and to develop action plans on how to address workforce issues. SkillsActive define workforce development as 'education, training and development of paid and unpaid staff and means developing skills to ensure that all staff have the relevant skills, the ability and the confidence to carry out their role effectively' (Greater Sport 2007).

Learning Activity 12.2

Find the workforce development plan for your region (generally found on County Sports Partnership websites). Summarise their key strategic priorities.

As part of this attempt to upskill, the government directed Sector Skills Councils to establish National Skills Academies as centres of training excellence. The National Skills Academy for Sport (NSAS) is, as with most of the government's skills initiatives, an employer-led organisation with the aim of providing a single, coherent approach to skills training and ensuring higher quality standards, better career opportunities and a more professional approach to training (NSAS 2009).

Learning Activity 12.3

Visit the National Skills Academy website and identify what is available for your region and the career you wish to undertake. http://www.sportactivensa.co.uk/home.ashx

---

Although SkillsActive are responsible for leading workforce development, the complexity of the sports labour market means that they need to undertake this with a range of partners from each occupational area. The following sub-sections will examine the current situation in sports management, coaching, sports science and health and fitness.

Sports management and sports development

As has been identified, a key problem for the professional aspirations of sports development and management has been the existence of two competing professional bodies (ISPAL and ISRM), meaning that there is no one authoritative voice for the sector. Moreover, only 2 per cent of those currently working in the sector are members of ISPAL or ISRM (Chartered Institute of Sport Project Working Group 2009). However, the push by DCMS to improve skills within the sector has led to ISPAL and ISRM undertaking discussions to develop a Chartered Institute for Sport (CIS) (Varnom 2006). The proposed remit is for a UK-wide body, responsible for those working in sport and physical activity, facilities (indoor and outdoor) and major events and sports tourism. The joint working group between ISRM and ISPAL identified that having a chartered status will provide enhanced respect and influence for sector, particularly within government and industry. It will also enable more and better partnership working, and it will raise the image and profile of the sector (CIS Working Group 2009).

Learning Activity 12.4

Access ISPAL and ISRM web pages to find out the latest on the development of a Chartered Institute for Sport:
http://www.isrm.co.uk/cis/
http://www.ispal.org.uk

Health and fitness

As has been discussed, health and fitness as an occupational area has grown substantially in the last decade, and, as with sports management and development, it has particularly focused on professionalising the workforce. A key part of this has been the establishment of the Register of Exercise Professionals (REPs). This is a licence to practise which was introduced to improve the image of the health and fitness industry, improve skill levels, reduce staff turnover and improve levels of pay for fitness professionals (Lloyd 2005). An overview of REPs is shown in in the box below.

Register of exercise professionals

The REPs Mission Statement is:

*To ensure that all exercise professionals are suitably knowledgeable and qualified to help
safeguard and to promote the health and interests of the people who use their services.*

The Register of Exercise Professionals (REPs) is a system of self-regulation for all instructors, coaches, trainers and teachers involved in the exercise and fitness industry. The REPs creates a framework within which individual instructors can achieve the highest standards of professionalism, linked to best practice in the exercise and fitness industry. Registration is achieved and maintained through the gaining of qualifications and training which are nationally recognised and which are linked to the National Occupational Standards for exercise and fitness.

The REPs exist because they are the only way to demonstrate independently that fitness professionals are competent and qualified to do their job. The Register is a central feature of the professionalism of the industry, and is essential to giving customers, users, the public and partners in the medical professions, the necessary level of confidence in the quality of services provided by fitness professionals.

Registration signifies that an exercise and fitness professional has met certain standards of good practice. The REPs encourage a properly qualified base of exercise professionals who:

- have gained recognised and approved qualifications;
- can demonstrate competence in their working environment;
- are committed to Continuing Professional Development (CPD);
- have appropriate public liability insurance for the level at which they are working;
- demonstrate commitment to the industry Code of Ethical Practice.

Each year SkillsActive undertakes a 'Working in Fitness' survey that identifies some of the issues facing the fitness workforce. It provides extremely useful information on the composition of employment in the fitness sector and includes salaries and terms and conditions. It also collects information on levels of qualifications, training and professional development amongst fitness employees as well as examining career intentions (SkillsActive 2009).

Learning Activity 12.5

Access the Working in Fitness Survey (2009) and identify the main issues for the Fitness industry raised by the survey's findings.
http://www.skillsactive.com/resources/research/working-in-fitness-2009

Coaching

sports coach UK is the national body that oversees coaching, it was established in 2001 from the former National Coaching Foundation. Part of its remit is to facilitate the professionalisation of coaching in order to address some of the issues that were highlighted earlier in the historical analysis.

In 2001 the Coaching Task Force was established to review coaching and coach education. It found that there was an over-reliance on volunteers and there was a need for more paid opportunities for coaches. Moreover, it also identified the need for a clear career structure which included a framework of nationally recognised qualifications, the issue being that each governing body qualification had its own levels and there was little consistency between qualifications required by different sports (DCMS 2002a).

As with the other sports occupations, coaching is working towards becoming a professionally regulated vocation, using the UK Coaching Framework to enhance the quality of coaching and provide qualified and skilled coaches (scUK 2008). In order to do this, coaching faces some key issues mainly stemming from the major transformation that will be required for a sector historically founded on volunteers (Taylor and Garrett 2008).

A sport that has been identified by scUK as 'trail blazing' in its workforce development plans is swimming. Its development framework for teaching and coaching in England 2009–13 is an example of good practice for workforce development in coaching and can be found at the following address: http://www.britishswimming.co.uk – click on the Institute of Swimming (IoS) page.

Sports science and sports medicine

This occupational area has become increasingly important with the use of Lottery funding to support high performance sports. Also sports such as football and rugby have gradually increased their use of sports science to improve performance over the last decade. This has led to employment opportunities in the English Institute of Sport, sports clubs, national governing bodies, universities and colleges. Moreover, the use of exercise to address health issues such as obesity and heart disease, and the growth of the health and fitness industry, means that there are opportunities for exercise scientists in primary care trusts and health clubs.

There are a number of organisations that are important in relation to employment in this area. The UK Sport Sports Medicine and Sports Science team, which is linked to UK sports, provides an overall strategy to support and develop sports medicine and sports science practitioners. An example of their work is the Fast-Track Practitioner Programme (FPP) which is a one year scheme which is 'designed to accelerate the professional development of young practitioners who demonstrate the potential for employment within the high performance sports. With continuing professional development, these individuals will grow into the next generation of high performance system practitioners' (UK Sport 2009c).

There are two main professional bodies that relate to this area of work. The British Association of Sport and Exercise Sciences (BASES) was founded in 1984 as a professional body to represent those involved in sports and exercise sciences in the UK. Another important body is the British Association of Sport and Exercise Medicine (BASEM) which was founded in 1953 and is the official UK representative to both the European Federation of Sports Medicine Associations (EFSMA) and the International Federation of Sports Medicine. BASEM focuses on both the promotion of physical activity as a basis for good health and also provides expertise in sports medicine to enable optimisation of all levels of athletic performance.

Chapter Review

This overview of the sports labour market has identified the massive expansion both in the sports labour force, but also the range of occupations within the sports sector. Despite this range, the recurring themes both historically and across those sectors are the need to professionalise in order to improve the skills of the workforce, but also to improve sport's status as a serious occupational area. Many of the initiatives that have been highlighted in this chapter are only in the early stages of their implementation so there is much change still to come for sports workers. Consequently it is crucial for those studying and who wish to develop careers within sport to be constantly updating themselves on the effects of such initiatives.

After reading this chapter and attempting the learning activities you should now be able to answer the following questions:

1   What are the key changes in the sports labour market from 1920 to the present day?
2   What are the main influences on the sports labour force of

    a   The Conservative government (1979–1997)?
    b   The Labour government (1997 onwards)?

3   Choose two sports occupations. How do they aim to professionalise their workforce?

Chapter 13
The sports labour market:
the voluntary sector

Learning Objectives

This chapter is designed to help you:

- understand the role and importance of the voluntary sector, specifically focusing on the nature of the voluntary workforce;
- examine the issues surrounding the recruitment and management of volunteers within the sports industry.

Volunteers are one of the key drivers of change necessary for sport to achieve its target of getting more people participating in sport and physical activity. In the UK, sports related activity is the most significant area in which volunteering takes place (Nichols and Shepard 2006: 205), providing the volunteer workforce on which UK sport is so reliant. The aim of this chapter is to illustrate the importance and value that the home nation sports councils attach to the voluntary workforce that underpins so much of their work. It will also discuss the changing nature of the sector and the key challenges faced by many sports organisations who are finding their pool of volunteers steadily diminishing. This trend may be set to change as the most recent data coming from Volunteering England is that in the current economic climate, with more than 2m people currently unemployed, there has been there has been a dramatic increase in the number of people looking for opportunities to volunteer (Volunteering England 2009). These requests are not specifically for sport but sports organisations may see an improvement in their numbers. It is within this context that the following chapter will explore the voluntary sector and the contribution it makes to the labour market.

The role and importance of the voluntary sector

The voluntary sector, also termed the not for profit sector, plays a vital role in the delivery of sport, as illustrated on Figure 13.1. Sports clubs are crucial to grassroots sport as they are responsible for the bulk of provision for those participating in sports requiring a formal structure (Nichols et al. 2004). A fundamental characteristic of those clubs is that they are run by volunteers. The voluntary sector is also crucial in the delivery of health, societal and community outcomes in relation to government policies of active citizenship, young peoples' participation in sport, social inclusion and the promotion of sport for health benefits (Sport England 2004a: 9, Nichols et al. 2004). Finally, national governing bodies, who are a key part of the voluntary sector, are critical for the development of elite sport (Nichols et al. 2004). Watt (2003: 62) argues that many volunteers share the commitment of the participants and devote their lives enthusiastically to the organisation and support of sport, in much the same way as participants do on the playing field.

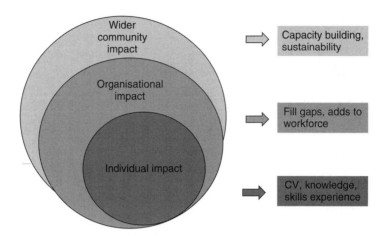

Figure 13.1 Illustrating the value and impact of volunteering

Internationally, Shin and Kleiner (2003: 63) studied non-governmental organisations in North America and Australia, and they concluded that volunteers improve the financial efficiency of organisations and bring innovation and social cohesion to those organisations; consequently they continue to be one of the most valuable resources to amateur sports clubs. For example, the equivalent of 10 per cent of Australians, 5 per cent of Canadians and approximately 11 per cent of the English population volunteer for sport organisations (Cuskelly et al. 2006). This would suggest that volunteers provide the foundation stone of lifelong participation that helps to build our sporting nation (Sport England 2004a: 14) and those in other sporting countries.

As volunteers are the lifeblood of the volunteer sector it is crucial to define volunteering before going on to examine volunteering in each of the home nations. The definition of volunteering used to underpin this chapter is:

Helping others in sport and receiving either no remuneration or only expenses. This includes those volunteering for organisations (formal volunteers) and those helping others in sport but not through organisations (informal volunteers).

(Sport England 2004b: 2)

Learning Activity 13.1

Read Taylor, P. (2004) *Driving up Participation: Sport and Volunteering*. Sheffield Management School: University of Sheffield and answer the following questions:

1   What are the main characteristics of 'informal' organisations such as voluntary sports clubs? (p. 105)
2   What is the one distinguishing feature between informal and formal organisations identified in the research? (p. 106)
3   What problems and pressures are identified which the author thinks voluntary organisations will face in the future? (pp. 106/107)

England

The Institute for Volunteering Research (IVR) recently published data showing that 87 per cent of local volunteer centres had seen an increase in enquiries about volunteering opportunities over the last six months (Volunteering England 2009). As mentioned in Chapter 1, these requests are not all for sport but it would appear that in an economic recession many people are looking to improve their re-employment opportunities by gaining voluntary experience. Some of those volunteers will be helping to sustain the 100,000 affiliated sports clubs in England. The sporting sector makes the single biggest contribution to total volunteering in England, with 26 per cent of all volunteers citing 'sport' as their main area of interest (Sport England 2004a: 14). Most recently the Active People Survey 3, commissioned by Sport England, recorded that 4.6 per cent of the adult population of England, which equates to 1,947,600 people, are doing at least one hour a week of volunteering in sport. Despite this being a slight decrease from the 2007/08 survey it still represents a significant contribution by the voluntary sector workforce that is at the very heart of UK sport (Sport England 2009a). It is estimated that volunteers contribute 1.8m hours of unpaid support every week of the year which equates to over 54,000 full time jobs (Volresource 2009).

The national volunteering development agency for England is Volunteering England, which was established in 2004. It is partly funded by grants from the Office of the Third Sector (part of the Cabinet Office) and the Department of Health. Funding also comes from corporate supporters such as PriceWaterhouseCoopers, charitable foundations, sponsorship and income generated through membership and events. Volunteering England supports sport by working with national sport organisations to improve the quality and quantity of sport volunteering (Volunteering England 2009). There is a myriad of voluntary sports organisations in England; Volunteering England's website provides specific links to a range of volunteering opportunities in sport – http://www.volunteering.org.uk/WhatWeDo .

A key issue for sport volunteering in England is the 2012 London Olympic Games in London. London 2012 (2009) estimate that 70,000 volunteers will be needed to help put on the Olympic and Paralympic Games. They are putting together a specific volunteer development programme, which will start recruiting in 2010, to ensure volunteers have the appropriate training ready for the games. Their website provides further information on the volunteer development programme and how to register your interest – http://www.london2012.com/get-involved/volunteering/index.php.

Learning Activity 13.2

Hosting the 2012 Olympic and Paralympic Games in London will provide a tremendous incentive for all young people to participate in a whole range of positive sporting, volunteering and cultural activities.

Consider the potential opportunity created by hosting in the Games in 2012. How would you maximise on the opportunity and create projects and programmes for young people to get involved in their local communities?

Role and importance of the voluntary sector in Scotland

Volunteers are also at the heart of Scottish sport. In 2005, **sport**scotland estimated that there were some 146,000 people involved in sport as volunteers. Most volunteers were involved in coaching but there were other vital 'behind the scenes' roles performed by volunteers – for example, raising money, book-keeping, serving on committees, providing transport, washing strips, keeping disclosures up to date and doing administrative tasks (Volunteer Development Scotland 2008: 1). They play a vital role in encouraging and supporting people to get involved, and stay involved in sport (**sport**scotland 2009d). The lead agency is Volunteer Development Scotland which co-ordinates a network of centres to ensure that everyone who wants to volunteer have opportunities near to where they live.

Project Scotland is a national charity which was launched in 2005 with the objective of helping young people across Scotland realise their potential through volunteering. Since 2005 it has placed over 2,900 young people into structured and rewarding placements with over 300 non-profit organisations including environment, education, sport and the arts (Project Scotland 2009).

Project Scotland is a registered charity and therefore relies on donations to keep it going. Current supporters include BSkyB, John Menzies PLC, Scottish Gas and Lloyds TSB Scotland Plc. The skills that young people gain whilst volunteering can contribute to the development of the four capacities within Curriculum for Excellence (Scotland's new school curriculum for 3–18 year olds) enabling them to become a confident individual, an effective contributor, a successful learner and a responsible citizen (Project Scotland 2009).

As with the London Olympics, the success of the Commonwealth Games in Glasgow in 2014 will depend to a large extent on volunteers, with some 15,000 volunteers required (Glasgow City Council). Glasgow City Council (2009) perceives volunteering for the games as an opportunity for volunteers to develop the skills and confidence that will benefit their work, family and community and a chance to change lives.

Wales

The Sports Council for Wales estimates that there are 51,000 people who regularly volunteer an average of two hours a week, resulting in 1,244,000 volunteer hours per year. It could be inferred that these volunteer hours equate to £12.9m (Sports Council Wales 2009). Volunteers have been seen as critical to the Welsh Assembly's strategy for sport in Wales, Climbing Higher. In order to achieve its objectives they set out the need to 'encourage and support volunteers, leaders and coaches in increasing the level and quality of participation in communities' (Welsh Assembly Government 2005: 18).

To develop the sporting infrastructure in Wales, the Sports Council Wales (SCW) has acknowledged that developing people is essential. The bedrock of the domestic sports structure is the voluntary sports clubs and they provide a means of transforming physical activity into competitive sport. 'Increasing participation in sport will only be sustainable through vibrant voluntary clubs which can keep young people engaged in activity into adulthood' (SCW 2005: 25).

*More participation requires more volunteers, paid leaders and coaches ... volunteering needs to be
attractive to those who give up their time but there are gains to be made in terms of building new
skills that will be valuable in other contexts.*

(SCW 2005: 19)

The Climbing Higher report also identified the importance of ensuring that volunteers have strong
qualifications and continuing professional development. Consequently, the Welsh Assembly has also shown
a financial commitment to investing £3.7m into the Coaching Plan for Wales. This programme targets
teachers, volunteers and other sport professionals to match training and qualification standards to the needs
of individuals at all levels of participation (SCW 2005: 3).

By investing in a co-ordinated training and development programme for volunteers, sports leaders and
coaches, the aim is that the administration, organisational and motivational skills, as well as the 'softer'
people skills that are developed, can be deployed in and outside sport to improve the skills set particularly of
young people across Wales. This is an area of work that SCW sees as a priority and they have built a strong
partnership with SkillsActive to ensure that the issues are to be satisfactorily addressed (SCW 2005: 19).

The umbrella organisation for voluntary organisations in Wales is Wales Council for Voluntary Actions
(WCVA). A useful website from which to find volunteering opportunities in Wales is Volunteering Wales
http://www.volunteering-wales.net.

Northern Ireland

There are approximately 5,000–6,000 clubs in Northern Ireland affiliated to governing bodies of sport
that provide opportunities for participation in sport and physical activity at local and competitive levels.
Each of these organisations draws upon a pool of highly committed volunteers and operationally they are
volunteer dependent (VDA 2009: 3).

The Volunteer Development Agency in Northern Ireland defines volunteers and volunteering as
'individuals and the work or action they undertake for the benefit of others or the community (outside the
immediate family) undertaken by free choice and not directly in return for wages' (Volunteer Development
Agency 2007: 2).

Recent research found that there were an estimated 30,569 people over 16 involved as volunteers in
sport in Northern Ireland with over 14,000 of these as coaches (Volunteer Development Agency 2007: 3).
Over 78 per cent of Northern Ireland sport-associated volunteers are giving time once a month and most are
doing so on a weekly basis, with over 92 per cent of sports clubs/governing bodies unable to operate without
volunteer support. The research by the Northern Ireland Volunteer Development Agency stressed the
importance of recruitment and support for volunteers in sport, given that they will be the largest personnel
resource that is involved in delivering the Strategy for Sport and Physical Recreation 2007–2017. In order
to achieve 'a culture of lifelong enjoyment and success in sport', as stated in Sport NI Strategy for Sport and
Physical Recreation 2007–2017, there is an acknowledgement that workforce development is important
and resourcing and support for volunteers is an essential objective. The economic value of volunteering in
2007 was £433m for informal volunteering (outside an organisation) and £504 formal volunteering (under
the auspices of an organisation), which totals £937m per year (Volunteer Development Agency 2007: 5).

The organisational value can be summarised by the fact that 77 per cent stated they could not operate without the support of volunteers and 67 per cent of organisations agreed with the statement that volunteers bring special qualities to an organisation (Volunteer Development Agency 2007: 8).

Why do people volunteer?

Cuskelly et al. (2006) note that there is little agreement about volunteer motivation, apart from the view that it is complex and multifaceted. Wang (2004) argues that the motivation to volunteer is generally seen as a multidimensional construct. Using empirical research of volunteers for the 2000 Sydney Olympic Games, he suggests that motivation for sports volunteerism comprises five distinct components which are identified and summarised below.

Altruistic values – represent a person's intrinsic beliefs in helping others and contributing to society. Thus a person with altruistic values does so for the welfare of other people and does not expect a complete quid pro quo.

Personal development – the volunteer seeks the opportunity to gain new knowledge, skills and experiences. This may include the opportunity to learn job-related skills to enhance labour market value.

Community concern – reflects a volunteer's sense of obligation and/or involvement with their communities.

Ego enhancement – people volunteer to maintain or enhance positive feelings about themselves, which would include feelings of pride and self-esteem.

Social adjustment – relates to developing/maintaining relationships with other people or engaging in activities that important others view favourably.

Although Wang's five components of motivation provide a useful framework from which to understand volunteers, a key limitation was the setting used to collect his data – the Sydney Olympics. Cuskelly et al. (2006) argue that voluntary behaviour is complex and the importance of the situational context must be considered.

Reflection Point 13.1

How might the motivations of those volunteering for sport events differ from those volunteering for sports clubs? Why do you think this is the case?

Doherty (2005) undertook research into sports club volunteers in Ontario, Canada and from this she developed a model of motives for volunteering in sport shown in Figure 13.2.

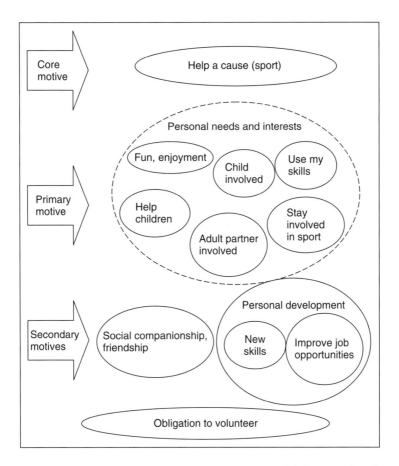

Figure 13.2 A model of motives for volunteering in sport
Source: Doherty (2005)

Doherty (2005) believes that the *core motive* for volunteering in sport is to 'help a cause' and that this is common (and most important) to all volunteers, reflecting the altruism in volunteering. Figure 13.2 indicates that below this are *primary motives* for volunteering in sport which are 'personal needs and interests'. It is at this level that there is some variation among sports volunteers, as shown by the range of items in the bubbles. Finally, 'social' and 'personal development' motives constitute secondary motives for sport volunteering. Doherty identifies that there is some variation among volunteers with regard to the relative importance of motives at this level. For example, personal development through new skills and experiences is typically a stronger motive for sport volunteers than social reasons. Doherty also suggests that secondary motives are different depending on age. Learning new skills and improving job opportunities are a particularly important motive for younger volunteers, as well as social reasons. She also suggests that motivations shift over time so that 'sport volunteers tend to get involved for themselves, and tend to stay involved for the organization' (Doherty 2005: 32). That is because the longer the volunteer is with an organisation the more they identify with, and feel a part of, the organisation.

Learning Activity 13.3

Undertake an interview with someone who is a volunteer in sport and find out their motives for being involved.

How do their motivations compare with Wang's (2004) components of motivation and Doherty's (2005) model of motivation?

In the UK, Nichols et al. (2005) identify that there are three types of sport volunteers within the voluntary sector who they suggest are motivated for different reasons.

Key volunteers – this group of people are motivated by a shared enthusiasm for the sport, social benefits and the desire for the club to be successful. These volunteers have a major role in running clubs therefore there is a heavy reliance on these people (Nichols et al. 2005).

Shorter term volunteers – these are the group of people that are primarily motivated through creating opportunities for their children and themselves. This relates to Doherty's personal needs and interests.

Young people – this group is motivated by their interest in sport, altruism and, as with Doherty's study, a desire to enhance their CVs to increase their employability.

In the UK there has been a focus on encouraging young people to be involved in volunteering. The Russell Report in 2005 detailed recommendations for delivering a step change in youth volunteering in the UK – a step change in diversity, quality and quantity. The Russell Commission responded to the clearly expressed desire of young people to find meaningful ways of contributing to their communities. It called for targeted campaigns to recruit volunteers for voluntary and community sector organisations at a national and local level; to promote the benefits of volunteering, targeting specific groups of young people, particularly those who are currently under-represented in volunteering, and/or promote specific types of volunteering opportunities; and to challenge the media to help create new public attitudes to young people's volunteering by celebrating and recognising their achievements. It also outlined in its report that 'it should be natural for young people to volunteer and natural for organisations to either offer young people the opportunity to volunteer or support them in doing so' (Russell Commission 2005: 6).

Learning Activity 13.4

Think about volunteering and young people and make a list of what you consider to be the benefits of volunteering both to the young person and the club or sport organisation.

Who volunteers?

Nichols et al. (2005) report that a number of studies of sport volunteers have shown that they tend to be from higher socio-economic groups and have children. This is reflected in research on swimming which found that volunteers tended to be married with children. Furthermore, they were likely to have been swimmers themselves (Burgham and Downward 2004). This profile was reflected in research on volunteers in other countries leading Doherty (2006: 106) to suggest that sport volunteers are 'unique among volunteers in general'. However, Coleman's (2002) study of cricket in the UK found that the characteristics of volunteers varied according to the level of job that they were undertaking. He found that a higher number of county cricket managers were retired, compared to those volunteers referred to in Nichol et al.'s study. Moreover, 72 per cent of volunteer county cricket managers were empty nesters, in that they had no dependent children, compared to 67 per cent of volunteers at club level. Consequently, Coleman argues that that sport volunteers are not one homogeneous group.

Key issues in the volunteer workforce

A major issue for the voluntary sector is the difficulties of recruitment and retention, leading to a shortage of volunteers (Cuskelly et al. 2006, Taylor et al. 2006). In the UK, 74 per cent of sport clubs identified that there were not enough people willing to volunteer and in 65 per cent of clubs work is being left increasingly to fewer people (Nichols et al. 2005). Particularly worrying are reports that there has been a reduction in younger cohorts of volunteers (Burgham and Downward 2004), meaning that the future of voluntary clubs will be difficult. However, as has been identified earlier in this chapter, young people have been increasingly targeted to get involved in volunteering. There are a number of reasons for the shortage but they relate to two key areas: the changing nature of the voluntary sector and the nature of those who volunteer. Each of these is discussed below.

Changing nature of the voluntary sector

A major issue for voluntary organisations, both in the UK and in other parts of the world, is the pressure to professionalise (Taylor et al. 2006). There are three major reasons for this: first, the impact of government in terms of their attempt to use the voluntary sector to implement policies; second, the changing nature of the sport and leisure market; and third, increasing legislation.

At the start of this chapter it was identified that a key role of the voluntary sector was the implementation of government policies relating to active citizenship, young peoples' participation in sport, social inclusion and the promotion of sport for health benefits. In order to obtain funding voluntary organisations have to meet government policy objectives, for example equity and child protection policies (Nichols et al. 2005). This is exemplified by Garrett, who maintains that, in England, Lottery funding is used to ensure that voluntary sports clubs 'behave in a way that is congruent with sport policy or reward them if they are already behaving in this way when they apply' (2004: 16).

Nichols et al. (2005) make the point that using the voluntary sector in this way creates a tension between enabling it to continue to flourish independently and making it accountable for the public funding it receives through performance indicators that relate to government objectives. In an earlier paper Nichols et al. (2004: 51) make a telling observation when they state that:

> Rewards and benefits of volunteering for volunteers did not extend to helping government meet its policy objectives of enhancing social capital or reducing social exclusion.

This view is reflected in Lusted and O'Gorman's (2010) study of grassroots football, which they argue is one of the most important sites for policy delivery given football's popularity. However, a key finding from their paper was that there was little consideration by policy makers either of the pressures placed on volunteers through being drawn into delivering government objectives, or of their resistance to the modernisation agenda.

Separate from the impact of government agendas, but also creating pressure on voluntary organisations to professionalise, is the changing nature of the sport and leisure market. The increasing importance of the commercial sector and the continued provision by the public sector of 'pay and play' facilities in sports such as badminton, squash and tennis (Nichols et al. 2005), and increasingly five-a-side football, has created greater competition with the voluntary sector. Nichols et al. (2005: 37) argue that the quality of the service at those alternative facilities has become a 'point of reference for sport participation'. This then creates pressure on volunteers to offer a comparable service, also leading to the need to professionalise. Consequently, this facilitates the transformation of sports clubs from 'mutual aid' organisations to 'service delivery' organisations (Nichols et al. 2005: 38).

Finally, Nichols et al. (2005) identify another key pressure to professionalise as coming from a society that is increasingly risk adverse and where there is an increased willingness to undertake legal action against organisations or individuals that are deemed to be negligent. This has led to increasing legislation creating greater bureaucracy for organisations and also volunteers.

All of these changes create massive pressures on volunteers in terms of time and also, in some cases, situations where club volunteers may perceive that they are exposing themselves to the possibility of legal action. Consequently, it is not really a surprise that there are difficulties in recruiting and retaining volunteers. This is reflected in Sport England's (2002b) findings that there is one lapsed volunteer for every two active volunteers.

The nature of the volunteer

Another key problem that makes recruitment and retention difficult are the pressures, outside volunteering, that are on the types of people who volunteer. Previously in this chapter, evidence was presented that volunteers tend to be from higher socio-economic groups and have children. However, at the same time those are the groups of people that are experiencing the greatest demands on their time (Nichols et al. 2005). Thus the identification at the start of this chapter, of the increased number of people looking to volunteer (Volunteering 2009) due to increasing unemployment, may not apply as much to sport due to the unique nature of the sport volunteer who may not fit into this group. Nichols et al. (2005) also argue that young people may be less likely to volunteer due to the increasing competition with other ways that they can spend their leisure time. Consequently, there may be a steadily diminishing pool of people from which to recruit volunteers.

The attempts to address the issues

The increasing pressure to professionalise and the need to improve the recruitment and retention of volunteers to address shortages has led to a view that volunteers should be managed as human resources (Cuskelly et al. 2006). This includes the development of more formal recruitment procedures offering training and development opportunities. Cuskelly et al. (2006) also identify the need to ensure good communication with volunteers and also provide meaningful experiences that match their needs. However, a study by Cuskelly et al. (2006b) of Australian rugby union clubs found that the relationships between volunteers and clubs are complex in that the volunteer is also the constituent body, co-worker, manager and client and not just human resources, as is the case in the public sector and for-profit organisations. Consequently, it is difficult to introduce systems that have been based on paid work organisations. This is likely to be similar to the situation in the UK.

In the UK a key approach taken by national governing bodies is the appointment of volunteer co-ordinators. An example is swimming where a National Volunteer Co-ordinator was appointed with the aim of increasing the numbers of volunteers, but also to provide clubs with advice on recruitment and retention issues (Burgham and Downward 2005). The appointment of such staff reflects the trend to employ paid staff in voluntary organisations (LIRC 2003). Roberts (2004) suggests that this could lead to tensions between paid employees and volunteers, as the paid employees will expect the organisation to be run professionally given that its success will impact on their livelihoods. Conversely, Lusted and O'Gorman (2010) found that in football there was a concern from voluntary staff that the new paid staff may not have the same dedication, commitment and sense of duty as amateur sports volunteers in the past.

Chapter Review

The aim of this chapter has been to explore the role and importance of the voluntary sector and to examine the issues surrounding the recruitment and management of volunteers within the sports industry. The voluntary sector is crucial in the delivery of health, societal and community outcomes at an organisational level (Sport England 2004a: 9, Nichols et al. 2004). In terms of the individual volunteer it also holds altruistic, developmental and social value (Wang 2004). Sport England (2004a: 14) would suggest that volunteers provide the foundation stone of lifelong participation that helps to build the sporting nation, and the examples given from all of the other home nations should help to demonstrate the value of the volunteer labour market across the UK sporting landscape.

However, the chapter has also identified that there are major problems in the recruitment and retention of volunteers, which are due to the attempts to professionalise voluntary sport and also the unique nature of the sport volunteer. It showed that in order to address recruitment and retention issues human resource processes have been introduced, although care needs to be taken as these may actually place further pressure on volunteers thereby exacerbating the problem.

After reading this chapter and attempting the learning activities you should now be able to complete the following task:

Discuss the extent to which voluntary sport organisations should be used to achieve government policy objectives.

Devise an action plan for a local sports club on how they can

- recruit more volunteers;
- reward them;
- retain them through training and development.

Use your own experiences to inform your plan.

Further Reading

For a background of the organisations and structures within which volunteers operate:
- Watt, D.C. (2003) *Sports Management and Administration*, 2nd edn. London: Routledge – Chapter 3, The Voluntary Sector.

For a comprehensive guide to further explore the issues surrounding nature, scope, value and management of volunteers:
- Cuskelly, G., Hoye, R. and Auld, C. (2006) *Working with Volunteers in Sport*. London: Routledge.

For international research on volunteers in sport have a look at the special edition of *Sport Management Review* (2006), Volume 9, which focuses on sport volunteerism.

Chapter 14
The professional athletes' labour market

Learning Objectives

This chapter is designed to help you:

- understand the structure of the professional athletes' labour market;
- assess how and why professional athletes are remunerated;
- make comparisons with other labour markets and professions;
- explore issues relating to the supply and demand of professional athletes.

Reports in the popular press often convey the large sums of money that professional athletes earn from their sports. Recently, the golfer Tiger Woods was reported to have exceeded the £1bn mark, making him the first billionaire athlete. Such reported high earnings are not limited to golf. Other sports such as American football, athletics, baseball, basketball, football and tennis are just a few other sports in which the top athletes are able to earn millions. Often when the role and function of professional athletes to society is considered, commentators are quick to argue that these athletes should not be remunerated so highly. When parallels are made with professionals such as teachers, nurses and surgeons say, the individuals in these professions earn significantly less than professional athletes. Furthermore, it is often argued that their contribution to society is far more significant. This chapter explores these and many other related issues. Why do professional athletes earn so much? In exploring this particular point, the various professional sports labour markets and the manner in which they are structured and organised are examined. We will also begin to explore the range of arguments as to whether professional athletes *should* earn so much.

Introduction

For some time now, there has been interest in the first sports man or woman to break the $1bn earnings mark. *Forbes*, a business magazine, regularly reports on earnings in different industries and has done so for the highest-earning professional athletes across different sports. *Forbes* reported that at the end of 2008, Tiger Woods' cumulative career earnings were $895m and that it was only a matter of time as to when he would break through the $1bn barrier. On 29 September 2009, Forbes.com announced this feat. As to whether this is true or not, only Tiger Woods and his accountant will know for sure, but the anecdotal evidence seems to suggest that this is the case.

Tiger Woods is just one of a multitude of athletes whose earnings from sport are extraordinary by many standards. In other individual sports like tennis, track and field, and city marathons, the likes of Maria

Sharapova, Venus and Serena Williams, Roger Federer and Paula Radcliffe are some of the leading earners. In professional team sports like football and basketball, names such as David Beckham, Cristiano Ronaldo, Kobe Bryant and LeBron James also lead the way. Table 14.1 shows the world's top 20 athletes by earnings in 2008. The table also serves to show which sports offer the potential for hyper-earnings. Golf and basketball feature prominently as sports offering high earnings; the distribution for the other sports is two with the exception of tennis and MotoGP (motor cycling) having one representation. Analysing this list of earners is quite illuminating and many of the issues raised here will be discussed later in this chapter. However, these headlines are interesting. Tiger Woods' position at the top of the earnings illustrates not only his excellence as a golfer but perhaps also his race. He is a black golfer in a sport that is white dominated. Another interesting point to note is Michael Jordan's position. Michael Jordan has long retired from professional basketball yet he not only dominates earnings in the sport, he is also joint second on the 2008 list of top earners. Another intriguing point is that there are only two representatives from football, arguably the most

Athlete	Sport	Position	Earnings (in millions of US$)
Tiger Woods	Golf	1	110
Kobe Bryant	Basketball	2	45
Michael Jordan	Basketball	2	45
Kimi Raikkonen	Formula 1 motor racing	2	45
David Beckham	Football	5	42
LeBron James	Basketball	6	40
Phil Mickelson	Golf	6	40
Manny Pacquiao	Boxing	6	40
Valentino Rossi	MotoGP motor cycle racing	9	35
Dale Earnhardt Jr.	NASCAR racing	10	34
Roger Federer	Tennis	11	33
Shaquille O'Neal	Basketball	11	33
Oscar de la Hoya	Boxing	13	32
Lewis Hamilton	Formula 1 motor racing	13	32
Alex Rodriguez	Baseball	13	32
Vijay Singh	Golf	16	31
Kevin Garnett	Basketball	17	30
Jeff Gordon	NASCAR racing	17	30
Derek Jeter	Baseball	17	30
Ronaldinho	Football	17	30

Table 14.1: The earnings of the world's top 20 athletes in 2008.
Source: Forbes.com (2009)

popular sport across the world, perhaps emphasising the fact that the wealth generated by football has to be distributed amongst a greater number of top footballers. Another illuminating fact is not who is in the list but who is not such as the absence of female athletes. This is an illustration that sport, whether participant or spectator, is male dominated. The female contenders to make an extended list are likely to emerge from tennis, golf or athletics. Maria Sharapova, who is the highest-earning female tennis player, is reported to have earned $22.5m in 2008 (Forbes.com 2009).

Table 14.1 is certainly enlightening; however, the facts here give rise to some much more interesting theories. For example, why is it that basketball is over-represented given that it is a sport predominantly played in the USA? Why does a retired athlete continue to out-earn those who are currently deploying their athletic skills? Why is it that the world's most popular sport is under-represented? These and many other questions will be addressed in the sections that follow.

Professional athletes generate their earnings from different sources. By and large, the dominant sources are earnings from participation, sponsorship and endorsements, and in some cases appearances. This is likely to be the case for athletes in individual sport and professional team sports. For many of these athletes, the revenues they generate from endorsements are likely to dwarf those generated from other sources.

Supply of athletic talent and labour

One of many starting points when it comes to understanding the professional athletes' labour market is the supply of athletic talent within a sport. For most sport, there is a pool of athletes and the size of the pool depends on the popularity of the sport; an issue that will be discussed in the following section. Any of these pools could be organised into a hierarchy where at the base is a mass of regular participants who enjoy participating but their athletic talents are far from exceptional. The next group of participants are more talented than the previous group but again their talents are not exceptional. They have a higher aptitude for the sport than the previous group and this might mean that they are able to compete at a slightly more competitive level. Above this group is another group of individuals who are more talented. And the scenario goes on and on until we arrive at the upper end of the hierarchy where the most talented athletes are grouped. In fact this group could be further disaggregated so that on the very top we have the most talented athlete in that sport at that particular point in time.

The process of organising athletes into a hierarchy in some sports involves a degree of subjectivity. For example, there are many thousands of professional footballers and perhaps millions of amateur footballers across the world, but what measures could and should be used to determine how they should be ranked? Some sports do in effect have ranking systems. The fact that most professional football leagues in most countries are hierarchical means that professional footballers will be allocated to these leagues based on their athletic ability. Although this is likely to be an imperfect way of deciding how good footballers are, it does aid such decisions. At the highest level, governing bodies such as FIFA and UEFA often oversee votes to decide the best world and European footballers respectively. In some team sports, such as basketball and baseball, there are a series of measurements that are often used to judge how good players are. Such measures even allow comparisons to be made between players who play different positions. Consequently, it is easier to compare Michael Jordan to Magic Johnson than it is to compare Pele to Bobby Moore. These mechanisms, whilst imperfect, allow judgements to be made on who the best athletes are.

For some sports, the allocation of talent to the hierarchy is more objective. In individual sports, players are normally ranked by the number of points they accumulate from competition over a specified time period. Examples of such sports include men's and women's tennis (see atpworldtour.com and sonyericssonwtatour.com). In some sports, the talent of the players can to some extent be measured in monetary terms, and this is the case in golf. In some instances, the number of major honours could be used as a measure of how good athletic talents are. Irrespective of how talent is measured, it is possible to produce a hierarchy of talent. The questions simply remain as to what criteria should be used and how far down should the hierarchy go. Table 14.2 illustrates the case of golf. The table shows a hierarchy of the best 258 players for the 11 months ending November 2009. As can be seen, the number of players is effectively a hierarchy or pyramid and the further down we go, we find the greater the number of players.

Upper limit ($)	Lower limit ($)	Number of players
12,000,000	10,000,001	1
10,000,000	8,000,001	0
8,000,000	6,000,001	1
6,000,000	4,000,001	4
4,000,000	2,000,001	30
2,000,000	1,000,001	52
up to 1,000,000	up to 1,000,000	170

Table 14.2: Distribution of earnings for the top 258 golfers on the PGA Tour from January 2009 to November 2009

However we care to organise the pool of talent in a given sport, there is one question that remains. What separates the very best athletes from the rest and are these qualities unique? Whatever these qualities or characteristics may be, be it Tiger Woods' precision and accuracy, be it Ronaldinho's ability to mesmerise opponents and audiences alike, or be it Roger Federer's ability to hit tennis shots that seem impossible and with incredible ease, what matters is their degree of exceptionality. Those who are connoisseurs and fans of basketball would concur that, at his best, Michael Jordan was truly an exceptional talent; the kind that has never before been seen in basketball and perhaps never will be seen again. Such was his ability as a player, his skills and attributes were truly unique; put another way, as an athlete, he was so exceptional that there was no substitute for him. A study by Hausman and Leonard (1997) concluded that Michael Jordan generated $53m for the National Basketball Association (NBA). The same also applies to athletes like Roger Federer, Tiger Woods, Ronaldinho and David Beckham. As professional athletes, their sporting skills and athletic talent are exceptional enough that, put another way, they have a monopoly on such skills. If many other golfers could match Tiger Woods' play, then what was exceptional could be readily duplicated and would no longer be exclusive. It is the unique talent of these athletes, combined with the high consumer demand (discussed in the section on page 183), that allows them to earn a premium over and above those earned by the rest of the field.

In some cases, the unique qualities that separate these athletes from others may not necessarily be exceptional sporting talent or athletic ability. There is no doubting the exceptional talents of Tiger Woods as a golfer having won 14 major titles. However, an additional unique factor that further separates him from the rest of the field is his ethnic background. In a sport that is white dominated and one where race barriers have been well documented, for a black golfer to break through is truly unique. Arguably if Tiger Woods were white, his sporting talent would no doubt be exceptional enough to generate substantial earnings, however, perhaps not to the current level. What Tiger Woods has is a number of unique qualities; in fact, he has a monopoly on these qualities and this is therefore reflected in his overall earnings. The same can also be said of Lewis Hamilton but to a lesser degree. Hamilton is regarded as an exceptional driver but is his driving talent unique? As a Formula 1 driver, he has to date won one driver's championship. Amongst the pool of drivers in the sport, this is nothing extraordinary. So why are Hamilton's earnings extraordinary? Some of his unique offerings, among others, are his age and ethnic background. Formula 1 is a sport in which experience, which can be proxied by age, matters and one in which black drivers are extremely rare. Consequently, he has a series of qualities which no one else is able to offer. Like Tiger Woods, he has a monopoly on these and as there is a situation of high demand, he too is able to earn extraordinary amounts. In essence, these athletes possess qualities, talent and skills for which there are limited or no substitutes; the *degree of substitutability* is low and in certain instances nil.

Is there any empirical evidence to support the theory which in this case suggests that the uniqueness of ethnicity (or, in the above cases being black), can generate extra remuneration? A study by Kanazawa and Funk (2001) found this to be the case but in reverse, in the case of white basketball players in the NBA. They found that television audience ratings in the NBA, controlling for other factors, were higher for games in which there were a greater number of white players. This preference by television audiences explained why white basketball players, controlling for how good they were, earned more compared with their black counterparts. A number of explanations for this difference in earnings were offered, one being that the relatively smaller number of white basketball players in the NBA meant that such players had a unique characteristic. As the NBA is a league dominated by black players, the limited supply of white players means that as a collective, they were able to earn more than non-white players of a similar talent. Whilst being a white player in the NBA is not unique, the supply is scarce enough for these players to earn a higher salary, particularly as viewers are willing to pay for such rarity. In this case, the *degree of substitutability* is not nil but low enough to merit higher than normal earnings for this group of athletes.

In the case of David Beckham, his uniqueness as a professional athlete may not be as obvious as those of Tiger Woods, Roger Federer or Lewis Hamilton. However, to be ranked fifth in Table 14.1 suggests that there is something unique about him as an athlete, which footballers are unable to replicate allowing David Beckham to be able to exercise monopoly power. In part, his ability to transcend football has created an aura that appeals to both football and non-football fans. To some extent, this unique offering is intangible. The emergence of new athletes like Usain Bolt also falls into this category of possessing and able to offer attributes that are unique. In his case, his sprinting talent is unrivalled: in the space of one year, he improved the 100 metre world record first from 9.72 seconds to 9.69 and then to 9.58, improvements of 0.31% and 1.14% respectively. These improvements, combined with his performances in other events, make Usain Bolt an extraordinary track athlete. His unique talent combined with other attributes provide him with a monopoly which should earn him extraordinary amounts now and in the future. This is, however, dependent on the demand there is. If Usain Bolt does not make the list of the top 20 high earners in sport, it is likely to be because of the relatively limited consumer interest (from live spectators, television audiences, commercial sponsors, etc.) that there is track and field compared with other sports such as golf, basketball, tennis and football.

> ## Learning Activity 14.1
>
> The degree of substitutability for the following athletes, to a small or large extent, is nil. What qualities do they have that allow them to generate substantial earnings over and above their rivals in the same sport?
>
> 1   Maria Sharapova in tennis;
> 2   Andy Murray in tennis;
> 3   Usain Bolt in track and field;
> 4   Vijay Singh in golf;
> 5   Michael Phelps in swimming;
> 6   Haile Gebrselassie in the road marathon.

For these high earning professional athletes and what they are able to offer, there simply is no substitution or there are limited substitutes; the *degree of substitutability* is nil or very low. It is analogous to a company having a rare commodity and it being the only supplier. Coupled with a high level of demand, such a company is able to exercise monopoly power and generate abnormal profits or extraordinary earnings.

So how do professional athletes compare with other professions? As a simple exercise, take the professions of teaching, nursing and law. Many would concede that these professions are important to society. In fact, it is not hard to find those who believe that the individuals who occupy these professions are more important to society than professional athletes. So why is it that professional athletes earn large multiples of the salaries in these professions? Relative to the pool of professional athletes, it is easier to replace teachers, nurses and lawyers; the degree of substitutability is high by comparison. Where substitutes are easy to come by, earnings are likely to be modest. Where substitutes are scarce or even non-existent, the degree of substitutability is nil and combined with high levels of demand, earnings are likely to be extraordinary.

Who needs professional athletes?

The broader issue of athletes' role within society compared with other professions was highlighted above, although to explore this issue in full is beyond the scope of this chapter. However, of greater relevance is the issue of the direct demand for these athletes' labour. Take individual sports like golf and tennis – in theory, it is possible for golfers and tennis players to directly organise events. However, the (monetary and non-monetary) costs of doing so are just too great to be practicable. Athletes will, amongst other tasks, have to fulfil the following:

- communicate with one another to organise the structure of the event;
- organise the tournament schedules and venue;
- decide which players should take part;
- engage in marketing, advertising and promotion;
- sell tickets for the event;

- manage the event's operations once the tournament starts;
- deal with safety and security issues at the venue;
- distribute prize money.

Athletes will find such administrative tasks burdening. In fact, so demanding are these functions, in practice it will be impossible to organise a series of events at the level that modern day sports consumers are accustomed to. The alternative, which is more efficient for the athletes, is to delegate their rights. For example, on deciding to enter a tournament, golfers and tennis players delegate their rights to the organisers of the tournaments. It is the organisers who in return shoulder many of the tasks noted above and they are compensated through the sale of tickets, broadcast and other media rights, sponsorship and endorsement deals, and other benefits. Furthermore, the athletes agree to abide by various terms and conditions which will often include media access at press conferences and other events. The delegation of these rights means that instead of athletes organising their own competition, professional and well-established event organisers do so. The benefits to the athletes far outweigh the various costs; likewise for the organisers, the benefits they accrue outweigh their costs. And given the number of tournaments that can be held in say a calendar year, many events and organisers can be accommodated until capacity is reached. Beyond this point, tournament organisers have to compete fiercely against one another for the best athletes. Demand from tournament and competition organisers is one principal source of demand for professional athletes.

Organisers need to know which athletes to admit to their tournaments in order to offer their various consumers the best sporting competition possible. Without information on how good athletes are, tournaments are likely to descend into uncompetitive contests as organisers will not know who to admit and, where appropriate, how to seed the entrants. For this, organisers turn to the representative organisations like the Association of Tennis Professionals (ATP) in men's tennis, the Women's Tennis Association (WTA) for women's tennis, and the Professional Golfers' Association (PGA) for men's golf, to mention a few. These bodies, to a small or large extent, organise, manage and promote the athletes, sanction tournaments and produce rankings for the players. Athletes delegate their rights to these bodies in return for these important functions. Tournament organisers are now able to work with these representative bodies, have their tournaments sanctioned, and use information such as the rankings of players to create tournament draws. In some instances, there is more than one representative body to whom athletes can delegate their rights, and these bodies may compete against one another. For example, darts and boxing have different bodies within their sports with their own stables of athletes, their own ranking systems, and their own sanctioned tournaments and competitions. In these instances athletes have to make a decision as to which body they delegate their rights to. In any case, the demand for athletes by tournament organisers is only complemented by those of the bodies that represent them (the athletes).

The delegation of rights by athletes to others in individual sports applies to professional team sports. In professional football for example, players delegate their rights to clubs and the national association (for international matches). The benefits the players accrue from doing this include being on the teams' rosters and having league and other matches organised for them. To a large extent, the clubs and the various bodies provide the sporting infrastructure in which professional teams are able to operate and in return they extract a proportion of the revenue before paying players their share in wages, salaries and bonuses. In professional team sports, the delegation and assigning of rights from players to clubs has not always been in the players' interest. Only in recent years have footballers been able to accrue the large sums that are reported in the popular press. Prior to this, the clubs had been able to exert monopsony power over players. A monopsony is when there is a single buyer and many sellers in the market. Up until the 1960s, there was a maximum wage that operated in English football and no matter how good a player was, his earnings could not exceed this. The maximum wage was introduced in 1901 and was set to £4 per week. Many players in fact received more than the maximum wage through bonus payments which were against the Football Association's rules. By 1958, the maximum wage had risen to £58 per week. For a review of the historical developments of wages in English football, see Dobson and Goddard (2001).

The current market for professional team sports is organised so that players are very well compensated for delegating their rights to clubs. The main reason for this is that policies which worked against the interest of players have in recent years been abolished, many of them for legal reasons. In Major League Baseball (MLB) in North America, a reserve clause operated from the late nineteenth century to 1975. The reserve clause meant that once a player had signed a contract with a team, that team owned his registration for the rest of his career. Similarly in English football, a retain and transfer system was operated from 1891 by the Football League until it was abolished in 1979. The system limited a player to his current club, and he could only move to another club with his club's consent (Thomas 2006). Clubs could retain players when their contracts expired and offer new contracts, trade their registration to other clubs or cancel their registration and make them free agents. Under the retain and transfer system, clubs had full control over players' registration. This control and power contributed to the limited earnings of players during this period. The abolition of the retain and transfer system in 1979 meant that once a player's contract expired, he could move to another club for a fee only if an agreement was reached between the two clubs. Without an agreement and payment of a transfer fee, players were not able to move. In 1995, the European Court of Justice ruled against this in a landmark case popularly referred to as the Bosman Ruling (see Dobson and Goddard 2001). Many of these policies are constraints which limit the earnings of players. Since their removal, earnings in professional team sports like baseball, basketball and football have increased substantially. Although there are some policy restrictions in some sports, i.e. salary caps in NBA and the NFL, players are very well remunerated nowadays.

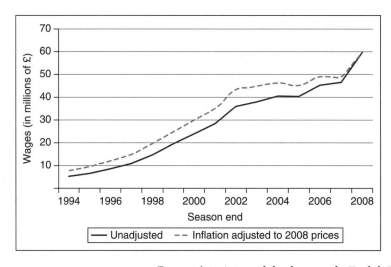

Figure 14.1 Average club salaries in the English Premier League
Source: Deloitte, various years

The removal of these policies in professional team sports combined with the demand by professional sports clubs has led to a dramatic escalation in wages. Figure 14.1 shows the annual salaries of clubs in the English Premier League from the 1994–5 season to the 2007–8 season. The rise over this 15 year period is substantial and is just one measure of the demand there is by clubs for the services of professional football players. The mean figure of £60m in the 2007–8 season is rather small when compared with the highest club wages in that season: Chelsea at £172m, followed by Manchester United and Arsenal with £121m and £101m respectively.

Learning Activity 14.2

Table 14.3 illustrates the wages costs of 19 of the 20 clubs in the English Premier League during the 2007–8 season. Using additional information about the number of players employed by the clubs (see Sky Sports Football Yearbook) or making appropriate assumptions, what are you able to infer from the wages paid by these clubs? For each club, identify up to three players who are likely to be the highest paid on the team roster.

Club	Salary costs (in £m)	Club	Salary costs (in £m)
Arsenal	101	Manchester City	54
Aston Villa	50	Manchester United	121
Birmingham City	27	Middlesbrough	35
Blackburn Rovers	40	Newcastle United	79
Bolton Wanderers	39	Portsmouth	55
Chelsea	172	Reading	33
Derby County	26	Sunderland	37
Everton	44	Tottenham Hotspur	53
Fulham	39	Wigan Athletic	38
Liverpool	90		

Table 14.3: Salary costs in the English Premier League, 2007–8 season

Case Study
The salary–endorsement ratio

The majority of professional athletes generate their earnings from a number of sources. For most, these can be classified into two categories: salaries and endorsements. For salaries and in the case of athletes in individual sports, this will on the whole comprise earnings from tournament prize funds. In some cases, athletes may also be remunerated for participating in certain tournaments. For example, organisers of big city marathons will often invite top athletes to participate, offering them appearances fees. For those athletes in professional team sports, this will be predominantly from the salaries paid by their team. Another major source of income is endorsements or sponsorship. Athletes are often paid to endorse brands or products which may be sports-related or non-sports-related. Endorsements of sport brands, shoes, apparel and equipment are very common. Other sports-related goods are also very common, e.g. sports drinks. Earnings from endorsing non-sports-related goods and services feature a great deal too. From restaurants to insurance services and banking, athletes are often used to promote and communicate the benefits of these companies' offerings.

How much athletes generate from these two major sources vary and a major distinction is their sport. For top athletes in individual sports such as tennis and golf, earnings from endorsements are likely to dominate that of salary or earnings from prizes. For those athletes in professional team sports, it is likely to be the other way around. Table 14.4 shows the top 10 athletes from the USA by earnings in 2008, as reported on the Sports Illustrated website. What is noticeable is that for those in individual sports the salary endorsement ratio is above one, and for team sport it is less than one, with the exception of LeBron James, one of the biggest stars on the NBA.

Rank	Athlete	Sport	Total ($m)	Salary: endorsement ratio
1	Tiger Woods	Golf	99.7	1:11.9
2	Phil Mickelson	Golf	53.0	1:7.3
3	LeBron James	NBA	42.4	1:1.9
4	Alex Rodriguez	MLB	39.0	1:0.2
5	Shaquille O'Neal	NBA	35.0	1:0.8
6	Kevin Garnett	NBA	34.8	1:0.4
7	Kobe Bryant	NBA	31.3	1:0.5
8	Allen Iverson	NBA	28.9	1:0.3
9	Derek Jeter	MLB	28.5	1:0.4
10	Peyton Manning	NFL	27.0	1:0.8

Table 14.4: Top 10 US athletes by earnings in 2008
Source: Sports Illustrated.com (2009)

One of the main reasons for this is that sponsoring firms have to spend a significant part of their budget on sponsoring the professional teams themselves and therefore have to decide which is more efficient, to spend their revenue on the club or the player. To some extent in team sport, the resources used to sponsor a team are arguably a form of indirect sponsoring of the teams' players. Only the sponsoring firm has less freedom on how they use the athletes to promote their brand or product. So while Coca-Cola sponsor the England Football team, they have little freedom on how they make use of players like David Beckham and Frank Lampard, two of the England players who are sponsored by Pepsi-Cola, a rival company.

Consumer demand for athletic labour and talent

So far, the preceding sections have documented the very high earnings, and in some cases hyper-earnings, of professional athletes. In doing so, we have partly explained the reasons for these high earnings and, in particular, noted the zero or very low degree of substitutability. However, perhaps of greater importance is the demand by consumers for athletic talent. Professional sports markets, individual and team sports, have their success rooted in the fact that there is consumer demand for the sport. The more spectators there are, the more these athletes earn, although in some sports, there are labour market practices which mean that athletes do not generate as much earnings as they could.

Traditionally and empirically, the earnings of athletes could be linked to the number of spectators that pay to view sports in arenas and stadiums. As this was the principal means of meeting consumer demand, there was a limit on how much sports leagues or tournament organisers could generate in revenue and in turn how much athletes could earn. In some instances the capacities of the stadiums and arenas limited the number of paying spectators whose demand could be met. Theoretically, to satisfy more consumer demand, sports leagues and tournament organisers would have to build bigger arenas and stadiums, expand the number of teams in the league so that more matches could be played, provide extra competitions using a different format perhaps, schedule more tournaments, or increase the number of competitors able to enter tournaments. This approach to satisfying consumer demand means that athletes have to work more by participating in more competitions and events; their earnings become a function of the number of competitions they participate in.

However, the symbiotic relationship between sport and the broadcast market has made athletes more efficient at what they do. Without television and broadcasting, to satisfy the extra demand by consumers, athletes would have to play more matches or more competitions given the limited number of spaces there are in arenas and stadiums. However, with broadcasting and television, this is no longer the case. Broadcast technology means that extra consumer demand can be satisfied without the need for professional athletes having to participate in extra competitions or tournaments. This is in fact what makes professional athletes so very productive. Comparing athletes with teachers, there is an equally high demand for teachers, given the demand there is for education worldwide. However, as demand for education goes up, the limited size of classes means that there is a limit to how much demand individual teachers can satisfy. Extra demand must be satisfied by scheduling more classes and employing extra teachers. In the case of professional athletes in today's market, extra demand need not be satisfied by scheduling extra competitions and events, it is simply satisfied through televising existing ones to wider audiences. Hence, greater levels of productivity are achieved by using existing sports events to meet extra demand through broadcasting. Professional athletes are for this reason comparatively more efficient than teachers when meeting extra demand. In fact, the professional athletes are similar to film stars in this respect, in that they do not have to play extra matches to satisfy more demand. The high demand by consumers and the manner in which this demand is met explain partly why professional athletes are highly remunerated.

Chapter Review

This chapter has examined the professional athletes' labour market and while professional athletes can be placed into two categories, individual and team sports, their earnings are equally very high, particularly for those in the top echelons of the sport. This chapter notes that one of the reasons for the high remuneration of athletes is the structure of the labour market. Unlike many other professions, top athletes possess unique qualities which in many cases cannot be replicated. In some instances these attributes are purely sporting. In others they are personal attributes which although may not offer any innate advantage to playing sport, can be used to further enhance an athlete's unique offering. Further issues noted within the examination of the labour market include how athletes delegate rights, thus allowing the market to operate more efficiently, generating greater revenue using the existing resources and talent available. For this reason, athletes' rights are traded and league and sports organisers are able to use these to produce sports competitions and tournaments which in turn are sold to sports consumers.

Historical aspects of labour markets were also examined. In particular the reserve clause that operated in MLB in North America and the retain and transfer rule in English football. Both labour market practices had the effect of minimising the wages that were paid to the athletes of these sports. Such practices were abolished, many as a result of legal challenges that were mounted in the highest courts, e.g. the Bosman ruling in the European Court of Justice.

A fundamental issue also noted in the chapter is the manner in which professional athletes are able to satisfy consumer demand. Unlike other professionals, the market for professional sport is such that, with the aid of broadcast technology, athletes are able to satisfy extra demand without having to increase the number of competitions or tournaments they engage in, although this does not necessarily mean that they do not participate in more sporting competition. However, broadcasting technology, particularly television, means that wider audiences across the globe can view various sports and the athletes of these sports. Hence, Tiger Woods need not increase the number of tournaments he plays to earn more. Tournament organisers and broadcasters can simply organise broadcast transmission of existing tournaments to wider audiences, Tiger Woods and his counterparts becoming the richer for it.

After reading this chapter and attempting the learning activities you should now be able to answer the following questions:

1 In the UK doctors and nurses are employed locally by NHS Primary Care Trusts but are on a central contract negotiated nationally. In theory, nurses and doctors are employed by the same employer, the NHS. Conversely, professional footballers can be employed by one of hundreds of football clubs in England, Europe and further afield. What are the likely consequences for remuneration in these labour markets?

2 Firms who sponsor professional athletes will in return expect athletes to fulfil obligations. Tabulate the (theoretical) cost and benefits to both parties: the sponsoring firm and the athletes. Having evaluated these cost and benefits for each party, do the benefits outweigh the cost?

3 Salary capping is a widely-discussed concept in professional team sport and one that has been discussed widely in the context of European league football. What are the likely effects of a salary cap on the market for professional football players and on the owners of professional football clubs?

Further Reading

- Dobson, S. and Goddard, J. (2001) *The Economics of Football*. Cambridge: Cambridge University Press.
- Hundley, H.L. and Billings, A.C. (eds) (2010) *Examining Identity in Sports Media*. London: Sage.

- Quirk, J. and Fort, R. (1997) *Pay Dirt: The Business of Professional Team Sport*. Princeton: Princeton University Press.
- Szymanski, S. (2009) *Playbooks and Checkbooks: An Introduction to the Economics of Modern Sports*. Princeton: Princeton University Press.
- Wladimir, A. and Szymanski, S. (eds) (2006) *Handbook on the Economics of Sport*. Cheltenham: Edward Elgar.

References

Active People Survey (2008) *Sport England Research*. http://www.sportengland.org/research/active_people_survey/ Active_people_survey_2.aspx, accessed January 2010.

Adidas (2009) Andre Agassi and Adidas enter agreement. http:// www.press.adidas.com, accessed November 2009.

Andreff, W. and Szymanski, S. (eds) (2006) *Handbook on the Economics of Sport*, Cheltenham: Edward Elgar.

Armistead, C. and Pettigrew, P. (2004) Effective partnerships: building a sub-regional network of reflective practitioners', *The International Journal of Public Sector Management*, 17(7): 571–585.

Audit Commission (1989) *Sport for Whom?* London: HMSO.

Audit Commission (1990) *Preparing for Compulsory Competitive Tendering*. London: HMSO.

Audit Commission (2006) *Public Sports and Recreation Services; Making Them Fit for the Future*. http://audit-commission.gov.uk/reports, accessed 20 November 2009.

Baade, R. and Matheson, V. (2002) Bidding for the Olympics: fool's gold? *Transatlantic Sport: The Comparative Economics of North American and European Sports*. London: Edward Elgar, pp. 127–151.

Bache, I. (2003) Governing through governance: education policy control under New Labour, *Political Studies*, 51: 300–314.

Barcelona Football Club (2009) http://fcbarcelona.com/eng. accessed 21 November 2009.

Bacon, W. (1990) Gatekeepers of public leisure: a case study of executive managers in the UK, *Leisure Studies*, 9(1): 71–87.

Bacon, W. (1996) Accredit to the industry, *The Leisure Manager*, Febuary/March.

Baimbridge, M., Cameron, S. and Dawson, P. (1996) Satellite television and the demand for football: a whole new ball game, *Scottish Journal of Political Economy*, 43(3): 317–333.

Barnes, M. and Sullivan (2002) Building capacity for collaboration in English Health Action Zones, in C. Glendinning, M. Powell and K. Rummery (eds) *Partnerships, New Labour and The Governance of Welfare*. Bristol: Policy Press.

BBC (2002) *Beckham Caught in 'Cola Wars'*, Saturday 9 March. http://news.bbc.co.uk/1/hi/england/1863402.stm, accessed November 2009.

BBC (2006) *Child Obesity Doubles in Decade*. http://news.bbc.co.uk/1/hi/health/4930264.stm,accessed 28 August 2009.

BBC. (2007) *Olympics Budget Rises to £9.3bn*. http://news.bbc.co.uk/1/hi/uk_politics/6453575.stm, accessed 16 December 2008.

BBC (2009) *Smokers Offered Money to Give Up*. http://news.bbc.co.uk/1/hi/scotland/tayside_and_central/7465908.stm, accessed 22 October 2009.

BBC (2009a) *Meadows Rewarded with Cash Boost*. http://newsalerts.bbc.co.uk/sport1/hi/athletics/8328123.stm, accessed 30 October 2009.

Beech, J. and Chadwick, S. (2004) *The Business of Sport Management*. Harlow: Pearson Education Limited.

Bloomfield, J. (2004) *Australia's Sporting Success: The Inside Story*. Sydney: USWP.

Bloyce, D. and Smith, A. (2009) *Sport, Policy and Development: An Introduction*. London: Routledge.

Bourdieu, P. (1986) *Distinction: A Social Critique of the Judgement of Taste*. London: Routledge.

Bramham, P. (2008) Sports policy, in K. Hylton and P. Bramham (eds) *Sports Development: Policy, Process and Practice*, 2nd edn. London: Routledge, pp. 10–24.

Bramwell, B. (1997) Strategic planning before and after a mega-event, *Tourism Management*, 18: 167–176.

British Cycling (2008) *Multi-Million Pound Sky deal for British Cycling*. http://www.britishcycling.org.uk/web/site/BC/bcf/News2008/20080724_Sky_Deal.asp, accessed 10 November 2009.

British Cycling (2009a) *2009 Road World Championships Selection Criteria*. http://britishcycling.org.uk/gbcyclingteam/article/Gbr20090605-2009-Road-World-Championships-Selection-Criteria--0, accessed 10 November 2009.

British Cycling (2009b) *GB On Track for 2008 Olympics*. http://www.britishcycling.org.uk/web/site/BC/gbr/News2007/20070325_Dave_Brailsford.asp, accessed 10 November 2009.

British Olympic Association (2008) *Role of the BOA*. http://www.olympics.org.uk/contentpage.aspx?page=19, accessed 16 December 2008.

British Olympic Association (2009a). *Mark Lewis-Francis, MBE* http://www.olympics.org.uk/athleterecord.aspx?at=5546, accessed 7 November 2009.

British Olympic Association (2009b) *Role of the BOA*. http://www.olympics.org.uk/contentpage.aspx?page=19, accessed 7 November 2009.

BSkyB (2009) *Announcing Team Sky – A Professional British Road Cycling Team*. http://corporate.sky.com/media/press_releases/2009/team_sky.htm, accessed 14 November 2009.

Buraimo, B., Simmons, R. and Szymanski, S. (2006) English football', *Journal of Sports Economics* 7(1): 29–46.

Buraimo, B. and Simmons, R. (2008) Do sports fans really value uncertainty of outcome? Evidence from the English Premier League', *International Journal of Sports Finance*, 3(3): 146–155.

Burgham, M. and Downward, P. (2005) Why volunteer, time to volunteer? A case study from swimming, *Managing Leisure* 10: 79–93.

Cabinet Office. (2008) *Tessa Jowell MP – Minister for the Olympics and Paymaster General*. http://www.cabinetoffice.gov.uk/about_the_cabinet_office/tessa_jowell.aspx, accessed 16 December 2008.

Campbell, C. (1995) The sociology of consumption, in D. Miller, *Acknowledging Consumption: A Review of New Studies*. London: Routledge, pp. 96–126.

Carrington, B. and Leaman, O. (1982) Work for some, sport for all? *Journal of Sport and Social Issues*, 22(3): 275–298.

Cashman, Richard (2002) *Impact of the Games on Olympic Host Cities: University Lecture on the Olympics*. http://olympicstudies.uab.es/lectures/web/pdf/cashman.pdf, accessed 9 November 2009.

Central Council of Physical Recreation (July 2007) *Historical Background* http://www.ccpr.org.uk/dyncat.cfm?catid=4351, accessed 16 December 2008.

Central Council of Physical Recreation (2008) *About CCPR*. http://www.ccpr.org.uk/, accessed 16 December 2008.

Change4life (2009) http://nhs.uk/change4life, accessed 28 October 2009.

Chartered Institute of Sport Project Working Group (2009) *Chartered Institute of Sport Progress Update*. http://www.isrm.co.uk/resources/mem_consult120509.pdf, accessed 2 November 2009.

Cheshire and Warrington Sports Partnership (2009a) *What We Do*. http://www.cwsportspartnership.org/about-us/what-we-do, accessed 22 November 2009.

Children and Young People's Unit (2006) *Our Children and Young People: A Ten Year Strategy for Children and Young People in Northern Ireland 2006–2016*. Belfast: The Office of the First Minister and Deputy First Minister.

Clark, T. and Clegg, S. (1998) *Changing Paradigms, The Transformation of Management Knowledge for the 21ˢᵗ Century*. London: Harper Collins.

Coakley, J. and Pike, E. (2009) *Sports in Society: Issues and Controversies*. London: McGraw-Hill.

Coalter, F. (1990) The politics of professionalism: Consumers or citizens? *Leisure Studies*, 9: 107–119.

Coalter, F. (2004) Stuck in the blocks? A sustainable sporting legacy, in A. Vigor, M. Mean, and C. Tims (eds) *After the Gold Rush: A Sustainable Olympics for London*. London: Ippr and Demos, pp. 91–108.

Coalter, F. (2007) A *Wider Social Role for Sport: Who's Keeping the Score*? Routledge, London.

Coalter, F. and Potter, J. (1990) *A Study of 1985 Graduates from Sport, Recreation and Leisure Studies*, London: Sports Council.

Coleman, R. (2002) Characteristics of volunteering in UK sport: lessons from cricket, *Managing Leisure*, 7: 220–238.

Collins, M. (2004) Driving up participation: social inclusion, in Sport England *Driving up Participation: The challenge for sport*. London: Sport England, pp. 61–67.

Collins, M. (2008) Public policies on sports development: can mass and elite sport hold together? in Girginov, V. (ed.) *Management of Sports Development*. Oxford: Elsevier.

Collins, M. (2009) *Examining Sports Development*. London: Routledge.

Crabbe, T. (2000) A sporting chance? Using sport to tackle drug use and crime, *Drugs: Education Journal of Sport Management, Prevention and Policy*, 7 (4): 381–391.

Crompton, J.L. (1995) Economic impact analysis of sports facilities and events: eleven sources of misapplication, *Journal of Sport Management*, 9: 14–25.

Crompton, J. (2001) Public subsidy to professional team sports facilities in the USA, in C. Gratton and I. Henry (eds), *Sport in the City: The Role of Sport in Economic and Social Regeneration*. London: Routledge.

Cuskelly, G., Hoye, R. and Auld, C. (2006) *Working with Volunteers in Sport*. London: Routledge.

David Lloyd Ltd (2009) http://davidlloyd.co.uk, accessed 1 November 2009.

DCMS (Department for Culture Media and Sport) (2002) *A Sporting Future for All*, London: DCMS.

DCMS (2002) *A Strategy for Delivering the Government's Sport and Physical Activity Objectives*. London: DCMS.

DCMS (2004) *Bringing Communities Together Through Sport and Culture*. London: DCMS.

DCMS (2008) *Playing to Win: A New Era for Sport*. London: DCMS.

DCMS/DCSF (2008) *PE and Sport Strategy for Young People Leaflet*. London: DCMS/DCSF.

DCMS/DES (2002) *A Sporting Future for All: The Role of Further and Higher Education In Delivering The Government's Plan For Sport*. London: HMSO.

Deloitte (various years) *Annual Review of Football Finance*. Manchester: Deloitte.

Department of Culture, Arts and Leisure (2007) *Sport Matters – The Northern Ireland Strategy for Sport and Physical Recreation 2007–2017*. Belfast: DCAL.

Department of the Environment (1975) *Sport and Recreation*. London: HMSO.

Department of Health, Social Services and Public Safety and Department of Education (2005) *Fit Futures: Focus on Food, Activity and Young People*. Belfast: DHSSPS and DoE.

Department of Health (2009) *Be Active, Be Healthy: A Plan for Getting the Nation Moving*. London: Department of Health.

Department of National Heritage (1995) *Sport: Raising the Game*. London: HMSO.

DfES/DCMS (2003) *Learning through PE and Sport: A Guide to the Physical Education, School Sport and Club Links Strategy*. London: The Department of Education and Skills.

Directgov (2009a) *Northern Ireland Assembly* http://www.direct.gov.uk/en/Dl1/Directories/DG_10012122, accessed 24 October 2009.

Directgov (2009b) *Government Departments and Agencies*. http://www.direct.gov.uk/en/Governmentcitizensandrights/UKgovernment/Centralgovernmentandthemonarchy/DG_073446, accessed 18 November 2009.

Dobson, S. and Goddard, J. (2001) *The Economics of Football*. Cambridge: Cambridge University Press.

Doherty, A. (2005) *A Profile of Community Sport Volunteers*. Parks and Recreation Ontario and Sport Alliance of Ontario, Canada.

Doherty, A. (2006) Sport volunteerism: an introduction to the special issue, *Sport Management Review*, 9 (2): 105–109.

Downward, P., Dawson, A. and Dejonghe, T. (2009) *Sports Economics: Theory, Evidence and Policy*. London: Butterworth-Heinemann.

EFDS (2009) *About Us*. http://www.efds.co.uk/page.asp?section=95&sectionTitle=About+us, accessed 18 November 2009.

English Golf Union (2009) http://englishgolfunion.org, accessed 20 November 2009.

English Institute of Sport (2009) *History of the EIS*. http://www.eis2win.co.uk/pages/EIS_History_Home.aspx, accessed 15 November 2009.

European Health and Fitness Association (2009) http://Ehfa.eu, accessed 19 November 2009.

Everton Foundation (2009) http://evertonfoundation.org, accessed 2 November 2009.

Fleming, I. (1996) The professionalisation of leisure management in Western Europe, *Managing Leisure*, 1: 248–251.

Flintoff, A. (2003) The school sport co-ordinator programme: changing the role of the physical education teacher? *Sport, Education and Society*, 8 (2): 231–250.

Flintoff, A. (2008) Targeting Mr Average: participation, gender equity and school sport *Sport, Education and Society*, 13 (4): 393–411.

Foley, P. (1991) The impact of the World Student Games on Sheffield, *Environment and Planning C: Government and Policy*, 9: 65–78.

Forbes (2009) www.forbes.com, accessed 2 November 2009.

Forrest, D., Simmons, R. and Szymanski, S. (2004) 'Broadcasting, attendance and the inefficiency of cartels', *Review of Industrial Organization*, 24(3): 243–265.

Fraser, A (2005) Olympics bill comes under attack, BBC.co.uk, accessed 23 November 2009.

Garrett, R. (2004) The response of voluntary sports clubs to Sport England's lottery funding: cases of compliance, change and resistance, *Managing Leisure*. 9: 13–29, January.

Gerrard, B. (2006) Financial innovation in professional team sports: the case of English Premiership soccer, in W. Andreff and S. Szymanski (eds) *Handbook on the Economics of Sport*. Cheltenham: Edward Elgar.

Girginov, V. (2008) *Management of Sports Development*. Oxford: Elsevier.

Glasgow City Council (2009) *A Games Legacy for Glasgow*. Glasgow: Glasgow City Council.

Gratton, C. and Henry, I. (2001) *Sport in the City: The Role of Sport in Economic and Social Regeneration*. London: Routledge.

Gratton, C. (2000) 'The peculiar economics of English professional football, *Soccer and Society*, 1(1): 11–28.

Gratton, C., Shibli, S., and Dobson, N. (2000) The economic importance of major sports events, *Managing Leisure*, 5: 17–28.

Gratton, C. and Solberg, H.A. (2007) *The Economics of Sport Broadcasting*, London: Routledge.

Gratton, C. and Taylor, P. (2000) *Economics of Sport and Recreation*, London: E and FN Spon.

Greater Sport (2007) *Greater Manchester Sport Partnership Workforce Development Plan*. Manchester: Greater Sport.

Green, M. (2004) Changing policy priorities for sport in England: the emergence of elite sport development as a key policy concern, *Leisure Studies*, 23 (4): 365–385.

Green, K., Smith, A. and Roberts, K. (2005) Young people and lifelong participation in sport and physical activity: a sociological perspective on contemporary physical education programmes in England and Wales, *Leisure Studies*, 24 (1): 27–43.

Green, M. and Houlihan, B. (2005) *Elite Sport Development: Policy Learning and Political Priorities*. London: Routledge.

Guardian (2009) Sheffield Eagles to share Bramall Lane with Sheffield United, Friday 16 October. http://www.guardian.co.uk/sport/2009/oct/16/sheffield-eagles-united-bramall-lane, accessed January 2010.

Hart, S. (2009) *Mark Lewis-Francis Loses Lottery Funding from UK Athletics, The Telegraph*. http://www.telegraph.co.uk/sport/othersports/athletics/6446406/Mark-Lewis-Francis-loses-lottery-funding-from-UK-Athletics.html, accessed 7 November 2009.

Hausman, J.A. and Leonard, G.K. (1997) Superstars in the National Basketball Association: economic value and policy, *Journal of Labor Economics*, 15(4): 586–624.

Healey, B. (2006) Sporting Chance Project, interview by L. Trimble 13 July 2006. Ormskirk: Edge Hill University.

Henry, I. (1993) *The Politics of Leisure Policy*. London: Macmillan.

Henry, I. (2001) *The Politics of Leisure Policy*. London: Macmillan.

Henry, I. and Bramham, P. (1993) Leisure and policy in Britain, in P. Bramham, I. Henry, H. Mommas, and H. Van der Poel (eds), *Leisure Policies in Europe*, Wallingford: CAB International.

Henry, I. and Spink, J. (1990) Planning for leisure: the commercial and public sectors, in I. Henry (ed.) *Management and Planning in the Leisure Industries*, Basingstoke: Macmillan.

Hill, M. (2007) *In Pursuit of Excellence*. London: Routledge.

HM Treasury (2009) http://hm-treasury.gov.uk/spend_index.htm, accessed 4 November 2009.

HM Treasury (2007) *2007 Pre-Budget Report and Comprehensive Spending Review*. http://www.hm-treasury.gov.uk/d/pbr_csr07_pn04olympics15.pdf, accessed 3 December 2008.

Hotchkiss, J.L., Moore, R.E. and Zobay, S.M. (2003) Impact of the Summer Olympic Games on employment and wages in Georgia. *Southern Economic Journal*, 69(3): 691–704.

Houlihan, B. (1997) *Sport Policy and Politics: A Comparative Analysis*. London: Routledge.

Houlihan, B. (2001) *Sport, Policy and Politics: A Comparative Analysis*. London: Routledge.

Houlihan, B. and Green, M. (2006) The changing status of school sport and physical education: explaining policy change. *Sport, Education and Society*, (1): 73–92.

Houlihan, B. and Green, M. (eds) (2009). *Comparative Elite Sports Development: Systems, Structures and Public Policy*. London: Butterworth-Heinemann.

Houlihan, B. and White, A. (2002) *The Politics of Sport Development: Development of Sport or Development Through Sport*. London: Routledge.

Hubbard, A. (2000) Time for a no-logo area, *The Independent*, 6 August.

Hylton, K., Bramham, P., Jackson, D. and Nesti, M. (2001) *Sports Development: Policy, Process and Practice*. London: Routledge.

Hylton, K. and Bramham, P. (eds) (2008) *Sports Development: Policy, Process and Practice*, 2nd edn. London: Routledge.

Hylton, K. and Totten, M. (2008) Developing sport for all?: addressing inequality in sport', in K. Hylton and P. Bramham (eds) *Sports Development: Policy, Process and Practice*, 2nd edn. London: Routledge, pp. 42–76.

Independent (2000) 'British Olympic swimmers cleared to wear bodysuits', Wednesday 7 June. http://www. independent.co.uk/sport/general/british-olympic-swimmers-cleared-to-wear-bodysuits-713856.html, accessed November 2009.

Jackson, D. (2008) Developing sports practice, in K. Hylton and P. Bramham (eds) *Sports Development: Policy, Process and Practice*, 2nd edn. London: Routledge, pp. 25–41.

Jeanrenaud, C. and Késenne, S. (2006) *The Economics of Sport and the Media*, Cheltenham: Edward Elgar.

Kanazawa, M.T. and Funk, J.P. (2001) Racial discrimination in professional basketball: evidence from Nielsen ratings, *Economic Inquiry*, 39(4): 599–608.

Kasimati, E. (2003) Economic aspects and the Summer Olympics: a review of related research, *International Journal of Tourism Research*, 5: 433–444.

Kesenne, S. (2007) *The Economic Theory of Professional Team Sports: An Analytical Treatment*. Cheltenham: Edward Elgar.

Kirk, D. (2004) *Sport and Early Learning Experiences*. Loughborough: Institute of Sport and Leisure Policy, Loughborough University.

Lagae, W. (2005) *Sports Sponsorship and Marketing Communications: A European Perspective*. Harlow: Prentice Hall.

Lawson, H. (2005) Empowering people, facilitating community development, and contributing to sustainable development: the social work of sport, exercise, and physical education programs, *Sport, Education and Society*, 10 (1): 135–160.

Learning and Teaching Scotland (2009a) *Scotland's New Curriculum*. http://www.ltscotland.org.uk/ curriculumforexcellence/index.asp, accessed 5 November 2009.

Learning and Teaching Scotland (2009b) *Physical Education, Physical Activity and Sport*. http://www. ltscotland.org.uk/curriculumforexcellence/healthandwellbeing/outcomes/physicaledactivitysport/ index.asp, accessed 5 November 2009

Lee, C. and Taylor, T. (2005) Critical reflections on the economic impact assessment of a mega-event: the case of 2002 FIFA World Cup, *Tourism Management*, 26: 595–603.

LIRC (2003) *Sports Volunteering in England in 2002*. London: Sport England.

Lloyd, C. (2005) Competitive strategy and skills: working out the fit in the fitness industry, *Human Resource Management Journal*, 15 (2): 15–34.

London 2012 (2008a) *Funding.* http://www.london2012.com/about/funding/index.php, accessed 16 December 2008.

London 2012 (2008b) *Olympic Board.* http://www.london2012.com/about/the-people-delivering-the-games/stakeholders/olympic-board.php, accessed 16 December 2008.

London 2012 (2008c) *Volunteering* (online) http://www.london2012.com/get-involved/volunteering/index.php, accessed 14 December 2009.

London.Gov. (2009) *Press release – Mayor and Dame Kelly Holmes announce new funding for young Olympic hopefuls.* http://www.london.gov.uk/view_press_release.jsp?releaseid=20884, accessed 25 October 2009.

Lusted, J. and O'Gorman, J. (2010) The impact of New Labour's modernisation agenda on the English grass-roots football workforce, *Managing Leisure,* 15 (1).

MacVicar, A. and Ogden, S. (2001) Flexible working in sport and recreation: current practices in Scottish public, not for profit and private leisure facilities, *Managing Leisure,* 6: 125–140.

Mastermann, G (2007) *Sponsorship For a Return on Investment.* London: Butterworth-Heinemann.

Mintel (2006) Sponsorship UK, *Mintel.* http://academic.mintel.com/, accessed 24 November 2009.

Mintel (2007) Health and Fitness Clubs, May, London: Mintel.

Mintel (2009) *Market Intelligence Reports.* http://mintel.com, accessed 20 October 2009.

Monopolies and Mergers Commission (1999) *British Sky Broadcasting Group PLC and Manchester United PLC: A Report on the Proposed Merger.* London: The Stationery Office.

Morrow, S. (1999) *The New Business of Football: Accountability and Finance in Football.* Basingstoke: Palgrave Macmillan.

Morrow, S. (2003) *The People's Game: Football, Finance and Society.* Basingstoke: Palgrave Macmillan.

National Assembly for Wales (2009) *Holding the Welsh Government to Account.* http://www.assemblywales.org/abthome/holding-the-welsh-government-to-account.htm, accessed 22 October 2009.

National Skills Academy (2009) *About Us.* http://www.sportactivensa.co.uk/aboutus.ashx, accessed on 1 November 2009.

Nichols, G., Taylor, P., James, M., King, L., Holmes, K., Gratton, C., Kokolakakis, T. and Garrett, R. (2004) Voluntary activity in UK sport, *Voluntary Action,* 6 (2): 31–54.

Nichols, G., Taylor, P., James, M., Holmes, K., King, L. and Garrett, R. (2005) 'Pressures on the UK voluntary sport sector', *Voluntas: International Journal of Voluntary and Nonprofit Organisations,* 16 (1).

Nichols, G. and Shepherd, M. (2006) Volunteering in sport: the use of ratio analysis to analyse volunteering and participation, *Managing Leisure,* 11 (4): 205–216.

Northern Ireland Assembly (2009) *The Work of the Assembly.* http://www.niassembly.gov.uk/the_work.htm, accessed 24 October 2009.

Office for National Statistics (2009a) *Census 2001: Preston.* http://www.statistics.gov.uk/census2001/pyramids/pages/30uk.asp, accessed 19 July 2009.

Office for National Statistics (2009b) *Census 2001: Wigan.* http://www.statistics.gov.uk/census2001/pyramids/pages/00BW.asp, accessed 19 July 2009.

ONS (2009) www.statistics.gov.uk, accessed 12 November 2009.

PAT 10 (1999) *National Strategy for Neighbourhood Renewal: Policy Action Team Audit: Report of the Policy Action Team 10: The Contribution of Sport and the Arts.* London: DCMS.

Powell, M. and Glendinning, C. (2002) Introduction, in C. Glendinning, Powell, M. and K. Rummery (eds) *Partnerships, New Labour and The Governance of Welfare*. Bristol: Policy Press.

Powerleague (2009) http://powerleague.co.uk, accessed 1 November 2009.

Project Scotland (2009) *About Project Scotland*. http://www.projectscotland.co.uk/aboutus/Pages/AboutProjectScotland.aspx. accessed 8 October 2009.

Public Sector Privatisation Research Unit (1992) CCT, the story so far, *Leisure Management*, 12 (5): 26–7.

Qualifications and Curriculum Authority (2009) *Physical Education Key Stage 4 – The Importance of Physical Education*. http://curriculum.qcda.gov.uk/key-stages-3-and-4/subjects/physical-education/keystage4/index.aspx, accessed 5 November 2009.

Reid, G. (2003) Charitable trusts: municipal leisure's 'third way'? *Managing Leisure*, 8: 171–183.

Reid, P. (2003) More than a game? The role of sports governing bodies in the development of sport education programmes, *European Physical Education Review*, 9 (3): 309–317.

Rigg, M. (1986) *Action Sport – Evaluation Report*. London: Sports Council.

Roberts, K. (2004) *The Leisure Industries*. Basingstoke: Palgrave Macmillan.

Roberts, K. (2006) *Leisure in Contemporary Society*. Oxfordshire: CABI.

Rovell, D. (2009) *Agassi Signs Adidas Deal after Long-term Deal with Nike*, www.sports.espn.go.com, accessed 22 November 2009.

Rowe, N., Adams, R. and Beasley, N. (2004) Driving up participation in sport: the social context, the trends, the prospects and the challenges, in *Driving up Participation: The Challenge for Sport*. London: Sport England, Chapter 3.

Royal and Ancient Golf Club of St. Andrews (2009) http://Randa.org, accessed 19 November 2009.

Russell Commission (2005) *A National Frameowrk for Youth Action and Engagement – Report of the Russell Commission*. Norwich: HMSO.

Scott, M. (2009) *Clive Woodward to Move from Coaching Elite Athletes to Those Left Out by UK Sport*. http://www.guardian.co.uk/uk/2009/mar/28/london-olympic-games-funding-clive-woodward, accessed 25 October 2009.

Scottish National Party (2009) *About SNP*. http://www.snp.org/about, accessed 22 October 2009.

Shin, S. and Kleiner, B.H. (2003) How to manage unpaid volunteers in organisations, *Management Research News*, 26 (2/3/4): 63–71.

Shipway, R. (2007) Sustainable legacies for the 2012 Olympic Games. *The Journal of the Royal Society for the Promotion of Health*, 127(3): 119–124.

Siegfried, J. and Zimbalist, A. (2000) The economics of sports facilities and their communities, *Journal of Economic Perspectives*, 14: 95–114.

SkillsActive (2009a) *Sport and Recreation*. http://www.skillsactive.com/sportrec, accessed 1 October 2009.

SkillsActive (2009b) Working in fitness 2009, FIA/SkillsActive. http://www.skillsactive.com/resources/research/working-in-fitness-2009, accessed on 2 November 2009.

Slater, M. (2007) *Woodward's Olympic Challenge*. http://news.bbc.co.uk/sport1/hi/other_sports/olympics_2012/7014144.stm, accessed 2 November 2009.

Social Exclusion Unit (1998) *Bringing Britain Together: A National Strategy for Neighbourhood Renewal*. Cmd paper 4045. London: HMSO.

Speck, I. (2009) GB change gear to chase Olympic glory, *The Daily Mail*, 3 November, p. 79.

Sport and Active Leisure Skills and Productivity Alliance (2006) *North West Sector Skills Agreement – SALSPA Action Plan*. London: SkillsActive.

Sport England (2003a) *Young People and Sport National Survey*. London: Sport England.

Sport England (2003b) *Sports Volunteering in England in 2002*. London: Sport England.

Sport England (2004a) *The Framework for Sport in England*. London: Sport England.

Sport England (2004b) *Young Volunteers: Making a Difference to Sport in England*. London: Sport England.

Sport England (2005) *Understanding Participation in Sport: A Systematic Review*. London: Sport England.

Sport England (2006a) *Understanding Participation in Sport: What Determines Sports Participation Among 15–19 Year Old Women?* London: Sport England.

Sport England (2006b) *Understanding the Success Factors in Sport Action Zones: Final Report*. London: Sport England.

Sport England (2008) *Sport England Strategy 2008–2011*. London: Sport England.

Sport England (2009a) *Active People Survey* 3. http://www.sportengland.org/research/active_people_survey/active_people_survey_3.aspx, accessed 15 November 2009.

Sport England (2009b) *One Million Fact* Sheet 2. http://www.sportengland.org/research/active_people_survey/active_people_survey_2.aspx, accessed 11 October 2009.

Sport England (2009c) *Funding Sport in the Community*. http://www.sportengland.org/funding/funding_sport_in_the_community.aspx, accessed 11 November 2009.

Sport England (2009d) *About Us*. http://www.sportengland.org/about_us.aspx, accessed 18 November 2009.

Sport England (2009e) *What We Do*. http://www.sportengland.org/about_us/what_we_do.aspx, accessed 18 November 2009.

Sport England (2009f) *Support for Rising Sports Stars*. http://www.sportengland.org/media_centre/press_releases/rising_sports_stars.aspx, accessed 18 November 2009.

Sport Industry Research Centre (2007) *The Economic Importance of Sport in England and in the nine English regions: 2003*. London: Sport England.

Sport Northern Ireland (2002) *Strategy on Sport for Young People 2002–2011*. Belfast: Sport NI.

Sport Northern Ireland (2009a) *Investing in Sport*. http://www.sportni.net/iis/InvestinginPerfSport2009–2013.htm, accessed 24 October 2009.

Sport Northern Ireland (2009b) *Recognised Governing Bodies of Sport operating in Northern Ireland*. http://www.sportni.net/links/ni_gov_body.htm, accessed 24 November 2009.

Sport Northern Ireland (2009c) *Corporate Plan 2008–2011*. Belfast: SNI.

Sporting Equals (2009) *What We Do*. http://www.sportingequals.org.uk/about-us/what-we-do, accessed 1 November 2009.

Sports Business (2009) www.sportsbusiness.com, accessed 19 November 2009.

sports coach UK (2008) *The UK Coaching Framework: Executive Summary*, Leeds: Sport Coach UK.

sports coach UK (2009a) *What We Do*. http://www.sportscoachuk.org/index.php?PageID=1&sc=1&uid=, accessed 18 November 2009.

sports coach UK. (2009b) *The UK Coaching Framework: The Coaching Workforce 2009–2016*. Leeds: sports coach.

sports coach UK. (2009c) *UK Coaching Certificate Information*. http://www.sportscoachuk.org/index.php?PageID=3&sc=9&uid=, accessed 24 October 2009.

sports coach UK. (2009d) *The UK Coaching Framework: History and Vision*. http://www.sportscoachuk.org/index.php?PageID=2&sc=5, accessed 24 October 2009.

Sports Council (1969) *Professional Training for Leisure Management*. London: Sports Council.

Sports Council (1991) *Coaching Matters: A Review of Coaching and Coach Education in the UK*. London: Sports Council.

Sports Council Wales (2005) *Framework for the Development of Sport and Physical Activity*. Cardiff: SCW.

Sports Council Wales (2007a) *About Us*. http://www.sports-council-wales.org.uk/about-us, accessed 18 November 2009.

Sports Council Wales (2007b) *PE and School Sport*. http://www.sports-council-wales.org.uk/getactiveinthecommunity/active-young-people/pess, accessed 5 November 2009.

Sports Council Wales (2007c) *5 × 60*. http://www.sports-council-wales.org.uk/getactiveinthecommunity/active-young-people/5x60, accessed 5 November 2009.

Sports Council Wales (2007d) *Welcome to Dragon Sport*. http://www.dragonsport.co.uk/en/About_Us/Operation_Delivery/, accessed 22 November 2009.

Sports Council Wales (2009) *Code of Practice for Funding the Voluntary Sector*. www.sports-council-wales.org.uk/21637.file.dld, accessed 8 October 2009.

Sports Illustrated (2009) www.sportsillustrated.cnn.com, 6 November 2009.

SportsAid (2009a) *About SportsAid*. http://www.sportsaid.org.uk/about/, accessed 12 November 2009.

SportsAid (2009b) *What We Do*. http://www.sportsaid.org.uk/about/what_we_do/, accessed 12 November 2009.

sportscotland (2004) *The Economic Importance of Sport in Scotland 2001*. Edinburgh: **sport**scotland/SIRC.

sportscotland (2007) *The Economic Importance of Sport in Scotland 2004*. Edinburgh **sport**scotland/SIRC.

sportscotland (2009a) *Corporate Plan 2009–2011*. Edinburgh: **sport**scotland.

sportscotland (2009b) *What We Do*. http://www.sportscotland.org.uk/ChannelNavigation/About+us/TopicNavigation/What+we+do/, accessed 18 November 2009.

sportscotland (2009c) *The Origins of Active Schools*. http://www.sportscotland.org.uk/ChannelNavigation/Topics/TopicNavigation/Active+Schools/The+origins+of+Active+Schools, accessed 5 November 2009.

sportscotland (2009d) *Volunteering*. http://www.sportscotland.org.uk/ChannelNavigation/Topics/TopicNavigation/Volunteering/Volunteering.htm, accessed 8 October 2009.

Stevens, D. and Green, P. (2002) Explaining continuity and change in the transition from compulsory competitive tendering to best value for sport and recreation management, *Managing Leisure*, 7: 124–138.

Szymanski, S. (2009) *Playbooks and Checkbooks: An Introduction to the Economics of Modern Sports*. Princeton: Princeton University Press.

Taylor, B. and Garrett, D. (2008) *The Professionalisation of Sports Coaching in the UK: Issues and Conceptualisation*, Leeds: Sport Coach UK.

Taylor, P. (2004) *Driving Up Participation: Sport and Volunteering*. Sheffield Management School: University of Sheffield.

Taylor, T., Darcy, S., Hoye, R. and Cuskelly, G. (2006) Using psychological contract theory to explore issues in effective volunteer management, *European Sport Management Quarterly*, 6 (2): 123–147.

The National Lottery (2009) *See the Difference Your Money Makes*. http://www.national-lottery.co.uk/ player/p/goodcausesandwinners/goodcausesstory.ftl, accessed 17 November 2009.

The Scottish Executive (2007) *Reaching Higher Building on the Success of Sport 21*. Edinburgh: Scottish Executive.

The Scottish Government (2009) *Participation in Sport*. http://www.scotland.gov.uk/Topics/ ArtsCultureSport/Sport/Participation, accessed 22 October 2009.

Thomson, D. (2006) The retain and transfer system, in A. Wladimir, A. and S. Szymanski (eds) *Handbook on the Economics of Sport*. Cheltenham: Edward Elgar, pp. 630–635.

Tomlinson, A. (2007) *The Sport Studies Reader*. London: Routledge.

UK Sport (2008a) *UK Sport Mission, Priorities and Values*. http://www.uksport.gov.uk/assets/File/ Generic_Template_Documents/About_UK_Sport/UK%20SPORT%20Mission%20Priorities%20 and%20Values.pdf, accessed 16 December 2008.

UK Sport (2008b) Brief guide to UK sport. http://www.uksport.gov.uk/assets/File/Generic_Template_ Documents/About_UK_Sport/UK%20Sport%202%20pager%20updated%20new%20-%20Sep07. pdf, accessed 16 December 2008.

UK Sport (2008c) 'World Class Performance'. http://www.uksport.gov.uk/pages/world_class_ performance, accessed 16 December 2008.

UK Sport (2009a) London 2012 – *Sport by Sport Funding Breakdown*. http://www.uksport.gov.uk/pages/ summer_olympic_sports_-_london_2012/, accessed 17 November 2009.

UK Sport (2009b) *World Class Performance*. http://www.uksport.gov.uk/pages/world_class_ performance/, accessed 17 November 2009.

UK Sport (2009c) *Sports Medicine and Sports Science Programmes*. http://www.uksport.gov.uk/pages/ programmes/, accessed 2 November 2009.

UK Sport (2009d) *World Class Performance – How it Works*. http://www.uksport.gov.uk/pages/world_ class_performance_-_how_it_works/, accessed 17 November 2009.

Varnom, A. (2009) *The Challenge Ahead – A Statement from Andy Varnom on The Way Forward for ISRM*. http://www.isrm.co.uk/news/news_story.php?news_id=6, accessed 2 November 2009.

Veal, A. and Saperstein, H. (1977) *Recreation Managers in Britain: A Survey*, Working paper 56 Birmingham: CURS.

VisitBritain (2009) www.visitbritain.org, accessed 12 November 2009.

Volresource (2009) *Information for Voluntary and Community Organisations*. http://www.volresource.org. uk/briefing/sectstats.htm, accessed 8 October 2009.

Volunteer Development Agency (2007) *It's All About Time Volunteering in Northern Ireland*. Belfast: VDA.

Volunteer Development Agency (2009) *Needs Analysis with Olympic Sport Governing Bodies in Relation to Volunteering and Volunteer Management Summary Report*. Belfast: VDA.

Volunteer Development Scotland (2008) *Briefing Paper for MSPs Business Debat*. www.vds.org.uk, accessed 8 October 2009.

Volunteering England (2009) *Dramatic Increase in Number of Volunteers as Recession Takes Hold*. http:// www.volunteering.org.uk/News/mediacentre/2009+Press+Releases/Dramatic+increase+in+number +of+volunteers+as+recession+takes+hold.htm, accessed 15 November 2009.

Wang, P.Z. (2004) Assessing motivations for sport volunteerism, *Advances in Consumer Research*, 31: 420–425.

Wang, W, and Theodorald, E. (2007) Mass sport policy development in the Olympic City: the case of Qingdao – host to the 2008 sailing regatta. *The Journal of the Royal Society for the Promotion of Health*, 127(3): 125–132.

Watt, D. (2003) *Sports Management and Administration* 2nd edn. London: Routledge.

Welsh Assembly Government (2005) *Climbing Higher Strategy for Sport and Physical Activity*. Cardiff: Welsh Assembly Government.

Welsh Assembly Government (2006) *Climbing Higher Next Steps*. Cardiff: Welsh Assembly Government.

Welsh Assembly Government (2009a) *About Us*. http://wales.gov.uk/about/?lang=en, accessed 22 October 2009.

Welsh Assembly Government (2009b) *Sport and Active Recreation*. http://wales.gov.uk/topics/cultureandsport/sportandactiverecreation/?lang=en, accessed 23 October 2009.

Welsh Assembly Government (2009c) *Climbing Higher – Next Steps*. http://wales.gov.uk/topics/cultureandsport/publications/climbingnext/?lang=en, accessed 23 October 2009.

Williams, J. (1994) The local and the global in English soccer and the rise of satellite television, *Sociology of Sport Journal*, 11(4): 376–397.

Wolsey, C. and Abrams, J. (2001) *Understanding the Leisure and Sport Industry*. Harlow: Pearson Education.

WSFF (2009) *About Us*. http://www.wsff.org.uk/about/, accessed 18 November 2009.

Yates, A. (1978) *Recreation Management Training Committee: Interim Report*. London: HMSO.

Yates, A. (1984) *Recreation Management Training Committee: Final Report*. London: HMSO.

Youth Sport Trust (2009a) *About Us*. http://www.youthsporttrust.org/page/our-mission/index.html, accessed 18 November 2009.

Youth Sport Trust (2009a) *Our Mission*. http://www.youthsporttrust.org/page/our-mission/index.htm, accessed 18 November 2009.

Youth Sport Trust (2009b) *Sports Councils and National Governing Bodies of Sport*. http://www.youthsporttrust.org/page/Sport/index.html, accessed 18 November 2009.

Youth Sport Trust (2009c) *School Sport Coaching*. http://www.youthsporttrust.org/subpage/ss-coaching/index.html, accessed 20 November 2009.

Youth Sport Trust (2009d) *Special Educational Needs*. http://inclusion.youthsporttrust.org/page/introduction/index.html, accessed 20 November 2009.

Youth Sport Trust (2009e) *Playground to Podium*. http://inclusion.youthsporttrust.org/page/p2p-intro/index.html, accessed 20 November 2009.

Youth Sport Trust (2009f) *Gifted and Talented*. http://gifted.youthsporttrust.org/page/welcome/index.html, accessed 20 November 2009.

Index